Also by Thomas Simmons

THE UNSEEN SHORE:
MEMORIES OF A CHRISTIAN SCIENCE CHILDHOOD

A SEASON
IN THE AIR

A SEASON IN THE AIR

One Man's Adventures in Flying

THOMAS SIMMONS

FAWCETT COLUMBINE   NEW YORK

A Fawcett Columbine Book
Published by Ballantine Books

Portions of chapter three originally appeared in Parenting.
Portions of chapter four originally appeared in California Living
and California Childhood, edited by Gary Soto,
Creative Arts Book Company, 1988.

Library of Congress Cataloging-in-Publication Data
Simmons, Thomas.
A season in the air : one man's adventures in flying / Thomas Simmons.
p.   cm.
ISBN 0-449-90739-2
1. Simmons, Thomas.
2. Air pilots—United States—Biography.
3. Fear of flying.   I. Title.
TL540.S57A3   1993
629.13'092—dc20
[B]   92-55001
CIP

Manufactured in the United States of America
First Edition: September 1993
10 9 8 7 6 5 4 3 2 1

Contents

CONTENTS

Acknowledgments

I would like to thank my flight instructors at Shoreline Aviation in Marshfield, Massachusetts—Steve Grable, Donnie Whittle, and Larry Schramm—for launching me safely into the air while tolerating my rather extensive eccentricities. Keith Douglass, president of Shoreline Aviation, and airport commissioner George Harlow generously shared with me their knowledge of the history and lore of Marshfield Airport; Ann Pollard cheered me up, occasionally let me cheer her up, and made sure the planes I wanted to fly were fueled and ready to go. Lew Owen, the FAA-designated examiner for my private pilot practical test, took the craft of flying as seriously as anyone I have ever met; his critical eye during the flight test reminded me how much is at stake on every flight, and how safe flying is a matter of constant vigilance and care.

By a fortunate accident I came across Gerry Bruder's *Heroes of the Horizon: Flying Adventures of Alaska's Legendary Bush Pilots* while writing this book. Bruder's extensive anecdotal accounts of some of the early Alaskan pilots, including Sheldon

Simmons, helped me shape my own story while clarifying my somewhat dim impressions of the past.

Lisa Bankoff, of International Creative Management in New York, found a home for this manuscript with remarkable efficiency and grace. Joanne Wyckoff, my editor at Ballantine, was an ideal colleague, interspersing necessary silences with bouts of emphatic encouragement and attending to refinements of the manuscript with a deft touch.

To my father, who suffered so much for so long and still managed to trust in the possibility of joy, I offer my love and gratitude.

Thomas Simmons
Iowa City, Iowa
January 1993

*A SEASON
IN THE AIR*

A LITTLE MORE
THAN FEAR

*T*WA flight 61, nonstop from Boston to San Francisco, will begin boarding in about fifteen minutes. Four weeks have passed since the crash of United flight 232 in Sioux City, Iowa; I am about to leave with my wife, Lesley, and our three-year-old son, Nathaniel, to see our relatives in California. For months I have been savoring the prospect of this trip, this respite from my job at MIT. At least, I tell myself, if it all gets to be too much, I'll just go back to California and not return. Since I have no money to speak of, going back to California without a job is scarcely a real option, but I say it to myself as if it were. Yet now, fifteen minutes from boarding, I cannot drag myself out of the children's play area where I am watching Nathaniel. If I pretend to myself that nothing is happening, that no planes are leaving, that I'm not leaving, then I won't have to go.

I saw the crash, almost by accident, while flipping channels during the TV news hour on July 20, 1989. The slightly fuzzy tape, the stereotypical work of an amateur, caught the DC-10—a fine-looking plane, intact and strong—slowly rolling nosedown over a runway. I don't remember what the news-caster was saying. I knew what I was seeing. I saw the plane's right wing dipping down, so slowly that it seemed like t'ai chi: a dip that became, incredibly, more than a dip, a roll, and then a deeper roll to the right as the wingtip itself struck the ground in a puff of dust and then—who could have choreographed this?—the great plane nosing down so suddenly that even slow motion could not freeze its fate, the tail rising into the air like a skyscraper suddenly surging up sideways from the ground and falling again as the dust and flame mushroomed around it, the whole plane cartwheeling into smoke and fire as quickly and easily as a diabolical toy. And then the stark divisions, life and death: survivors hugging one another, stretchers with bodies covered in fresh plastic. As if coming out of shock, I began to remember snatches of what I thought I had not heard—United flight 232; disintegrating fan in the tail engine; hydraulic failure; Sioux City. "They almost made it"—112 dead, or something on that order; 187 survivors.

Over the past few weeks that crash has become an obses-sion playing itself at will over the airwaves of my mind when I am driving the car or walking down the street or just playing with Nathaniel. At first the crash itself frightened me—the appalling devastation, the sudden descent from grace to obscen-ity. Then a deeper fear took hold, even though it played itself out in those same images of collision and explosion. I realized I did not really know why I was so frightened. There had been other airplane crashes, I reminded myself, and worse ones. These had not obsessed me, although I could call them instantly to mind: flight 191, a DC-10 rolling out of control after an engine ripped away on takeoff from O'Hare in 1979, all souls lost; the Pacific Southwest Airlines 727, going down in flames after colliding with a Cessna near Lindberg Field in San Diego in 1978. Last week, admitting to myself that I had become phobic about flying, I began to consider finding a therapist who specialized in phobias. And yet, when I got right down to it, the flying phobia was not all there was to whatever was bothering me. I was not afraid of flying; I was afraid of living. As many risks as I took—riding motorcycles, giving up a job in California for a job in Massachusetts, getting married, having a child—I was still afraid of risk; I took no essential pleasure in the changes in my life, but feared them and sought ways to avoid them.

A few days before my job interview at MIT in 1987, I was riding my Honda motorcycle on a California freeway in the rain. No one is quite sure what happened, but for some reason the front wheel went into a wobble at sixty miles per hour. I hung on for a few strange, liquid seconds, completely aware that I was out of control, until the bike went down and then over, flipping me twice and then skidding along on the pavement until it, and I, came to a rest in the center lane of the five-lane highway. I was facedown, looking back toward traffic. And my mind was as clear as it had ever been. I thought: If there is a car there, I will die. As I looked up, expecting to die, I saw a row of cars at what turned out to be about a four-second distance from me. I thought: I could get up and run off the freeway. And I did. After running to the median, I blacked out for a few seconds, then found myself kneeling in the grass while a man in a maroon Jaguar XJ6 pulled over beside me, leaned out the window, and asked me if I wanted him to dial 411 on his car phone. "I think 911 would be more helpful," I remember saying. And then I knew that I was still alive and that the maroon XJ6 was not God's way of ushering me into heaven. But I was also vaguely disappointed: There was so much still to be done, so much to come back to. Yet I was deeply offended when a friend of mine suggested, ever so gently, that the accident was not entirely accidental. Of course it was an accident, I argued furiously. The highway was slick, the fiberglass lane dividers were slick, I hit a patch of oil. Two or three things conspired at once, and—bam!—there I was facedown in traffic. You call that intentional? Not intentional, my friend said; just—well—there was so much you were facing right then. It was a scary time. Maybe life wasn't exactly what you wanted. Bullshit, I said.

And yet I myself wondered a week after that, on a flight from San Francisco to Boston for the interview at MIT—a flight I did not want to take, although then I was not really afraid of flying. Was there no other way for me to treat life than to avoid it? Did I have to back into everything? But I'm not backing into this job, I argued with myself; I'm flying out, I've worked hard for it, I'm one of a handful of finalists. I deserve it; it's what I want. I thought about the motorcycle accident, which had left me miraculously unharmed, and how lucky I was to be alive, and as these standard ways of thinking flooded back through my mind I began to feel better. But somehow I still felt that I was avoiding something significant—something I needed to know about how to live.

What are you afraid of? the voice asks as I sit in the TWA terminal at Logan, trying to compose myself. I get up, a little shaky, and walk with Nathaniel and Lesley through the security checkpoint to the gate, where a couple of hundred people are already sitting, reading books, talking, waiting. A line of people who need boarding passes snakes along the well-waxed corridor; businessmen and -women are talking on the phones by the side wall. It is an antiseptic place, given over to life in abeyance; everyone here seems to be waiting for something to happen. Beyond us, only a few feet away, the Lockheed L-1011 sits at the gate, its tall rounded nose aimed straight at the window. Lesley, who knows how upset I am and worries even more because I cannot explain myself, takes Nathaniel over to the snack machines while I walk up to the window and stare.

Could it be this plane? Could this beautiful red-and-white machine, with its Rolls-Royce engines and time-tried avionics, with its virtually fail-safe hydraulic system, could this airplane fail? Involuntarily I glance at the people around me, as seemingly calm as if waiting in line at the supermarket: Flying is something everyone does, something that thousands of people do safely every day. Why should this flight, for them, be any different? This very flight, in fact, goes nonstop to San Francisco every evening, 365 days a year. Never in the history of flight 61 has there been a catastrophe, or even a significant problem. Never.

I envision the people around me boarding this flight, noisily stowing their luggage and strapping themselves in, waiting for dinner, eating chicken or fish at 35,000 feet, talking or reading or playing checkers with their kids when a vaguely muffled bang occurs, somewhere in the vicinity of the rear, and then the plane begins to shudder and buck, and there is a moment of silence, and then someone cries out in fear, and everyone knows. Everyone knows. For some reason the plane itself does not lose pressure, but as it begins to climb to the right, then dip to the left, then turn, level, climb again, then slide downward in a long, roller coaster descent, everyone knows that it is a plane out of control, or almost that; and everything these people have been, every relative they have waiting for them on the ground, every dollar they were about to earn or speech they were about to give or present they had for a niece or new brother-in-law, everything is irrelevant, is lost—or almost lost. For now there is a disaster in the making but there is also time, the second-worst enemy: no cataclysmic explosion, no pieces falling from the sky, but a metal tube in which two or three hundred people rock and roll through the sky, unable to lift a finger to redeem themselves, yet still human, still thinking, still planning and panicking—Oh my God, let this be over quickly, let the plane come apart; what will my children do; please let this be over; give the pilot a miracle; God, God, save me; God, let my son live. And we look at each other, sideways at first, then directly, pleading, and the ones who are not quite panicking cradle the ones who are; there is love and compassion and forgiveness here, and such tenderness, and all too late. But the pilot comes on the still-working intercom and announces, with a flat practiced calm, that the rear engine has exploded and the plane has lost all hydraulic pressure and the air traffic controllers have diverted them to Sioux City, since they can make only right-hand turns, and they think if they can just control the engines carefully enough they can turn and descend to a series of headings and altitudes that will take them right to the runway. But everyone must be calm. There are no guarantees, but the crew is experienced (and an extra pilot is on board, in fact, and now in the cockpit kneeling at the throttle controls as if before an altar, pulling and pushing the engine levers at the captain's command to control descent and direction) and the prospects for a safe crash landing are good. And there is time, so much time to fear and cradle and forgive, and then the ground is rushing up and the pilot is shouting "Left! Left! Left!" but it takes a few seconds for the right engine to power up and the right wing dips lower, lower—and then all prayers are scattered in a random segmenting of fire and rescue, the first-class and mid-coach passengers vaporized faster than the first syllable of "Agnus Dei," the cockpit crew and coach passengers forward of the wing and all the people in the tail sitting more or less miraculously at odd angles on the runway, their lives preserved.

For a brief second I cover my face with my hands, as if to wake up from a terrible nightmare. I look around. It seems to me that a few people are staring at me. "Uh-oh," I hear them saying to themselves. "He's gonna be a problem. Hope he doesn't sit near me." "Oh, for God's sake," I say to myself; the self-loathing almost liberates me from my terror, but not quite. Death is on my tail now, I can feel him, but he has been here all along, all through my time in this job in this life in Massachusetts, and I have not yet faced him, have dodged him and avoided him and bought time: But I am afraid of dying because I am dead here in this place, and I do not know how to bring myself back to life. And all that is left is catastrophe.

Instantly a mob of uncontrolled impressions floods back: nightmares about the ugly neighborhood where we live, words from my chairman suggesting my work is marginal and may place my job at risk, students who ask at the beginning of class if we'll be covering anything important today. Who was I before I became a professor at MIT? I was . . . It is time to go.

The first panic attack comes when I snap on my seat belt. Lesley and Nathaniel and I are in row 26, seats C, D, and E; I am in C, the aisle seat, because I want at least to be able to get up and walk to ease the claustrophobia. This time, however, even the aisle seat does not help. I try to distract myself by pulling out crayons and paper and drawing dragons with Nathaniel while we push back from the gate and begin to taxi. But after a few minutes my hands are shaking so badly that I cannot hold the crayons, and I am beginning to have trouble breathing. Nathaniel looks at me oddly, as a three-year-old looks at someone who simply does not make sense. Lesley glances over, takes the paper and crayons, and draws Nathaniel's attention to her. I reach down to my bag and pull out a small bottle of pills— Xanax, a powerful antipanic drug, which I had a doctor in California prescribe for me a few years earlier for a job interview at the *New York Times*. I have two kinds of Xanax with me—

the peach-colored ones, .5 milligram per tablet, and the white ones, .25 milligram. I'm pretty sure I grab the white ones—I'm still trying not to make a big deal of this—and I swallow one with a swig of some water I've brought with me. Even so, sitting back in the seat brings a wave of nausea: I have no escape. I am trapped in a long metal tube, which is this airplane but also my life, and I cannot get out.

We are rolling now—I am pressed back against my seat as the big engines roar to full power. Wanting to turn back, to get out, I still find the great surge of lift momentarily comforting: It sends me back to some earlier moment when I knew something about the pleasure of an adventure. But once we're in the air I'm trembling again. Nathaniel pats my arm; I smile at him weakly. I'm a terrible father. Lesley manages to look both concerned and miserable. She knows what kind of flight this is going to be.

But already the flight attendant is coming around with drinks, and—uncharacteristically—I take a bottle of champagne. I drink the entire small bottle, even though I haven't eaten anything in hours; when dinner comes around a half hour later, I refuse it, fearing further nausea. But I take a second bottle of champagne. And still I am trembling, waiting for the muffled explosion and the roller-coaster ride to doom, wondering how all these people—so many of them!—all around me can be so calm. I want these people to go away, but I cannot make them, nor can I make myself invisible. I am terribly embarrassed, knowing how I must look—sick, frightened, drunk—and in this state I down the second bottle of champagne. That is not enough; I reach for another Xanax.

When I come to, we have arrived in San Francisco. I have managed to spill part of the last bottle of champagne all over my pants; I did not notice. The flight attendant has cleaned up the bottle and the glass; Lesley has moved my tray table into the upright position. Nathaniel, blessedly, is asleep. And I? I actually feel fine, wonderful. I am giddy; we are here, we have arrived, and I am not dead! Although the flight attendant asks everyone to remain seated, with seat belts fastened, until we are parked at the gate, everyone is unbuckling and fumbling and reaching for luggage in the overhead compartments. The flight is over. We are in California. I stand up, remarkably steady as far as I can tell, and open the bin with Nathaniel's bag in it. A woman's coat falls out halfway; it belongs to the woman across the aisle from me. "Pardon me," I say with extreme formality, "I believe this is yours." "Thank you," she says, looking at me as if I were an alien. I think briefly about how I must have appeared to her for the past five and a half hours.

Lesley's father and stepmother greet us at the gate; in a few minutes we're outside, where the late summer air is crisp and delicious, almost edible. I love this place. I can breathe here, I can live here. I will never fly in an airplane again; I will never go back to MIT. I will wake up tomorrow morning, go over to Stanford, visit old friends, go for a long hike in the hills. I will take back my life.

In the morning, going through my luggage, I realize I did not take the white Xanax but rather the double dosage, the peach ones. I smile—first time I've ever done anything like that. It's not like me to confuse prescriptions, but then it's also not like me to take any kind of drugs along with booze. I laugh at myself a little—what was I thinking? I must have been scared. Oh well. That's all over. The pale, cool, delicious California sun sweeps in long beams through the house, and I can feel myself easing back into its embrace. Why was I gone so long? It's the beginning of a good day.

And it is, in fact, a good day until about four in the afternoon, when suddenly, without warning, I feel as if the entire weight of my life has dropped back down on me. Lesley and I and Nathaniel are sitting in a friend's living room, talking about MIT and graduate school and all the usual hell associated with academia. Nathaniel and I are playing with some Sesame Street characters on the floor. Suddenly I am exhausted, then terribly, terribly sad; I stop playing and sit cross-legged on the floor as Nathaniel, after tugging at my arm, goes over to Lesley for a second opinion.

"What's up?" she asks.

"I think I need to lie down," I say.

"Probably jet lag," she says. "You didn't have the best flight of your life."

"You can lie down in my bed," our friend Meg says. "Or if you want to take off, that's fine too. I'll see you in a couple of days."

Everything is fine here, peaceful, and yet what I most want to do is run: I want to run from this house, from this town, from Nathaniel and Lesley and her relatives; I want to hop in the car and drive north, past San Francisco and Mendocino to Fort Bragg and Crescent City, up into Oregon . . . what am I thinking? I am lost here, even here, and I have no energy left to cope. For some reason I am coming apart.

For two days I lie in bed at Lesley's father's house; people bring me soup and ask me how I am doing. When the house is quiet and everyone has gone out, I take the rental car and drive way, way out into the Pacific coastal range, a place I used to go to when I needed to escape. But now even that is not enough. It feels like a jumping-off point, the merest taste of a northern escape, and I cannot go north. I go back to the house and lie down again.

Somewhere in the back of my mind I remember hearing that Xanax is an addictive drug and that a continuous high dosage or an overdose will cause withdrawal symptoms. With-drawal—I wonder what that really means? Having been raised as a Christian Scientist, I never took drugs—not even aspirin or Tylenol—so all of this is relatively new to me. I never smoked dope or drank in college; withdrawal was something other peo-ple went through. But the question begins to shape itself more insistently, more personally: Is that my problem—the downside of Xanax? And what can I do about it? If that's the problem, I think, then I ought to be able to ease myself away from Xanax by going back on it for a little while, taking progressively smaller doses. So I do: three of the white pills one day, two the next, one the third day. And slowly, slowly, I come out of my depres-sion.

What do I need to change? Over the next week, as I spend time with Lesley and Nathaniel at the Point Reyes National Seashore and wander on beaches south of San Francisco, I begin to piece together some possible answers. Of course they seem to fly apart as soon as I attach words to them. I feel I am walking through a mine field of my own making. But it is better than a drug-induced depression, and better—much better—than the death I continue to fear.

But what am I afraid of? I am afraid of flying; I am afraid of being encased in a metal tube with a bunch of strangers, hurtling toward oblivion at any moment. But it seems that there must be reasons beyond the fear of catastrophe that compel me to stay away from airplanes. Perhaps an airliner is too good to be true. Not miraculous, but too good, the way a child in school can be too good. In an airliner everything must be in its place; order and politeness must prevail; people sit in their assigned seats, fasten their seat belts, eat (or be surrounded by eaters) at the appointed time, and don't make too much noise. They surrender control to others. Everything they might consider

13

important to daily life is temporarily taken out of their hands. And they learn to accommodate this. They comply.

As I say these words to myself, I see a strange confusion of images, all related to school—the place where I work, the schools I attended as a child, the teachers who badgered me to improve my handwriting or not to go to the bathroom so often or sit quietly until my mother came to liberate me at the end of the day. Maybe I am describing an airliner, but I am also describing my job and the way I have lived for years: I have been too good. I have been profoundly compliant. In kindergarten, when the teacher laughed because I managed to glue my construction paper flower petals into the shape of a turkey's tail, I burned inside and vowed to make a perfect flower; it did not occur to me then to question her judgment. Yet, almost thirty years later, when the man who hired me at MIT suggested significant inadequacies in my academic work, I still could not easily question his judgment: I was at fault.

These words fly into a pattern with the speed of a hurricane and fly apart almost as quickly. It should be obvious what I am trying to tell myself, but it is not; instead I go back into the usual round of self-recriminations. Should I quit my job? Leave my family? Become a hermit? And once again I am back in that strange dream time when fear is my closest companion, my impenetrable fog.

Somehow the days in California help. The long walks around the landscapes I love push the fear back and quell the questions of goodness and badness. I am who I am; I am other than what my job, my colleagues, and my family make me out to be. And I forget that so quickly in the ordinary course of a day! The night before our flight back to Massachusetts, I drink heavily and ease myself into a mellow sleep. In the morning, running on .25 milligram of Xanax, I help Nathaniel onto the plane and manage to avoid panic until midway through the flight. Nathaniel is napping; Lesley has learned to avoid me. I get up, walk back from row 24 past the galley and into the rear of the L-1011, where the roar of the third engine above me is palpable and yet a comfort, like a loud, unquellable beast. This is the smoking section. I walk slowly around the rear of the plane, past the lavatories, eyeing the people who have chosen to sit here. They look like me—a bunch of neurotics and loners, occupying separate seats in a part of the plane few people willingly choose, smoking, looking gray and sallow, reading fitfully, drinking, listening to music with eyes tightly shut. Huh, I say to myself—so there are other people who're afraid too. But these people aren't just afraid of flying. These people are hurting. They aren't hiding it. At ease among them, I sit down with them for most of the rest of the flight, thumbing through magazines, resting in the roar of an engine that terrified me two weeks ago on the flight out. Nothing will happen here, I say to myself; I am among friends. And yet they look stranger to me than any group of people I have ever seen. We are a bunch of Martians.

II.

*I*t is winter now, early February 1990, the low point of the season, the low point of everything that I have worked for. I have been revising my dissertation on modern poetry for publication as a book—one of the requisite behaviors of a young professor of writing or literature in the contemporary university, since publishing is the only real gauge of one's ability to keep a job. This remains true, I have discovered to my bewilderment, despite the considerable lip service given to teaching and advising students: It turns out that I am on a very shaky limb, and the question of whether I can make my dissertation a publishable book is beginning to haunt me.

The chairman of my program calls me in to explain that he is beginning my third-year job review. Why, I ask, is he doing this in my second year? He could say, "Because that's customary procedure at MIT"; instead he says, "Because if people aren't working out, we want them to know early." I leave his office shaking, thinking of my family, my wife without a job, our second child on the way, and that, if I lose this job, I may not be able to find another. Finding a job in a university is like finding a four-leaf clover. I go home after teaching my last class, unable to explain what has happened to me. Nathaniel and Lesley head out to the library; I pick up one of the magazines in the living room and begin to read.

The magazine is *Flying*. Intrigued with my love-terror relationship with airplanes, my mother-in-law gave me a subscription for Christmas. It was my turn to be intrigued. Was this a joke? A hint? I read aimlessly, annoyed with the jargon: What is an ARSA? A directional gyro? An NDB instrument approach? None of this makes sense, but I cannot quite let go of it. Beyond its nuisance value, it has some of the appeal of a foreign language. Then I flip another page and come to an ad for something called the General Aviation Task Force. The ad itself is simple—a small, low-wing, single-engine plane flying over a southwestern landscape, perhaps the Canyon de Chelly. It is a beautiful picture, full of peace and power.

I think about what my chairman said a few hours ago. There is an 800 number in the ad. I go to the phone, dial once, blow the number, wait, try again. A man answers.

"Well, it's just that, I saw your ad in *Flying*," I say. What am I saying? "And I was wondering, well, which airports near me might have someone who could take me up for a ride."

"Why don't you tell me where you live," says the friendly person out in the outer space of 800 numbers, "and we'll send you the names of a couple of flight schools nearby. One of them can take you for an intro ride, and you can see if it's something you want to do."

Something about his either-way-is-okay-with-me attitude calmed me down. I wasn't going to get a lecture about how wonderful flying was, and I wasn't going to wind up blurting out to him how terrified I was of airplanes—small planes even more than large ones. I gave him my address. He wished me good luck.

The packet he sent was tiny—much smaller than I had imagined, just a letter of introduction to the Task Force, a pamphlet called *Learning to Fly: A Few Facts to Get You off the Ground*, and a list of not five, not three, but only two schools in my area. I lived in Belmont, Massachusetts; Hanscom Field, a fifteen-minute drive away, had at least one flight school I knew about, and I was trying to gear myself up to go out there. I expected the Task Force report to bolster my confidence by referring me to Hanscom, but Hanscom was not on the list. There was one place in Norwood, a sprawling suburb twenty minutes south of Belmont by freeway, and another place called Shoreline Aviation in Marshfield.

"Where the hell is Marshfield?" I asked Lesley as she passed by, taking a break from her own writing. "You ever heard of it?"

"Never," she said. "What's there?"

"An airport, apparently."

"What are you thinking of doing?" she asked.

I didn't know. It was enough just to get out the road atlas and see if such a place as Marshfield even had a listing. It showed up in the index; I followed the combination of numbers and letters on the map as they led me well south of Boston and then east, east of Norwood, east of Weymouth, right out to the coast:

There it was, a coastal town just north of Plymouth. I knew nothing about it. When, a couple of days later, I asked colleagues at MIT what they knew about Marshfield, only two could recall even hearing of it; neither one really knew where it was.

I began to make up a list to myself: a place that no one I know knows anything about, by the ocean, with an airport. What could it look like? And why would anyone put an airport there?

"I guess there's no point in going down there," I said to Lesley. "Maybe I'll think about Norwood."

But I couldn't go to Norwood. I didn't even know why I was thinking about going to a small airport at all, but Norwood was a place where people bought cars, shoes, doughnuts, and all the other miscellany of ordinary life; it was just a place. I had been through it. It had no magic. But Marshfield—would it have marshes? Would it have a big terminal, shiny hangars, Cessnas landing at the rate of one a minute? I couldn't get any sense of it; I could only remember growing up in Avalon, New Jersey, rowing on endless summer days through the waterways among the marshy islands, and watching a black seaplane take off and land in the main channel near Townsend's Inlet.

No, no, no—I didn't want to fly. I hated flying. What was I thinking? But in our year and a half in the Boston area, Lesley and I had found only three or four coastal areas we liked: the northern Maine coast; the Parker River Wildlife Refuge, near Newburyport, an hour north of Boston; the Chatham shore; and the public beach at Duxbury. Maybe Marshfield would offer another alternative.

But when, a week later, the three of us piled into the car for a trip to the beach, I was feeling shaky and disoriented, almost as I had felt when I flew to California in the late summer. It was not the fear of flying that crippled me now, however; that was hardly in my mind. It was the routine of ordinary days, the desperate effort the three of us made to find something to do with too little money and too little time, while I worried about my allegedly poor performance at MIT and wondered whether I would even have a job in a year's time. We had huge debts, we had a child who slept badly, and we had each other—not the greatest consolation, considering how hard we both worked and how resentful we had both become. Wanting to fix everything, I took on too much; I crippled myself at MIT, and yet came home to find that I still did too little child care. There was no room, no way either to win or to escape.

I rolled that idea over and over in my head as we headed south, presumably for the Duxbury beach, with Nathaniel alternately crying and dozing in the back seat and Lesley trying not to think of things to say. At one point I almost turned the car around; I was too tired, too depressed, to go play on a beach. "Well I started out on Sunday," sang America on the radio, "but I got so damned depressed, that I set my sights on Monday and I got myself undressed. . . ." It made sense to me.

But then time passed, we traveled, and the road sign identified the next exit as Marshfield and Pembroke. We were crossing a long, low bridge over a wide marsh within which a narrow channel snaked back into woods and out, among kestrels and owls, toward the ocean we could not see. I took the exit.

"Where to?" asked Lesley.

"I don't know exactly," I said, trying to remember what I'd seen on the atlas. "In theory this road runs right down to the ocean. I guess we can just stay on it."

We could see the landscape beginning to settle down toward something lower, the ocean, just at the point when an airport sign pointed us toward a narrow road to the right.

"Huh," I said. "Might as well see."

What we saw was a road opening out into a mostly un-paved parking lot where an old red barn seemed to take up more than its share of the sky. Someone had installed a plate glass window and a white colonial-style front door, and the sign above it identified this as the home of Shoreline Aviation. I stood outside it for a while, taking it in. The day was sunny and cool, and the anemometer on top of the cupola turned with a distinctive lassitude; there was no wildness here, only a kind of settledness. Beyond the chain link fence, on the other hand, were things that gave me the fear of wildness: A plane I recog-nized as a Piper Tomahawk, a tiny low-wing trainer, sat next to the building, and beyond it an assortment of Pipers and Cessnas rocked in the breeze, well anchored with orange tie-down ropes. These were the machines I did not like, the ones that would fly. And yet I was here because of them.

"You want to wait here a couple of minutes?" I ask Lesley. She and Nathaniel walk toward the fence, looking at the planes; I fling open the colonial door with something approaching aban-don and look for the first reasonable person I can find. To the right are a couple of roughed-in rooms with pipes sticking out of the floor: bathrooms-to-be. To the left are pilots' offices, with large maps tacked to the walls. Two men, both younger than I, are sitting in the second office, talking about some kind of landing procedure. Not knowing what I want, I stand there for a second until the man behind the desk looks up. He is almost stereotypically handsome—closely cropped reddish blond hair, mouth and nose and chin as finely sketched as Clark Gable's, kind eyes. I feel a slight rush of envy.

"What can I do for you?"

"Well," I say, knowing my words sound too rushed and too quiet, "I called the General Aviation Task Force about maybe taking a ride with someone, and they gave me a couple of names, and one of them was Shoreline's, so I just thought I'd come down here and find out what the scoop was."

The scoop? Did I say that? What have I set in motion? I lean against the doorway. The guy in front of the desk turns around to take a look at me; the kind-eyed man stands up.

"Let me show you around," he says, waiting for me to clear the doorway without suggesting that I'm actually blocking his path. I like him.

"I don't really know if I want to fly," I say without really thinking. "I mean—"

"It's all right, it's all right," he answers, unsurprised. "I've got time. You want to look at a plane?"

"Do you have any Warriors?" Once, several years before, in California, I had seen something called a Piper Warrior, a low-wing four-seat single-engine plane that seemed to me a little wider and more planelike than the Cessnas that regularly zipped in and out of the Palo Alto airport.

"Warriors are pretty much all we fly for training planes," he says.

"Really?"

"Yeah, they're nice planes. My name's Steve," he says suddenly, offering a handshake.

"Tom." We pass the main room of the old barn, renovated with carpets and sofas and a display case full of headsets, hand-held radios, maps, and books about flying; somewhere a radio is blaring some pilot's position report, and some people are hanging around a counter and going over an enormous schedule book. Steve grimaces slightly.

"It gets a little busy down here on weekends, especially sunny weekends in the winter," he says as we head out to the ramp. "People haven't flown for a while. They get a little stir-crazy in the bad weather."

Listening to Steve, trying as usual to be polite and disguise my fear, I almost don't notice the airplane right in front of me. What startles me is how real it looks—graceful, metallic, solid: Its details leave my fantasies behind. A rakish antenna about a foot long extends from the top of the fuselage; two other antennae angle off from the top of the tail. There's another small antenna underneath the cockpit (what can all these antennae be for?) and another, much skinnier, near the base of the tail. The gray fuselage, clearly well cared for, gleams dully in the winter sun, showing the trace glares of wax; red and blue stripes angle sharply upward and across the tail, and foot-high numbers and letters across the fuselage proclaim this to be aircraft N4347H. Through the windows I can see the high-backed seats in the cockpit, but by this time Steve has already made his way around to the other side of the plane; standing on the wing, he waves me over. "Have a look," he says.

I come around, climbing onto the wing where a patch of something like thin asphalt marks the spot where it's okay to step. Warriors have only one door, on the right side of the plane; Steve has already opened it, and as I look in he hops off the wing to stand beside the plane. "Have you ever flown in a light plane before?" he asks.

"A couple of times," I say, thinking back on my tenth birthday, when my brother-in-law took me up in his Cessna 140, and on an afternoon many years later—September 26, 1978, the day after the PSA crash in San Diego—when I went up for an hour-long lesson in a Cessna 150 just to prove to myself that I could do it. I wound up airsick and full of loathing for Cessnas.

"Then you know something about it," Steve says cheerfully. "Why don't you hop in and see what you think? Just take your time. I'll be inside if you have questions." For some reason it feels colder now, and Steve has come out without a jacket; I'm bundled in my L. L. Bean parka, which suddenly seems cumbersome. "Why do all airplane numbers begin with *N?*"

"*N*'s the letter for all U.S. aircraft," Steve answers. "Other countries have different first letters." I climb into N4347H.

My heart sinks. The interior of the airplane, a kind of orange crushed velour, looks like a bordello. Who could fly around in something like this? But as I settle into the left seat, the pilot's seat, my curiosity about the plane takes over, and I stare at the strange assortment of instruments in front of me. There's something that looks like a speedometer off to the left, but also something I recognize as the altimeter, with a little barometer set into the middle of it, and a black-and-blue instrument with a little airplane in the center—I seem to remember this as an "artificial horizon," though "attitude indicator" also pops into mind: I'm clearly confused about all this. And yet, staring at these instruments, I feel a surge of . . . something—of lift, of departure, of control. Each one of these devices could tell me something useful about getting off the ground, about leaving, if only I knew how to read them and respond. "It's about leaving," one of the Apollo astronauts once answered when asked to summarize the purpose of NASA; this little plane is about leaving, too, and all of a sudden I want to leave. But where would I go? What do *I* mean by "leaving" anyway? I know virtually nothing about flying, and my only experiences in small planes have been tickets to prolonged motion sickness. It's ridiculous for me to be here. Still I sit, intrigued with the instruments, gripping the control yoke in my left hand and easing it backward and forward, turning it left and right, following the motion of the ailerons as if I were banking far above this airport and its earth. I slip back into fantasy as easily as slipping into sleep, until, glancing over at the old barn, I notice Steve looking out the window. This is no dream. I am in an airplane, and I want to go: All I have to do is say yes.

I think about the control yoke in my hand and the instruments before me, telling me what I am doing and what I can and can't do; I wonder what possible difference there could be, really, between flying this plane and flying as a passenger in a commercial airliner. Wouldn't my fear still be the common denominator? Wouldn't it all end in flames, one way or another?

The cool sunlight lies around me like an answer I cannot hear. Slowly I climb over the passenger seat and out the door, shutting it so the latch clicks almost soundlessly. Steve has gone back to his paperwork in the pilots' office; I pause on the way out to thank him.

"Give us a call if you want to fly," he says. I nod, feeling as if I have once again trapped myself between fantasy and reality. I will never be able to choose flight. I wave good-bye, using my most confident smile, and leave feeling hollow. Yet for the rest of the afternoon, as Nathaniel and Lesley and I play on Duxbury Beach, I follow the flight path of all the planes in and out of Marshfield, and feel a rush of happiness when they descend behind trees onto the runway or vanish in the brilliant expanse of sky.

Chapter Two

GATE HOLD

One of my greatest fears about flying in airliners actually has nothing to do with flying. It has to do with the infamous gate hold, in which a fully loaded jet is held at the gate because of airspace congestion or bad weather. As in the air, I'm stuck in a metal tube full of strangers, but even worse, I go nowhere. If flying is hell, then the gate hold is limbo, a kind of embodied nothingness. And yet the method of the gate hold is what I turn to when some version of congestion or bad weather shows up in my life. I delay, hoping not to make the trip at all, thinking to avoid trouble by sitting still. But of course I am trying to trick myself, thinking I have some kind of security when I do not. There is no gate to my life, and even delaying is a way of moving. I stand on the brakes, hoping to keep my place, and whatever it is that's out there wraps around me like a great wind, unimpressed with my anxiety.

Two weeks have passed since I went down to Marshfield; already I have made the airport an interesting memory, a mere safe place. I think of myself from time to time sitting in the

Warrior. Huh! How did it feel? Better than that Cessna back in 1978. But there was an important difference: I wasn't on the ground very long in the Cessna. Presenting myself at the general aviation terminal in Palo Alto, California—a small, so-called portable building—I met the man who would be my flight instructor for the day: He was sixty-five and had just retired from Pan Am, where he had captained 747s on routes across the Pacific. He was an old-school pilot, exquisitely trained and gruff, and he saw me immediately as the beginning of his postretirement career. He was smart and imperceptive; he did not see that I was terrified.

"So what brings you here?" he asks as we sit down to do a half hour ground school, an introduction to the Cessna and its flight instruments.

"Oh, I've always thought about flying," I say, meaning something more like "I've always thought about crashing." Somehow that voice in the back of my head makes my more polite, public voice seem a little ineffective, so I add the clincher: "My father was a flight instructor in the navy during World War II." Among people interested in flying, this detail about my father's life always wins their favor; in some ways it is the only detail that has any such effect.

"Really?" says the instructor. "How about that? I was too. Where was he stationed?"

"Pensacola," I say, and whip out the fragments of my father's stories like pictures from a wallet: the old two-seat military trainers and the carrier landings, the forced ditchings and the practice ditching tank in which cadets were strapped into an open cockpit—an old half hulk of a plane—and fired down into a tank full of water. It was up to them to get themselves out, although two navy divers were standing by if, unable to extricate themselves, they began to drown. My father had mentioned these things as he might have talked about old love affairs that had gone wrong. Now I add my own imaginings, my extrapolations, and questions, until it seems as if the instructor and I have known each other a long time. When he notices that my hand is shaking as I fill out the information card for the Stanford Flying Club, the organization through which I am presumably going to become a pilot, I simply tell him I was up late the night before finishing a paper for one of my classes. It isn't true.

"Let me take you out to the plane," he says, motioning toward the ramp where a row of white, striped planes stands gleaming in the California sun. "We'll be in a Cessna 150," he says, pointing it out to me as we walk. "It's a basic trainer, and a great little plane. Some people think it's on the small side. But I think you might as well learn to get comfortable in a small plane. No airplane is really big, when you get right down to it. The important thing is to think of the plane as an extension of your body, as if you had wings, and so, in some ways, the smaller the better."

"An extension of my body"—I pause in front of the 150. It's a two-seat, high-wing aircraft, and my head just brushes the underside of the wing as I stand next to it. What strikes me most is how narrow it is. Peering through the side window, I see two seats that look like jump seats from a small foreign sports car. This is where the pilot and copilot sit? Somehow I remember my brother-in-law's Cessna 140 being quite a bit larger, but I was only a child then; of course it seemed bigger to me. The problem here is that this plane doesn't look anything like an extension of my body. It doesn't look like a body at all. It is hard and angular and precise, and already I don't like it. But I want to know why people decide to fly—or rather, how they do it without fear—and by the time my mind flips over to this rationale, the instructor is already untying the plane from the

27

ground, removing the heavy ropes that hold the wings and tail steady. Released from that downward tension, the plane bounces slightly, rocking in the dry, cool breeze. It wants to go—or would, if it were a body.

The instructor pops open the door on my side of the plane—the left side. "Hop in," he says cheerfully. He goes around to the other side—this plane has two doors—and hops in himself, adjusting his seat and buckling the double safety harness over his shoulders before I've even begun to figure out where the seat adjustment lever is. I'm stunned at the instrument panel: It's like looking at a textbook in a foreign language, and it's also quite high, so that—at five feet eight inches—I have some trouble seeing over the top of it. The rest of the ramp, and the other airplanes, are half hidden by the range of dials and gauges before me. How does anyone see to taxi this thing?

A chuckle draws my attention away from my side of the plane to his; he's reached behind the seat to grab my safety harness. "I'm sorry," he says. "It may take me a while to remember to start from scratch. Look"—he eases the double harness over my head so that it crisscrosses my chest, buckling into a latch between my legs. It's a little snug; I feel pulled back in my seat, as if I were already on the way to some aerobatic maneuver. I suck in my breath for a second, staring straight ahead. The instructor looks a little perplexed.

"Too tight?" he asks. "Let me loosen it a little. But you don't want it too loose, you know. And you have to tighten up when we simulate an emergency landing."

"A what?" I say.

"Oh, we'll be doing a lot of important, basic stuff today," he says. "It's okay. It's perfectly safe, and you'll like it. But the whole point is safety—knowing what to do if there's trouble. Remember yesterday."

28

How could I forget yesterday—two planes screaming in pieces down to the ground five hundred miles south of here. That's why I'm sitting in this airplane, although I can't tell him that. But maybe he's guessed.

I'm about to say something reassuring to him, but he's already pulled a checklist out of a side pocket in this tiny box of a plane; he's fiddling with knobs and adjusting dials on the instrument panel.

"For this first lesson I just want to get us into the air as fast as possible," he says. "So let me wait until next time to go over all this stuff. Basically I'm just getting the engine ready to go and tuning the radios to the right frequencies." As he says this I hear a loud pop, and the small airspace within the cockpit suddenly fills with noise—"three-seven-tango three miles out," "cleared to land, right-hand pattern," "whiskey foxtrot ready to go at three-zero." Who's talking, and what are they telling each other, and why are they so loud? The instructor turns down the volume just a little and grins at me. "We're in a pretty crowded airspace here, so we're going to have to watch for other traffic very carefully. That's one of your big jobs today—tell me if you see other planes."

"No problem," I say, relieved at having a mission of my own; but then the engine starts, and the earthquake I've always wondered about seems to emanate from the front of this small plane. The noise ricochets back and forth through the cockpit like a small war; the whole plane vibrates as if it were on the moving platform Stanford uses to simulate radical ground motion.

"Sure wants to fly, doesn't she?" he yells over the noise of the engine and the radio. "This is a tower-controlled airport, so we have to call Ground Control to get permission to taxi. Then, when we're down at the end of the runway and we're sure the plane's running okay, we'll switch to the tower frequency and get permission to take off."

Ground Control? Who are they? Where are they? Why do we have to talk to so many people? Are they all talking to each other? Does anyone know where everyone else is? Is that what happened in San Diego—sheer knowledge overload, a human and technological meltdown?

We're moving. The nose of the plane dips down slightly, although I still can't see anything closer than twenty feet, and we begin a slow turn to the left. I can feel the left rudder pedal depressing; assuming something is wrong, I try to counteract it by pressing down on the right pedal. The instructor smiles as the plane begins to straighten out, and we head directly for the general aviation building.

"See, in an airplane, you steer with your feet," he says. "On the ground, the rudder pedals are connected to the nosewheel, so when you push on the left one you go left, when you push on the right one, you go right. Pretty clever, huh? You try it."

And suddenly I'm attempting to control this loud, rattling non-beast, which begins to veer all over the ramp as I push first with my left foot, then with my right, attempting to find something like a straight route. There's a delay of about a second between the time I push the pedal and the time the plane actually begins to turn, so I'm always late: I'm beginning to do S-turns toward the taxiway. I'm sweating now: Whatever this thing is, it cannot be controlled. Or at least I can't control it.

The instructor has such a confident grin—not even directed at me, but more at himself, or at what he knows about airplanes, or at how students always respond. It's a grin about control; he's smiling because *he* knows everything is under control.

"You'll get the hang of it," he says. "Everyone does. Well,

most people do." Then, taking over, he makes a series of quick transmissions on the radio, idles the plane down the taxiway to the end of the runway, and begins what he calls a "run-up."

"We have to make sure everything's working okay," he yells over the deafening noise of the engine, which he has just cranked almost to full power. Every part of my body is trembling. He's checking the RPM gauge, he's flipping the ignition switch half on and half off ("checking the magnetos," whatever they are), he's looking to see if there's enough "vacuum pressure" and if the ammeter is functioning; he flips a switch to check the carburetor heat (the engine's going to be plenty hot pretty soon, I tell myself rather absently, beginning to detach myself from this experience; why does the carburetor need extra heat?). Then, all of a sudden, he cuts the RPMs down to idle, changes radio frequencies, and calls the tower to tell them we're ready to depart. They clear us, and we pull onto the runway.

"As we're pulling on, why don't you check above us and behind us to make sure no joker's coming in over our clearance," the instructor says as he lines the plane up with the runway centerline.

"Does that ever happen?" I ask. The motion of turning around in my seat, looking up and back, makes me feel nauseated.

"Everything happens," he says simply, opening the throttle. No time passes, and we're a quarter-way down the runway; I flatly do not believe—no, actively resist—the idea that we're lifting off. I don't want this. I know enough about airplanes now; I want to go back. But then, as in the airliners I've flown since childhood, there's a slight sensation of lift, my stomach rises in a not-unpleasant way, and I remember all those old associations of departure and escape. This feeling lasts for about two sec-

31

onds, when I suddenly realize why this is not an airliner. For one thing, it yaws wildly—a gust catches us at about a hundred feet and the tail swings hard to the left, then back to the right as the instructor tromps on the left rudder pedal. This bouncing, yawing motion, so fluid and unpredictable and unlike anything that's supposed to be scary—a roller coaster, a fun house ride—leaves me frozen in the left seat, looking straight ahead into the clear sky. What did the poet Rimbaud say about eternity? It was, he said, "the sea allied with the sun." I see the sun now off to my left, still high in the sky, but no sea—just the marshes of the San Francisco Bay, where, I recall, a fellow student went down in a Bellanca Decathalon with his girlfriend one Saturday morning a couple of years ago. The plane rolled over and crashed, landing upside down in the marsh; both of them drowned.

"You doin' okay?" the instructor shouts over the roar of the engine. Having to turn my head to look at him makes me realize how queasy I feel. He picks up on this, which surprises me. "We're not gonna be going too fast, so you can actually open your window there," he says, pointing to the latch at mid-level on the door. I didn't realize the window would open; the powerful rush of cool air makes me suddenly grateful, as if this were not entirely a hostile environment. At about the same time, the air smooths out: We're at about 2,500 feet now, heading for 3,500 feet and turning west over the Pacific coastal range, one of my favorite landscapes. Oddly enough, I've never seen it from the air, since all of my approaches to San Francisco International Airport in airliners have followed a different path. Suddenly I begin to relax a little, looking down to see the valleys and ridges, the roads I've traveled, Highway 84 and Alpine Road looping over to the sea. And there—as I look up—is the sea itself, the second half of Rimbaud's equation, running out to the horizon as if there were nothing in the world to do but watch and look and love. I'm astonished at how beautiful it is today.

"Okay, simulated engine out," the instructor says cheerfully.

"What?"

"The engine just died," he says. "First rule in a small plane is knowing where to put the plane when the engine dies. You've only got one engine; it's gonna die sometime. Now, where're you gonna put the plane?"

"You mean on the ground?"

"Of course I mean on the ground," he says, looking at me as if I were beginning to worry him. "That's where it's going anyway. You might as well have some say in the matter. Now, where're you going to put it?"

All of a sudden my favorite landscape looks extremely ominous. There are almost no flat spaces below us; rolling hills, tight narrow valleys, and ridges lined with live oaks spread out below in a deadly vista. I'm scattered. Looking eastward, I see Skyline Boulevard, but it's hard to find a stretch of it that's straight enough to serve as a runway. The plane's engine is idling, barely running, making its slight noise as a warning of the emergency that could be happening; we're losing altitude so quickly that the ground, which once seemed meditatively distant, is now rushing at us like an enormously obese, unwelcome acquaintance. Glancing off to the right, I spot something that looks like a plowed field, perhaps a vineyard, with furrows running perpendicular to us—east-west. "Right there," I say.

"That's about as good as you'd get here," he says. "Good choice. We'd have just enough room for a bank to land parallel to the furrows. Remember that—don't land across the furrows, or you're dead." Now, a couple of hundred feet above the ground, he adds the power back in, the engine roars to life, and we climb back up to the practice altitude. I'm shaking at what has just happened—at how my landscape has become my enemy, how my best guess and riskiest compromise has become my best friend, and how none of this was what I expected; but we're on to other things.

"The four fundamentals of flight," he shouts at me over the whine of the newly empowered engine and the wind rushing through my window, "are straight-and-level flight, climbs, descents, and turns. This obviously is the climb"—he points to the altimeter, which does indeed note that we are going up, and to some other device called a "vertical speed indicator," which says we're going up at a rate of about 700 feet a minute. The quantity of numbers is beginning to blur in my mind. "We did a descent a few minutes ago. The most important thing about the descent was that we had a constant glide speed. This plane won't fall out of the sky like a rock, as you just saw. It's really very safe." Why does he keep telling me this? "But to stay up as long as you can with an engine out, you need to keep that airspeed needle right on the best glide speed. Now let's level off and putter along for a while."

At just below 3,500 feet he pushes the nose over slightly and turns a control wheel in the lower front of the cockpit. "Elevator trim," he says. "This will help keep us level. Here, you try it. You've got the airplane."

All of a sudden the plane, which had seemed relatively stable in his hands, becomes a strange, bouncy, fun house car in mine. The nose begins to rise; I push it back down, but while I'm turning the trim wheel I feel as if I'm falling forward and notice I've put the plane in a shallow dive. Pulling back on the control yoke, I feel my stomach zoom toward my mouth, and as the altimeter needle passes above 3,500 once again I'm trimming the plane frantically, trying to level it out. We roller-coaster around like this for several minutes until, noticing what must have looked like something more than discomfort on my face, the instructor takes over again.

"Okay, two simple things," he says. "First, you've got a horizon out there. If you line it up so that it crosses the lower third of the windshield, you'll be pretty close to straight and level. Remember, look out of the airplane. Don't just follow the instruments. There's a world out there—use it when you're flying. The other thing is to level the plane first with the yoke, then trim it so that you just have to touch the yoke lightly to keep it level. Don't keep chasing level flight with the trim wheel or you'll be going all over the place, like you just were."

All this helpful advice is beginning to weigh on me the way the first day of any school always did—too much coming in, no place to escape to. But wasn't this supposed to be an escape? If so, maybe we should play a little. I hear myself saying this, a comment slightly out of character, as the instructor says, "Now, about turns . . ."

"Can I ask a question?"

He looks surprised. "Sure. Fire away."

"You know how in *Twelve O'Clock High*, when those B-17s are all in formation, and the German fighters come down on them from above—you know how those fighters kind of fall out of the sky sideways? How do you do that?"

"Easy," he says. "It's just a slip. Look—turn the control yoke hard to the left without using your rudder pedals."

Following his instructions, I find myself suddenly more or less on my side as the airplane simply rolls left and begins to fall out of the sky. For some reason I glance at the instrument panel; all the instruments seem to be going wild. I feel a little pressure on the control yoke, and notice the instructor pulling us back a little from the steepness of the turn. But we fall a good two or three hundred feet until he encourages me to pull the plane back to level flight. As I do, the nose pitches up suddenly, and I feel as if I've just jumped off a tall building with a bungie cord.

"Didn't want you to do more than a sixty-degree bank there," he said. "We're not legal for more than that."

"What do you mean, 'not legal'?" I ask.

"We're supposed to have parachutes aboard if we go past sixty," he says cheerfully. "FAA regs. Anyway, that was a slip. Aileron without rudder. Technically it's an uncoordinated turn, but that's how those guys fell out of the sky sideways."

We try a couple more slips, then a few so-called coordinated turns, where I push on the rudder and turn the control yoke at the same time; the plane stays more or less level in the sky. We do two complete circles—one to the left, one to the right—and then the instructor glances at his watch. "Time to go back," he says. "Why don't you take us back to Palo Alto."

For the first time I smile—the lesson is almost over, everything will be easy from here, the tension is gone. And then I realize that I feel more nauseated than I have felt in years. It comes over me in such a wave that I grip the control yoke in a sudden burst of rigidity, hoping not to vomit all over the instrument panel: What will I do? I don't even have a sweater or a jacket to throw up in. As I tighten my grasp on the yoke, the plane begins to climb, and the instructor, who's been taking in the view, suddenly looks over in uncharacteristic concern.

"You okay?" he asks.

"Not really," I say.

"Huh," he says. "Well, we went over a lot today. Just take it easy. Here, let me open a vent on my side too." I get another blast of cool air, which helps a little, but I'm not sure I'm going to be able to avoid messing up the cockpit. My embarrassment is becoming almost as acute as my fear of vomiting. But we're almost to the airport now; we've crossed Highway 101, heading into a right-hand traffic pattern that takes us at about 1,000 feet out over the southern tip of the San Francisco Bay. I can see the runway, the airport, the little planes; I'm almost home. I can breathe a little more easily. Now I only feel tired.

"Why don't you line the plane up with the runway and try to get it as close to a landing as you can," the instructor says. "I think you might be pretty good at it. I'll just take over when we get right up to the threshold."

"Okay," I hear a voice in me say. Wherever that voice is, it's no longer connected to my body, for as we reduce our power, add flaps to steepen our descent, and slow our airspeed, I find that I actually cannot line the plane up with the runway. In fact, I seem to see two runways. Lining up with one, I shake my head and see the other, not right next to it but about 10 feet apart—where am I? I take my right hand away from the throttle for a second to wipe my forehead, and in that moment I feel the plane come firmly into line, all the controls clear and precise; looking over at the instructor, I find him glancing at me repeatedly as he brings the plane into line with the runway a few seconds before we actually touch down. He says nothing for a few seconds, staring straight ahead, then tries one more tack.

"Why don't you slow it down," he says as we roll down the runway, approaching the marshes at the other end of the field at what seems to me a rather fast clip. I press hard on the tops of the rudder pedals, remembering as if by some panic reaction that those are the brakes once we're on the ground. The nose dips down; the plane begins to wobble left and right.

"Not so hard, not so hard," the instructor cautions. "We don't want to do a ground loop." But by that time my strange, erratic efforts have slowed us down, and I push on the left rudder pedal to ease us off the runway. I turn too soon, and we almost go off onto the grass, but the instructor's ready right foot keeps us just barely on the paved surface, and soon we're back at the ramp near the general aviation terminal. I sit in the plane for a second, taking a deep long breath, as the instructor slips out and comes around to open my door from the outside.

"That was a pretty damn good first lesson," he says, looking me straight in the eye. Is that why he wanted to come around to the other side of the plane—so I'd still be sitting in the pilot's seat, as if I were actually the pilot and he were the knowing outsider, intent on reassuring me? I'm thinking too much about this, I think, shaking my head and remembering how queasy I still feel. Thanking him, I unlatch my seat belt and step unsteadily out of the plane. He reaches in behind me to gather the Flying Club folder he brought with him, along with a book in which he records the time we actually spent flying—nine tenths of one hour. It seemed like two or three hours to me.

"I need to ask you a question," I say. He pauses from checking various numbers and waits, somehow a little too expectantly.

"Toward the end of the lesson, well—you know—I didn't feel so great," I say, feeling stupid that I can't actually bring myself to tell him I was one yaw away from barfing all over his beautiful plane. He looks at me for a few seconds, taking me in more than he has so far today, trying to gauge what to say.

"You know, some guys, they just bring a plastic bag up with them," he says. "It all depends on what you want to do. The fact is, you did really good airwork for someone who's never flown a plane before. You did good airwork for someone who *has* flown a plane before. Think about it. I'll see you next week."

"Thanks," I say, thinking of a little plastic bag. I shake his hand. As I begin to walk away, he calls after me. "You ought to stop at the flight shop on the way out and pick up a logbook," he says. "You're going to need to keep track of your flight time."

"Okay," I yell back. "Take it easy." I feel a funny numbness in my chest, and my legs are trembling the way they do when I've been walking or bicycling too long. Without much thinking, I make my way to the flight shop, buy a logbook, and throw it in the back of my car. When I get back to my apartment, I crawl into bed and stay there through dinnertime and well into the evening. Later, feeling safer, I step out onto the patio to look at the stars. They are reassuringly far away, and the live oak and laurel trees at the edge of the yard are reassuringly close; this is the earth. I do not feel at all like eating. I crawl back into bed and sleep until morning, when I awake in a rush of gladness at being alive. My nausea, however, does not depart for two more days.

About a week later, at my more or less weekly dinner with my mother and father, I mention my first lesson.

"Going up again?" my father asks. He works hard to be nonchalant, from which I detect some degree of astonishment. I was the frightened child, the too-good child, not the one who took up flying.

"No," I say. "I felt too sick."

A long pause.

"How did you avoid getting sick when you were in the navy?" I ask him.

"I never got sick."

Once again our conversation begins to disintegrate on the shoals of our mutually exclusive personalities. But then, surprisingly, he asks a question.

"What exactly did you do on this first lesson of yours?"

I describe the emergency procedures, the climbs and descents and turns, the slips like the ones in *Twelve O'Clock High*, and my futile attempt to line the plane up with the runway. My father's eyebrows rise slightly with each detail, until his expression crosses the border from interest to alarm.

"He did all that with you? No wonder you felt sick. We didn't do all that with navy cadets on the first lesson. Goddammit," my father swears, calling on some emotion that seems to me to come out of nowhere, "you've got to know how to judge your students and ease them into it. Flying's no simple thing. It's not easy. It can be scary as hell. You have to be gentle." He goes back to his eating.

I stare at him for a moment. What did my father know about being gentle? He was in many ways a hard man, given to long silences and sudden rages; he laid down the law in our family, and when my brother and sister transgressed his rules he did not ask them about their motives; he punished them. Few words passed between him and them that were not angry or sullen, and few words passed between him and me at all. Even when present, he was distant, an absence waiting to happen. What could he be trying to tell me now? What he said was straightforward; what it meant was not. Although I roll his words over and over in my mind for the next few days, I cannot really make sense of them.

II.

My dream of flying—or of being freed from fear, the fear of my own absurd death—imploded under the loudness, discomfort, and complexity of this first effort, but there was another dream before this, and as I stay away from Marshfield, blurring my memories of sitting in the Warrior and wobbling around in the Cessna, I begin to have flashbacks of that dream, as if it were a puzzle I had shoved into a back shop of my mind and left as a jumble, not knowing it might reassemble itself. I was in high school; I was in a car with my parents; I was holding a model airplane. But that made no sense: I had been too old for model airplanes in high school. The plane was blue and white, an old high-wing thing, and it fit in the palm of my hand. I roll the plane around in my mind as if it were a hologram, and the dream falls into place.

In September 1972, just before I began my junior year of high school, my parents and I were coming back from a trip to Lake Tahoe. While they sat in the front seat of our old Chevrolet Chevelle discussing the miles of almond orchards and other safe topics, I sat in the back, buried under the weight of my own reflections.

By the end of the previous year I had understood that I was going to be one of the students tracked for "success" in the school, by which I knew I was destined for advanced placement classes and Ivy League college applications. Somehow this was not simply because I was smart but because, as usual, I was good. At the same time I was learning more about goodness. To be good was to meet or exceed other people's expectations; it was to live out their dreams for you in your own life. When, every now and then, I confronted this reality of my behavior, I was not really surprised. I was simply astonished at how I excelled at it. I could not exactly frame any words of discontent or disturbance, partly because I was doing so well and partly because, when I made other people happy, they liked me; I was not lonely, and I did not really have to think about who I was. I was what they wanted me to be; that was enough. This was true even in a religious sense, when I went to Christian Science Sunday school and learned that I was not what I thought I was. I was not material, but spiritual. I was not bad, mad, angry, variable in love or hope, but pure, perfect, and eternal. I was good. The goodness my religion reinforced in me was inseparable from my sense that other people dictated what goodness was, and that I would have to find and follow those dictates in order to be good—to be a decent part of the human community.

The problem was that the stakes kept getting higher. To continue to demonstrate my academic virtue, I realized that I would have to begin the round of standardized tests that constitute the statistical antechamber to distinguished colleges—the PSAT, the Preliminary Scholastic Aptitude Test, and then the SAT. Although the PSAT was not required for college admission, it was the yardstick by which National Merit Scholars were chosen, and virtually all of my friends were planning to take it in October. I, too, had signed up for it, but unlike most of my friends I feared it deeply. I would wake up in the middle of the night, not afraid that I would not get a good score but afraid of the whole idea—of questions that could be answered with someone else's calculated multiple choices, of scores that would say publicly something about my intellectual dexterity, of people who would begin to look at the numbers I racked up instead of at me. I had nightmares of computer-read answer sheets, in which the little penciled dots became silhouettes of me, with nothing in the center. I began to think I had been critically wrong about what I thought I was supposed to be doing in school. I had thought I was to read the works of Salinger and Dostoyevski, to learn about the formation of labor unions and what they did for the working poor, to figure out retrograde motion in the heavens, to write, to place myself in a world of knowledge and possibility. And perhaps this was true; but in a narrower, more immediate reality, I was supposed to demonstrate intelligence in a way that would be quantifiable and marketable. And my teachers, the ones who had urged me so strongly to follow my instincts and find myself in my work as a writer and photographer, could not stop this process; even as they urged me to be different, they were committed to the whole routine. All they could do was tell me that it wouldn't matter as much as I thought; that tests and test scores and college admissions forms couldn't harm me. And yet I saw what happened to the seniors who applied to Harvard or Stanford and didn't get in—the sense of disappointment, of having been diminished as human beings—and I knew that somewhere under this elaborate system was an enormous, harmful lie, and I could not get to it because I could not really explain or even admit it to myself. I was trapped in my goodness and my determination to succeed at what seemed fundamentally pointless.

On the trip back from Tahoe, my parents decided to stop at the Nut Tree, a strange California institution off Highway 80. It had started in the 1930s as a roadside stand, selling almonds and other produce garnered from the Central Valley farmlands that stretched away from the road to a fecund infinity. Over decades it had grown into a hybrid in which something like an upscale Howard Johnson's was grafted onto a miniature Disneyland. The place had an enormous parking lot and a narrow-gauge railroad that took visitors to and from the main restaurant and gift shop, as well as on a general tour of the property. It even had an airport, so that people en route to and from Tahoe could zip in, eat in the main restaurant or any of several take-out stands, and head back into the skies. There was a small amusement park for children, with clowns and—it seems in memory at least— some animals, although since I always reacted to the place as if it were a circus I cannot be sure I actually saw a clown leading a pony there. It might simply have been an appropriate delusion. My parents—or at least my father—found the place vivid and quaint at the same time.

I ordered a milkshake for dinner and left the table as soon as I could. But then, because my parents were still eating, I went for a walk around the arcade of shops. In the gift shop, as I moved idly among the Nut Tree mugs and the pictures of How It Was In The Old Days, I came upon a shelf of small airplanes—presumably for the children of the pilots, to give them something to play with in the back seat of the Cessna or Piper while Mom and Dad were trying to navigate back to San Carlos or Modesto. These were no cheap little generic things; they were scale models of noteworthy planes, handsomely boxed, with brief histories of the aircraft and its most celebrated moments (stacks of the *Spirit of St. Louis* and Amelia Earhart's Lockheed Electra took up about half the shelf). What caught my eye was a funny white plane with a blue stripe from engine to tail. A high-wing plane, it had an oversized radial engine in the front, a heavy-looking rounded tail, and big tires on heavy struts. I turned the box over to read the description on the bottom. This was a 1947 De Havilland Beaver, officially a "light utility transport" used primarily in rugged country, particularly Alaska. A bush plane. Although later versions came with a turboprop, the earlier ones had a Pratt and Whitney piston engine and ferried people and gear up and down Alaska from Juneau to Whitehorse to Fairbanks to Barrow to Anchorage and out to the Aleutians. Many of the planes were fitted with floats and skis to land where there was no runway or, for that matter, no land at all.

I turned the box back over, looking at the plane. It was about five inches from nose to tail. The wide, long, white wing gleamed in the fluorescent light of the gift shop. I had not thought about flying for many years. I had even stopped asking my father to tell stories of his exploits as a flight instructor, because the stories came more haltingly now and in truncated versions, as if they were too far back—and perhaps too power-ful—to have any real bearing on the present. But I wanted this airplane. And I did not know why.

When I paid for it, pulling the lone five-dollar bill from my pocket and scrounging around for twenty-five additional cents to cover the tax, I walked out with something magical, and I felt happy, the way I used to feel at Christmas when no one stormed out of the room in a rage. My parents were just coming out of the restaurant, and I must have seemed to them suddenly like the ten-year-old boy they remembered, the one who col-lected Matchbox cars and G.I. Joes; they walked into a time warp.

"Whatcha got there?" my dad said.

"A De Havilland Beaver," I said.

"I didn't know you still liked toys," my mother said. It was an absentminded comment, not judgmental, but a little con-fused.

"Well, I just saw it," I said, "and . . ."

"You always liked souvenirs, even back when we used to travel in New Jersey," said my mother, who was rapidly heading somewhere else in her mind. I was beginning to feel as if I were shrinking.

"A Beaver, huh?" my father said. "Let me take a look." He glanced at the plane, then flipped the box over. "Great plane," he said. "A lot of these up north. Really tough. You could get in and out of anywhere with one of these. Haven't thought about a Beaver in a long time." He handed it back to me with no other comment, yet his words meant that somehow this had been a good choice. I wanted more.

"Did you ever fly one?" I asked.

"Me? No—never did," he said. "Come on, let's go. We've got a ways to go, and it's late."

That was it—a classic father-son conversation, starting in a wilderness, going nowhere. But I had the plane. And as I sat in the back of the darkened car, holding it and flying it back and forth at a politely low altitude, so that my parents wouldn't notice what juvenile things I was up to, I realized that I wanted to be a bush pilot. It was an absurd realization, because I knew nothing about flying and very little about Alaska; my only exposure to the country was William O. Douglas's *My Wilderness*, which I read as solace during moments of misery in seventh grade at Westtown School in Pennsylvania. Westtown had been an earlier experience of academic overkill, a place where to be loved I had to be good, which meant I had to perform better than anyone else; I was sick much of the year there. But in moments of panic I used to creep down to the lower level of the library, where the books on America happened to be, and read Douglas's accounts of the Washington coast and Brooks Range in Alaska. I would never go there, I knew, but I could at least know that places existed where people lived in close contact with something more than a book. The irony of this line of thinking escaped me, but now—at the age of fifteen—I thought I remembered something about a route from Anchorage to Fairbanks via the Susitna Creek, a 200-mile notch between mountains rising to 18,000 feet, and I looked at the De Havilland Beaver waiting in my hand. Could it take me there? Could I take it there? And what was there beyond Fairbanks—or south or east of Anchorage? I had heard of Lake Louise; there must be a seaplane base there, and Beavers were a snap on floats.

I would never be a bush pilot. I was too attuned to my prescribed future to confuse that fantasy with anything like reality. Yet, in some imaginary parallel universe, I felt so strongly that I already was a pilot that the Beaver stayed on my desk for months, through the PSAT and the SAT and the college applications, hovering at the head of my pads of lined paper as I began writing poetry and experimenting with stories and essays. Like a talisman from a time of crisis, it lost its magical quality as the future became actual: I fell in and out of love, I stayed in school, I devoted myself to poetry and to the work of writers I admired. I began to pull away from Christian Science; I also fled back to it in moments of terror or guilt. These experiences aimed me from high school toward college, and whatever had caught my attention that day on the way back from Tahoe receded into some farther valley of my range of fantasies. If I thought I was a pilot, I was also much more clearly a poet, and I could prove my identity as a poet in ways I could not as a pilot. By the end of my senior year in high school the Beaver was simply a toy. I did not need it or the escape it connoted. It was, I told myself, a delayed reach back to childhood, a last grasp at something I had not earned or wanted or, for that matter, deserved. Sometime over the next year or so it disappeared, as things do when they lose too much meaning, and though I occasionally thought about it, I never found it again.

III.

*A*nd yet I see that plane now, in February 1990, even more clearly than I saw the Cessna from the Stanford Flying Club as I turned away from it in 1978 and vowed I would never fly in small planes again. What is it about the current moment that brings me back to that darkened rear seat of the car, my parents for the time being well separated from me in the front seat, while I held in my hand the metal bird that would carry me away?

Under the pressure of great fear or love one becomes, at least for a time, a different person; the self that begins to collapse under the strain of the moment actually compresses into something harder, more striated, more variable, and no one knows who will emerge from the crisis, no matter how much that person may resemble the former one. In the car with my parents in 1972, I slipped into a dream, not of escape, but of a self more lively, more attuned to adventure, more literally breath-taking. On this dream I skidded through my fear of the academic and social expectations that might have crushed me, and when I found myself stronger than I thought, I let the dream go; it was an expedience, not a fundamental change in who I was, I told myself, and all I had really needed was a set of imaginary possibilities to comfort me. But the dream of that self was not an expedience, and although I left it behind it did not leave me; it knew how skillfully I devoted my life to imprisoning myself in roles that were too narrow and upright, too rigid and duty-bound, to let me live. It knew how often I died each day, and why therefore I was so afraid of death.

That dream is here again, sailing back and forth before me like a bush plane waiting for the right moment to land, and I watch it, scared once again. Between it and me lies a chasm of disaster, or rather disasters—fears of catastrophes I can name, terrors of airplanes and crashes and claustrophobia but also vaguer terrors of letting myself go, of losing something and perhaps—or perhaps not—finding something else. Evading this moment of self-confrontation without losing it entirely requires an almost instinctive story, a way of seeing what I can't see head-on, and the story itself takes the form of a crash: I am afraid that I have already crashed, that I am the pilot on the ground with darkness coming on, frost forming on my face as the search plane swings back and forth, lower and lower, unable to find a trace of my wreckage and, I suddenly realize, unable to land. How long will it be before the pilot realizes the impossibility of rescuing me and flies away? There will be no more dream then.

On such a night in December 1938—where had I heard this story?—Sheldon Simmons, one of the few Alaskan pilots whose exploits were news in the Lower Forty-eight, flew away in a fury from the cargo ship *Patterson*, which had run aground that day near Cape Fairweather, about 130 miles northwest of Juneau. Simmons had made his reputation by ferrying passengers and cargo in weather that had grounded other pilots; he had made a practice of rescuing downed and injured fliers and their passengers, and the Coast Guard called on him regularly when the worst happened. This time even Simmons seemed fated to lose, however. The eighteen survivors of the wreck of the *Patterson* were huddled on a spit of land near the cape, while three Coast Guard cutters rode the high seas nearby, helpless to assist. Simmons air-dropped food and other supplies to the survivors, but could find no place to land; the terrain around the cape was rocky and heavily forested, and the waves that kept the cutters at bay also prevented him from attempting a water landing. For three days he went back and forth over the site, knowing the men below risked death by exposure, fuming at the limits of terrain and equipment that seemed to leave him no options.

Gradually, however, he realized that, at high tide, the biggest waves crashing ashore made a kind of lagoon that lasted a few minutes before subsiding. If he could touch down in a float plane just after the wave hit, he might be able to deliver a guide to the survivors and rescue the injured men. Picking up a guide, flying back to the wreck, Simmons swung low back and forth, getting his timing right, touching down just as a wave rolled across the land and became a lagoon whose life span was about as long as it would take him to run from one end of it to the other.

49

The other men loaded the two injured survivors aboard Simmons's Lockheed Vega as another wave formed and broke, and when it spilled itself into a lagoon the grounded Vega floated free. In that instant Simmons gave the plane full power, stepping it up onto the surface of the shallow water and knowing that any miscellaneous boulder or tree trunk would destroy the plane, his passengers, and him. He was in the air in a few seconds, free and clear, heading back to Juneau, and no one died.

He was not related to me, at least as far as I know, but his story came to mind as I thought of the pilot out there who could not reach me, the pilot I had invented for myself so many years ago. There were limits, and there was luck; you might die, or live miserably in a kind of death, but you might also see a pattern, a break in the waves, a lagoon, and touch down to rescue injured souls. But first you had to fly.

I head back to Marshfield one Thursday in mid-February after a morning of teaching at MIT. It's a brilliantly sunny day, and as I leave Route 3 for Route 139, the road into town, I'm startled at the clarity of things—trees etched hard against a luminous sky, ice catching the light like small beacons on the marshes, the North River making its dark way to the sea. Marshfield is pretty and sad, a place the collapsing Massachusetts economy has hit hard; Route 139 is lined with buildings for lease, and places that have an old-time look to them, like Feinberg's clothing store, are shutting down. Yet as I pass the main intersections in the town and head out toward the hardware store, Papa Gino's Pizza, and the McDonald's, the marshes come back into view and the landscape seems to widen and shrink at the same time: The scale goes from up to out, and I sense the ocean nearby as the terrain eases down to flatness, making even the buildings seem smaller and more provisional. A plane—a Piper Warrior—goes by overhead. Shivering a little, I watch for the brown-shingled Airport Sub Shop, which marks the turn for Old Colony Lane.

Through breaks in the low scrub I can see the hangars, and as I come around a slight bend the red barn stands out against the sky like some 3-D picture in an old Disney Viewmaster. It's all here, all still the same. The sign still says "SHORELINE AVIATION," the Piper Tomahawk still sits near the fence along with the old Cessna 180, the taxiways and runway extend out beyond my line of sight. Nothing has changed; there has been no delay, no gate hold; I have all the time in the world. I sit in the car for a few minutes, listening to an old favorite song on the radio, then go inside.

Steve comes in at about the same time through the back door, the door to the ramp and the planes. He's carrying his David Clark headset and talking to someone who listens and laughs—a student, probably, the one he's just come down with. Their rapport is easy, filled with mutual pleasure. Suddenly it seems a long time since I've been here, and I feel unaccountably angry.

Steve notices me, remembers I've been in before, and waves across the room; he's not done with the student yet. They're going over something—I can hear things like "slow flight" and "approach stall," and figure I'd better leave them alone. I want to talk to Steve, although I don't really have anything to say. What will I say? Why am I here anyway? The question jars me, and I turn as if to leave, not having an answer: I feel ashamed. But a couple of people are gathered at the large ledger book on the main counter, where people sign up to fly at various times with various instructors. I go over for a look. The vertical columns represent different airplanes, recorded according to the last three digits of their call numbers—"949," which someone is calling "niner-four-niner"; "47H" and "50F,"

which come out as "four-seven-hotel" and "five-zero-foxtrot."
Even letters and numbers have a slightly foreign sound here.
The horizontal columns represent times of day: Shoreline opens
at eight A.M. and schedules pilots all day and through the night
if someone needs a night flight. I lean over the counter to look
at the entries, while a woman with short, graceful hair and lively
eyes confers with one of the other fliers about times.

"Want to schedule a flight?" she says to me. I realize I've
been staring at the book for a couple of minutes. I laugh mirth-
lessly.

"Oh, I don't know," I say. "I'm just kind of curious about
flying."

"This is the right place to be curious," she says. "We get
people who just come in and sit over there on the couch,
watching the planes." She turns away to photocopy something
behind the counter.

"So what's an intro flight?" I ask, trying to be conversa-
tional. She's busy.

"It's just a half hour flight with an instructor," she says, her
back to me. "You spend a half hour on the ground doing a
preflight inspection of the plane, then you fly—go over fundamentals, get a feel for it. We try not to do too much all at once."

I think about my first lesson in the Cessna twelve years ago.
This woman seems so reasonable, so . . . normal.

"Do you fly?" I ask.

"Oh, yeah," she says, as if it were nothing. "My husband
owns the place, and we fly all around—the kids, too. I'm working on my private license now."

"Hey there." Steve has wandered over, and flipping the
schedule book around—I've been looking at it upside down—
he looks over his time. "Want to go up sometime?"

Gate hold. What do I want to do? Why am I here if I don't want to fly?

"Sure," I say. "But it makes me a little nervous."

Steve's smile is luminous. "It makes almost everyone nervous at first," he says. "I don't have any time today, but why don't you go over the book and pick a time that sounds good. I'll be here. Talk to you later." He heads into one of the offices at the side of the building, and I realize how much I still feel on the outside. Not only have I not committed myself to a flight; I'm not even sure why I'm here. Steve won't talk me into anything I don't want to do. He's clearly not out to drum up business. Suddenly I notice the place seems busier; two other men dressed like instructors—black pants, white shirts, black ties—have come in with students, and someone else seems to be arranging to take one of the planes up by himself. The point here is not to stay on the ground but to leave; leaving means figuring things out, learning, going on. Staying on the ground is just . . . nothing, is just waiting to be picked up by a pilot who can't see you and isn't even sure you've crashed.

The schedule book is still turned toward me. I look into next week: Steve is free all day Monday.

"I think maybe I'll schedule an intro flight for Monday afternoon," I say much too quietly to the woman behind the counter.

"What time?"

We settle on two, she writes it in, and I'm back in the car, driving home as if I were driving on two-by-fours over the Grand Canyon. I'm jumpy and astonished and caught between memories and dreams.

IV.

Although sunny, Monday is a wildly windy day, and the flight is canceled. I'm relieved, and yet I schedule another one, unable to break the habit or back down. This time it's the next-to-last day of February—a week away. I have too much time to think about it, and protect myself by being more the person I have become—the good teacher, the good father. I spend lavish amounts of time commenting on students' essays, I hold extra office hours, I take Nathaniel to the Science Museum, I make dinner, I wash the dishes. It's good to be needed, to be in a predictable space with predictable habits; I'm safe here. And yet, in moments when the thought of Marshfield catches me by surprise, I'm not so much afraid of flying as plunged suddenly into despair about my life.

February 27 dawns gloomy and cold, with a thick cloud cover; I sigh again in relief. Whatever it is that's going on inside of me, at least I won't have to face the air today. But I go on down to Marshfield anyway, in part because I know it's safe: I can show up without fear of having to fly. What I don't realize is that a cloudy day doesn't necessarily mean trouble from a pilot's point of view. I'm shocked when I drive down Old Colony Lane and see a plane taking off into the gloom. Then I know I'm done for: I've set myself up for this one.

Steve is dashing out the ramp door as I arrive; he turns to talk to me for a second. "I've got a check-ride today," he says in a hurry, "a flying test. You're going to go up with Larry—he's in the office there. Have a good flight!" Steve's out the door.

I wander over to the office and peer in. A man with tightly curled, reddish hair is staring intently at a book of flying rules; I can see "AIM/FAR 1990" on the spine, which turns out to be an acronym for "Airman's Information Manual/Federal Aviation

Regulations." Aim far. The man looks up, smiles slightly—nothing like Steve's smile.

"You're Tom?" He is serious, studious. I nod.

"I'll be taking you up today," he says, getting up from the desk to shake my hand. "My name's Larry. I guess you've already talked to Steve. Sorry about the switch. He had to do a check-ride today."

"That's okay," I say, not meaning it.

"We'll be in five-zero-foxtrot," he says, walking over to the rear of the counter to pull out a blue binder. "This is the manual, with some required papers and the keys. Let's head out to the plane; we'll do a preflight and go over the instruments, and I'll tell you a little about this book. You ever flown before?"

"Once," I say. "Well, twice, but the first time was a long time ago."

"That's okay," he says, clearly meaning it. "It's good to have a little experience. But we'll still start from scratch."

"Well—" I want to explain. My stomach is twisting around despite the Pepto-Bismol I took an hour ago.

"Let's go," he says, and we head out the ramp door into the cold light of a Marshfield February. At the edge of the ramp, a Piper Warrior with the call sign N2150F—"five-zero-foxtrot"—rocks slightly in the chilling breeze.

Chapter Three

GOING UP

*A*s we walk out to five-zero-foxtrot, I hear crunching under-foot and realize I'm walking through a patch of ice. Ice—I didn't even think about that. Sensations seem to be coming into my head from some slightly distant place. A couple of hundred yards away, the runway looks clear of ice and snow, although plowed snow is piled in a hundred frozen hummocks along the edge. The taxiways are clear; there are patches of ice on the ramp, and just beyond the barn the other two Piper Warriors hover over a sheen of icy snow, their wheels half hidden as if caught in a winter lake. I'm freezing.

Larry has been talking as we've walked; now he stops for me.

"Anything wrong?"

"No, no," I reassure him quickly—no cracks in my facade.

"Steve told me you came down once before to see what the plane is like, so let's treat this more like a first lesson than an intro flight, at least on the ground," he says rapidly, confi-dently. We're on the right side of the fuselage; Larry steps up on the wing and, popping open the door, reaches inside to tug at something on the floor between the seats. This makes the flaps—metal rectangles on the trailing edge of the wing—drop well down below the wing.

"We're going to do a preflight," he says, coming back down to ground level. "That means we're going to go all around the airplane, look at all its systems, make sure it's safe to fly. There's a right way of doing it, and you do it the same way every time. It becomes a habit, like brushing your teeth."

Larry pulls a long, clear plastic tube out of the pocket of his nylon flight instructor's jacket.

"This is a fuel tester," he says. "But first—before we look at anything else—what do you think we need to make sure this plane can fly?"

Trick question; I'll bite. "Fuel," I say.

"No," says Larry. "Paper. We need lots of paper. Specifically, we need an airworthiness certificate in the aircraft, a registration, a radio operator's license, and an operating manual with weight and balance information for this particular aircraft."

Oh, no, here it comes; my mind is beginning to spin, and we haven't even left the ground. I'd forgotten how complicated flying is. For some odd reason I flash suddenly on the times when I was a Boy Scout—once for three months when I was twelve, and again a couple of years later for four months. What drove me away both times was what I came to call "Boy Scout knowledge"—a mishmash of nature lore, knot tying, camp making, meteorology, and assorted ritual skills that seemed to me largely contrived and pointless. Was flying going to be Boy Scout knowledge? I look annoyed, and Larry, who's clearly in a businesslike mood, signals a pause with his hands.

"Listen, there's a lot to learn, it's true, but it's not that hard. For example, all that stuff I just told you? How are you gonna remember it? You're not, right? Sure you are. Just think A.R.-R.O.W.—airworthiness, registration, radio license, operating manual, weight and balance. Arrow, arrow, arrow. See? Now you already know what the FAA says you have to have in the plane." He motions me over to the right side of the fuselage.

"We always start the pre-flight at the same place," he says. "I like to start here because it's where you just happen to be after you set the flaps. First we check the flaps to make sure the cotter pin's in the main linkage." He points to a rod extending from somewhere in the wing and attached to a bracket on the flap hinge. The cotter pin is there; we're okay so far. Larry also presses up against the lower edge of the flaps to make sure they don't accidentally retract. We go slowly around the plane after that, checking all the screws in the aileron hinges ("What's an aileron do again?" I ask Larry. "I'll show you in a few minutes," he says), making sure the metal skin of the wing is not cracked or bent or dented. Like most planes, the Warrior holds fuel in the wings, so we open the cap on the top of the wing to check the fuel.

"See that little tab in there?" Larry asks. I look in and see bluish fuel brushing the top of a small metal tab a few inches down from the top.

"Each wing tank holds twenty-five gallons," he says. "Leaving aside about two gallons riding around in the engine and the fuel lines, you get twenty-four usable gallons of fuel in each wing, or forty-eight total. We use hundred-octane low-lead; that's blue. If you see anything other than blue fuel in the tank, tell one of us. The tab marks the seventeen-gallon level—means you've used about seven or eight gallons. We try not to let the fuel fall below tab level."

Each wing, as it turns out, also has a fuel strainer on the

bottom. The strainer looks like a little upside-down *T*, and Larry presses against the *T* with his fuel tester. A stream of pale blue fuel runs out; a couple of little bubbles float to the bottom.

"That's water," he says. "That's what we're looking for. You want that out of your tanks before you take off, obviously. Water condenses inside the tanks, especially when it's cold, and sinks to the bottom. We strain it out here." He tosses the three or four ounces of fuel onto the ramp, fills the tube again, and looks. It's clear; no water.

As we keep going around the plane, checking the engine cylinders for cracks around the spark plugs and checking the oil level, draining the engine fuel strainer, checking the fuel in the other wing, examining the brakes, I feel caught in some odd drift or eddy between this lesson, which has scarcely begun, and my first one in Palo Alto. There the emphasis was on flying; the instructor wanted me in the air. I was terrified. And I'm not much less terrified now, despite my appearance, but there's something about Larry's approach that's comforting. The airplane is not an albatross—ugly mystery on the ground, elegant performer in the air; it is a complex machine made to perform reliably (I tell myself) as long as the pilot understands its possibilities and limits. There's something even more than knowledge at stake here, something like intimacy: In each test or check Larry does, I sense an ease, as if he were coming back into conversation with a friend he hadn't seen in a while. This is not Boy Scout knowledge, but something else—a rapport, a way of reassuring oneself.

It's easier to think this way while standing on the ground, outside the plane. We're back to the door after having examined the vertical stabilizer, the rudder, and something called a "stabilator"—the combined horizontal stabilizer and elevator on a Warrior, the device that helps the plane go up and down. "Hop in," says Larry. The two worst words in my current vocabulary. I comply.

Sitting inside the plane is like sitting inside a very small iceberg. I chafe my hands trying to warm them, and my parka seems to fill up half the plane. My breath forms small cirrus clouds around my head. Larry climbs in, forming his own clouds on his side of the plane, and pulls the door shut. The door has two latches—one on the side, one at the top—and each shuts with a distinctive click. I feel locked in. Larry sighs and looks at the instruments.

"They were supposed to preheat the engine for us," he says grumpily, "but they didn't. So this is going to be, not a cold start, but a *really* cold start. Let's go over the instruments for a second, though."

Some of these I already know, like the altimeter and the airspeed indicator; as Larry points out others, I remember suddenly what they looked like in 1978 when I was daring the Cessna to fall out of the sky. But now Larry is priming the engine, pulling a little handle out and pushing it in four times; the sound of gas spurting somewhere in front of us drifts back through the cockpit. Then Larry begins to speak the language of the checklist, and things start to happen.

"Master switch, on." Larry flicks the red switch in the middle of the instrument panel and a whirring sound fills the cockpit. I jump; he looks at me for a second. "That's just the sound of the gyros spooling up," he says. "Fuel pump on, mixture rich, two shots of throttle, throttle one-quarter-inch-open." He leans over to my side of the plane, puts the key in the ignition switch below my control yoke, and flips open a little plastic slot in my window. It's getting to be a very crowded airplane.

"Clear prop," he yells so loudly my ears ring. He looks around; no one is near the plane. He turns the key. The propeller begins to turn; the starter motor's *whaa-whaa-whaa-whaa-whaa* is almost as loud as Larry's yell. This is a noisy, cold, cramped, crazy place. I want to get out.

But the engine does not start. It doesn't start the first time, nor the second nor the third time Larry cranks the starter; it doesn't show the slightest interest in starting. Finally, after fiddling with the controls a few times, Larry gives up in disgust.

"Flooded," he says. "We'll just have to wait a few minutes."

In that moment I, who wanted so much to flee a brief time ago, begin for some reason to settle in. Everything happened so quickly in 1978; I could scarcely stop to think. But here, when it looked once again as if knowledge and power were going to spin beyond my grasp, and I was going for a ride in a device I could not understand or control, a little glitch came my way and brought a useful pause. I notice I haven't really been breathing for a couple of minutes; I feel faint. Larry begins to tell me about what Steve is probably doing on his test, his check-ride. Steve is getting the most advanced certificate there is, the air transport pilot's license. This is what airline pilots are required to have. Larry tells me he got his ATP a while back. Somehow, despite the guy back in Palo Alto, I didn't realize I was going to be flying with people who were qualified to fly airliners.

Some sun has been working its way through the overcast, and now—for the first time—I look outside the cockpit. The ice gleams brilliantly in streams of light like pale waterfalls from the sky. I like it here.

"Let's try again." Larry goes through the starting routine again, and this time the engine catches, chokes, thunk-thunk-thunks, climbs smoothly to its heavy idle throb. In a few minutes we've made it out to the run-up ramp, where Larry revs the engine up to 2,000 RPM, just as my first instructor did years ago. Now, however, Larry is yelling explanations above the roar.

"The engine has two magnetos, left and right," he says, pointing to the ignition switch, which instead of a car's "off-accessory-on" positions has "off-left-right-on." "In a car you have a distributor, and one spark plug per cylinder. In a plane like this you have two plugs per cylinder, connected to two separate magnetos. That way, if one magneto goes, you still have power."

"What's a magneto?" I yell.

"Engine-driven electromagnet," he yells back. I'm about to say "What?" but he adds, "The engine turns a magnet inside two coils which makes electricity which gets sent to the plugs. Got it?"

Before I can nod, he's on to other things. "We've got a vacuum gauge over here"—he points to the right side of the instrument panel—"to tell us whether there's enough vacuum or suction to drive the gyros. Should be a little above five inches of mercury." It is. We go through the ammeter, the annunciator panel—which lets us know if there's trouble with the alternator, the oil pressure, or the vacuum pressure—and the carburetor heat. Then Larry hands me the microphone.

"We want to make sure this works. So press the button on the side and say, 'Marshfield unicom, Warrior two-one-five-zero-foxtrot needs a radio check, please.'"

"What's Marshfield unicom?"

"A unicom is the radio at an uncontrolled field, which is what we are because we don't have a control tower," Larry explains patiently. "Someone in the red barn will answer you."

With some stuttering, I say what Larry tells me; it's the first time I've operated an aircraft radio. A voice comes back to me: "Five-zero-foxtrot, you're loud and clear." "Huh," I say to myself; at least I've learned one thing. But looking up, I see that

Larry has taxied us to the edge of the runway; what's about to happen is what I've been telling myself would not happen. I freeze.

Larry nudges me. "Now say, 'Marshfield traffic, Warrior two-one-five-zero-foxtrot back-taxiing for departure on runway two-four, Marshfield.' "

"What's back-taxiing?"

"It's what we're doing now," he yells as we turn the plane toward the short end of the runway and head that way. "Most useless thing in the world is runway behind you," he says. "We go down to the very end, turn around, and start our takeoff roll there."

I begin. "Marshfield unicom—"

"Marshfield *traffic*," Larry yells. "The unicom doesn't care where you are, but someone coming in for a landing might."

I begin again. "Marshfield traffic, Warrior two-one-five-zero-foxtrot is—" I draw a blank.

"Back-taxiing," Larry yells.

"Back-taxiing for takeoff on the runway, um . . ."

"Two-four," Larry yells. "Runway two-four."

"Runway two-four."

"Say Marshfield again."

"Um, runway two-four, Marshfield."

"Something like that." Larry sighs. "Actually, that was pretty good. This is runway two-four, by the way, because it's lined up with the two-hundred-forty-degree mark on the compass. You drop the last zero. Going the other way, it's runway six, or sixty degrees. The reciprocal. Right?"

He's given the engine full power and we're bumping down the runway. I grip the control yoke tightly, trying not to interfere as he eases it back; we're in the air. I'm in 1978. At around 700 feet we encounter what an experienced pilot would describe as "light chop"—a moderate, consistent bumpiness. I have premonitions of death. The nose of the plane rises and falls, the wings tilt, the tail yaws back and forth; every inch of this plane seems to be in contradictory motion, yet it continues to rise at a relatively constant rate, and in a minute or so we've passed through 1,000 feet on the way to some other altitude. My eyes are glued to the instruments. I haven't been able to bring myself to look outside yet.

"We'll be going up to two thousand feet," Larry yells, "and then you can take it for a while." I nod, watching the vertical speed indicator hover at about 800 feet per minute of climb. "Hey," Larry says, "you want to look outside?"

In crises, except those entirely of my own making, I tend to be thoroughly obedient: This is no exception. I pop my head up, which immediately sends a small wave of nausea through my body, and look around.

We're flying south, over a long spit of sand—Duxbury Beach—with Duxbury Harbor behind it. I'm struck at once by the complete absurdity of my presence here and by the beauty below me. A fishing boat is coming into the harbor past the lighthouse; its wake turns starkly white against the frigid darkness of the ocean. Within the rough rectangle created by Duxbury Beach and the land behind it, darker strands of water lead to creeks and rivers I have never seen on the ground. These run well back into the marshes through acres of forests, with houses scattered here and there like outposts. Larry points out harbors I've never heard of before—Green Harbor River, just south of the airport, where a small fishing fleet rides at anchor among docks and tiny islands that remind me of my childhood in Avalon. And beyond us, east of all this, lies the Atlantic Ocean, with only Provincetown between us and thousands of miles of water. Occasional rays of sun beam down on the charcoal sea, catching islands of whitecaps in a luminous archipelago. In spite of how I feel, I think I might some day be able to fly over the ocean forever.

Larry taps my shoulder. "Over there's Plymouth," he says. "That's the *Mayflower* down there, or rather the *Mayflower Two*"—he puts the plane in a 30-degree right bank so I can see the ship, but my stomach clinches and I lean way over to the left side of the plane. This is not what I want. Larry doesn't notice.

"Okay," he says. "Let's do some stuff. You asked about ailerons. Ailerons help turn the plane by changing the shape of the wing. If you turn the yoke to the left, the aileron on the right wing will drop down, giving that wing more lift. All lift has a horizontal component as well as a vertical component, so as the right wing lifts it also draws the plane around to the left. Unfortunately," he adds as he begins to turn the yoke to the left and I begin to feel dizzy, "turning just the yoke tends to make the plane's nose yaw in the direction of the upward wing, as you can now see." Sure enough—though I'm not sure how much longer I can keep paying attention—when Larry turns the control yoke to the left, lowering the aileron on the right wing, the plane begins to go left but the nose begins to go right.

"The lower aileron adds drag as well as lift," Larry says. "So to give it some help we add rudder, specifically left rudder." Larry gives a little kick to the floor, and suddenly the whole plane feels as if it's turning left, not just the cockpit. On the other hand, we've had about five different stomach-churning motions here in the last thirty seconds, and the air outside was not all that calm to begin with. I look at the clock on the instrument panel. We've been in the air not quite ten minutes. Only twenty to go. Barf.

We do a couple of other turns, using only ailerons, only

rudder, and then both; we do some climbs and descents. Toward the end, Larry does a demonstration of the three axes of the aircraft—the pitch axis, where the nose goes up and down, the roll axis, where the wings roll left and right, and the yaw axis, where the fuselage of the plane swings back and forth. I can't stand much more of this. Despite Larry's care on the ground, this is no better than the lesson in Palo Alto. The plane is cramped, loud, and uncomfortable; all its motions are uncomfortable; I don't really understand what's happening; I feel sick.

"Okay," Larry says. "Let's go back."

We're only about eight minutes from the airport, and we make the trip in silence until, turning to his final approach to the runway, Larry makes a 30-degree bank to the left. As my face goes white, I lean into the center of the plane, which puts my head right about at Larry's shoulder. He looks over, almost as if he were administering a test.

"That bother you?" he asks.

"A little." I'm lying.

"We'll be down in a second."

And now, fighting a crosswind, we're cocked sideways as we approach the runway, flying toward it but aiming more toward the hangars; are we going to land this way? The plane drops lower and lower, settling and rising as Larry gives it power to counteract the sudden downdrafts. We're almost at the runway threshold. The engine is idling, the nose is coming up, and suddenly Larry straightens the plane out—even though, at this point, I can't see where we're landing—and then the stall warning comes on. "EEEEEEEEEEEEEE!" sounds the buzzer, warning that we're only a few knots away from losing all lift on the wings, and I say to myself, "Oh, God, this is it!" when there's a slight bump and a squeak of rubber on asphalt, and suddenly we're down, puttering along on the runway to the nearest exit.

"Not bad," says Larry.

"Why did that stall warning come on?" I ask, trying to sound controlled.

"That's supposed to happen on a good landing," he says. "Ideally, you want the wing to lose all lift just a couple of inches above the runway, so it eases itself out of the sky. The stall horn is telling you that's happening—assuming, of course, you're only a couple of inches above the runway. If the horn comes on when you're fifty feet up, you've got a problem."

"You did okay," he says a few minutes later, after we've tied down the plane and come back into the barn. I thank him; he's off to another student. I stand at the counter, looking.

"You did okay." Of course I didn't feel that way. But I realize that's one phrase almost no one uses about me anymore. I never hear it at my job. To tell someone at MIT that he or she is "doing okay" is tantamount to an admission of weakness. I don't hear it at home; at home I hear how much more child care I should be doing, how we're short on money, how my wife's dissertation is going badly. It's a strange revelation to have when I'm feeling nauseated. Here's a place where, somehow, I did okay. Even if it's not completely true.

In the glass case below the counter are some of the tools and toys of pilots—Sigtronics headsets and intercoms, a Narco 830 hand-held aircraft radio with a special navigational device built in, books on flying, charts that show terrain and airports and navigational beacons all over the country. Another flight instructor, a tall Norwegian named Rod, is working behind the counter today.

"Can I take a look at that Narco?" I ask. "And also a chart for this area—which one is it?"

Rod gathers up the radio and a chart. "It's the New York chart—called a 'sectional.' Goes from Portland, Maine, down to

Philadelphia, more or less. A lot of territory." He hands me the radio carefully, then places the chart beside me on the counter.

The radio is beautiful—compact, cleanly designed. The radio in the plane was the one thing I more or less understood during the flight, and this too feels familiar: I could talk to other pilots or air traffic controllers with it, I could find out where I was if I were lost. I want it—somewhat unaccountably, since it won't do me much good on the ground and I don't own an airplane, and even if I did the airplane would already have a radio in it. But I want it. It's $350, completely unaffordable. Laying it carefully aside, I pick up the sectional chart.

The chart is new, crisply folded, and smells of fresh ink and heavy paper. I open it gently. There I begin to see a map of a world that looks somewhat like the one in which I live, but not entirely. Most obvious is Logan Airport in Boston, with a series of thick blue concentric circles around it: This is a TCA, a Terminal Control Area, the highest-priority airspace in the United States, and small planes like the one I just flew in can't even get into a TCA without special clearance from air traffic controllers. But there are other circles; a dashed circle surrounds the Hyannis airport on Cape Cod. The airport itself, identified as "Hyannis-Barnstable," has a series of frequencies and some other numbers whose meaning I can't identify. A pale blue line runs out from Hyannis to Martha's Vineyard and to Nantucket, both of which have circles around their airports and other circles, compass roses, as well. Circles everywhere, beginnings and endings and beginnings, across a craggy and oddly unfinished terrain of beaches and forests and suburbs and tall cities. Some-how—not unlike the attitude indicator in the airplane—the sectional chart makes sense to me.

"I'll take one of these," I say to Rod, paying for the chart and for my introductory lesson—a total of $40.25. "You comin' back?" Rod asks.

"Could be," I say, feeling deceitful. "I might see what it's like going up with Steve." There's something about Steve's love of flying that I need to know a little more about. It might make no difference at all, but then again it might. Rod and I check the schedule book; Steve has time a week from now. I book a slot, feel my heart sink, and go away with my chart and my longer list of questions.

II.

*I*n October 1985, after Lesley and I had learned from our doctor that she was pregnant, we went driving around Palo Alto and Stanford, where we lived. It was a remarkable autumn day, even for California: The pale sun seemed to invest itself in everything, every live oak and laurel, every weed stalk, so that the landscape glowed and hummed with light, an almost audible sensation. Weary from several years of graduate school, we were looking for a way back to some old adventure we had known just after college, and somehow—leaving aside fears for the future—we had locked into the passion that had once guided us. We were in love with each other again, in the high part of that cycle of love and loneliness that defined us, and love meant that we could go—just go: We could choose our way, and the world would rise behind us like a sustaining wave. We felt happy and free, without ever having to think what those words meant; they were not ideas but solid realities, like Sierra granite or Point Reyes chert. It was a good time, we thought, to have a child, not really believing that anything would happen.

And now that it had, now that Lesley was going to have a

baby, we were scared. We drove down Palm Drive, the ceremonial entrance to Stanford, saying nothing to each other, looking out above the palm trees lining the road to the university and the golden hills beyond. Suddenly, out of the corner of my right eye, I caught sight of something, and in the split second it took me to register motion a red-tailed hawk sailed out of one of the palm trees and glided right in front of our car, timing his glide so precisely that his left wingtip brushed our windshield. There was no time to brake; he was gone in an instant. It had been perfect. I had never seen such a thing, and when, in the next instant, I pulled over, I realized I was shaking. Part of me thought of the accident—the hawk crashing through the windshield, my loss of control, Lesley and I both killed or injured. But another part of me realized that what I had seen was absolutely what was meant, that the glide was meant to cross our path exactly at eye level, the wingtip meant to brush the glass without causing harm. I realized I had seen the hawk's outstretched primaries, the flash of red in the tail, even the intense indifference of his gaze—I had seen him as if he were a museum piece, and yet he had passed by in a fraction of a second.

"Did that mean something?" Lesley turned to me.

"We can't be superstitious," I said.

"But that was about something, wasn't it?"

"Yes," I said. "Well, maybe." But somehow we knew we were having a hawk-child, a child for whom the California red-tailed hawk would be a guardian. In the months that followed, we saw more hawks than we had seen in all the years we had lived in California. They circled above us when we hiked in the Los Trancos Preserve near Skyline Drive; they followed me in sequence, like Pony Express riders, as I drove past Crystal Springs Reservoir on the way from Palo Alto to Berkeley, where I taught. When Nathaniel was born in Stanford Hospital on the morning of August 5, 1986, a red-tailed hawk soared outside the room, then glided down into a live oak not far from the window, where he waited briefly, then flew away. The hawks stayed close by throughout Nathaniel's first year, and when we left Palo Alto in 1988 to move to Massachusetts, a hawk came down into the suburban neighborhood where we lived and took up a post in the birch tree outside Nathaniel's room. It was the first time we had seen a hawk so close to people, and the hawk stayed until the moving truck was full and we were packed into our old Subaru. As we pulled out of the driveway, we saw it raise its powerful wings and fly away.

I remember this all now, sitting in the same old Subaru at Marshfield Airport, as a kestrel crosses the runway some distance away, catching my eye as it heads toward the nature preserve next to the airport. I've never really been a bird-watcher, nor have I thought much about them as a species; I like them only because I like to watch them fly. But I have watched hawks and kestrels since Nathaniel's birth, and when they go by I pay attention. This one shows no interest in me, but as it flaps its wings once or twice and glides over the Cessna 150 and the Piper Archer at the near end of the field I have a kind of double image of planes and hawks, and I feel a momentary confusion, as if somehow I were off-center. I turn back to the chart in my hands.

I've flipped it open to the south side, which shows Cape Cod, Martha's Vineyard, and Nantucket—all easily accessible, I realize with some regret, from Marshfield, since I'll probably never have the stomach to get to any of them. But following the series of airports and circles around airports down the coast of Rhode Island and Connecticut, I come to an impossibly complicated patch of airspace over Long Island and Manhattan—it's outlined with a series of blue lines that look like alternator belts and compressor belts in a car with too much optional equipment—and then down to the bottom of the chart, just above Philadelphia. Until I was thirteen I lived in West Chester, about thirty miles from the city, and I remember my father taking me once or twice to Philadelphia International Airport to look at airliners. As a quality control manager for the textile division of FMC, he flew constantly down to the textile plants in West Virginia and the Carolinas, and he was one of United Airlines's first 100,000-mile fliers. In honor of this achievement the airline gave him, not frequent flier miles—the airline business was subtler then—but a plaque with a brass image of a Lockheed Electra circling the globe four times. He must have had connections with United and some of the smaller airlines, like Allegheny and Mohawk, because he could get us in to look around a plane just by waving and smiling at the right people. Some of the pilots and flight attendants knew him by name.

I remember him this way—waving and smiling at the right people, standing with me in the cockpit of an Electra at Philadelphia—but as I scan the sectional chart I stop at a different airport, Northeast Philadelphia, and it seems to ring a different bell. Nothing was ever very clear about my father, but Northeast Philadelphia seems almost synonymous with him, and I realize I connect it with odd bits of his past—names of aircraft like Waco and Stearman, old flying buddies like Gordy Hall, an airport called Summerton that used to be right across from Northeast Philadelphia and now no longer exists.

There was something frightening about my father, and those days he took me to the airport to look at airliners were never far from the days he left for work in his long black wool overcoat, bent and haggard, not coming home for days or perhaps coming home too soon, his eyes obscured behind some unnameable dark cloud. He had wanted to be a professor of engineering after World War II, but things had gone wrong; he slid continually into jobs he didn't want, keeping the family together, hovering at the edge of bankruptcy, never escaping, wanting to escape so much that everyone who held him was an object of hatred, even those of us he loved. He never flew when I knew him.

But sometimes I saw him, and still see him, as an eighteen-year-old with a brand-new pilot's license and a little plane, a 1938 two-seater Taylorcraft with a 40-horsepower Lycoming engine, a flying lawnmower, taxiing out to the grass strip at Summerton on a Sunday morning in early June. His mother had died the year before; his father was tough, unyielding, determined to be strong and convey that strength to his children. My father's younger sister, Miriam, withdrew, became more silent, mourned to herself, began to invent a new and wilder life. My father took his father's lesson to heart, kept grief at bay, but knew for sure he was alone. Although he admired and feared his father, there had really been no one for him besides his mother—until now; now there was everything that was beyond human, everything a little larger and better, the sky, the sun spreading across it like a very thin, warm, pale fluid, and the machine that would take him into that warmth. The airplane was not a substitute for grief, or for love received, but it was a way of giving love to himself, and that was something. Man-made but not human, it was not subject to the decay of the body, but lived on and on, almost infinitely repairable, with cylinders that could be rebored and piston rings that could be replaced. My father would not have to grieve over this machine.

One of the line boys at Summerton helped him start the engine by pulling the prop, and as the small powerplant coughed and whined and eased its way into a smooth idle, my father taxied the plane across the grass, feeling the slight bumps

73

through the tires as a child might feel them through his shoes. Revving the engine, checking the magnetos and adjusting the altimeter to field elevation, Warren would ease the Taylorcraft out onto the grass strip, add full throttle, and push forward slightly on the stick that came up through the floor. This would lift the tail just off the ground—the Taylorcraft was a "tail-dragger," with a third wheel in the tail instead of under the nose—and then, as the plane began to gather speed and fly, he would ease back on the stick and feel himself drawn into the air. He was free.

Turning east-southeast, climbing to 3,500 feet, he would begin the slow flight to south Jersey, to Avalon, where his father's and my mother's families both went to escape the Philadelphia summers. The morning haze at that altitude seemed impenetrable, the visibility no more than six or eight miles, and although he could pick out landmarks on the ground, he had at times the feeling that he was heading into some haze-hidden stratus cloud layer. There might be no way out. Yet it was an acceptable risk, probably an illusion, and anyway he had an engine he could trust and a few instruments that would help keep him from harm. And then, losing track of time and the ground for a few minutes, humming something from Count Basie to himself, he looked out at what had been haze and realized it was ocean, the pale sky blue of a sea that was not sky, heading out toward an infinity that was not infinity but only another kind of illusion. After this he was ready to come down, to think again about life and bodies and descents, and he made his way to another landing in another grass field; and then he went home. But that flight would stay with him all day, and through the week, until he could get away from school or work and come back to Summerton, where the line boy would prop his plane again and he would be off.

74

From early on he was a wounded man, and the sky took care of him. But if it is true that the wounded make the best teachers, I ask myself, what kind of teacher, what kind of professor, would he have been? How much did it matter that his life swerved so widely from the mark at which he aimed? Twelve years ago he spoke to me of the need for a gentle touch in a teacher, yet I can find no gentleness in my one memory of the time he tried to teach me something. As a ten-year-old I dreamed of owning a rowboat, and somehow, after searching fruitlessly for a rowboat cheap enough for him to afford, he found an old dinghy in someone's basement outside of Philadelphia. It was November, scarcely the time of year to take up rowing, but he and my mother and I went down to New Jersey the next weekend to try out the dinghy.

A nor'easter was moving in, and the wind gusted hard; the channel chop was sharp, with a faster current than I had ever seen. My father and I carried the dinghy down to the landing. Although I had been looking forward to being a passenger as he rowed, I was no longer sure that heading out in such weather was a good idea.

Motioning to me, my father pointed to the center seat.

"Get in," he said simply.

I was confused. This was beginning to look less like a lesson than—well, I wasn't sure. My dream of rowing had never included this heavy chop, these hard gusts, the cold spray of the whitecaps. As my father held the dinghy, I climbed into the stern seat, waiting for him to follow. He motioned me again to the center seat.

"What are we doing?" I asked.

"Grab the oars and pull," said my father. He began to push me out into the channel. The current spun the boat stern-first toward the marsh grass, so that he had to stand calf-deep in the freezing water and push the bow outward.

"What do I do?" I had to yell over the rush of the wind.

"Just pull harder on one oar to go that way," he shouted back. "To go right, pull right. To go left, pull left." He pushed suddenly with all his might. I was beam-first in the rough current.

I could hear my mother on the bank shouting at my father, but her warnings suddenly seemed distant and irrelevant. The boat wobbled wildly as I tried to spin it around, and when I banged the oar handles together they drew blood from my knuckles. Trembling with fear, I ran the dinghy aground on the marsh bank several hundred yards from where I started. I was out of reach of my parents, wet, and defeated.

I was also furious—furious at my own ineptitude, furious at my father and the tattered state of my dream. I had wanted this boat, I told myself; now I had to make it my own. As the whitecaps snapped against the gunwale, I talked myself through the simple maneuvers I would need to get off the bank and out into the channel. I waited; I seethed. Out of sheer anger I would not fail. A few seconds later I had clumsily twisted and pushed the boat off the bank. Stroke after stroke, some excellent, some inept, I struggled back to my starting point. By the time I dug the keel into the sand of the landing, I knew how to row.

My father was ecstatic. "You really pulled that one out, son," he said over and over. "I'm proud of you, sport. You showed a lot of courage." My mother, though obviously disturbed at what had occurred, patted my head in the way she reserved for my few great accomplishments. Yet I twisted away; I brushed them both off. We headed back to the house in a damp and shivering silence.

I had my boat, yes—that dream was no longer merely a dream. Nor was I simply a child of books and imagined adventures. The adventure I had just had was real and threatening. My life had been in my hands, and I alone had saved it. At least it seemed that way to me. And in that moment of discovery, that first taste of real freedom, I knew bitterness as well. Who was my father to propel me into a rising storm in a boat I had never tried before? What did his love mean? I stayed aloof from him for hours, unable to absorb the way he had let me go and yet prizing it as I would have prized a trophy. Whatever courage or strength he might have imparted to me then, I disavowed; I took my strength from the boat. It was years before I saw my father's method as something other than cruel—as a calculated risk, or even more, a gamble of love.

But it was a love based on parting; and while parting may be an essential component of all human love, it is not really the basis of it, not strong enough to hold what love affords. I needed, desperately wanted, a presence, not an absence. But my father, who had felt so much absence in his life, found his sense of place, not among people, but among the extensions of himself in the world—objects he could master, like airplanes and cars and boats, that made him feel as if parting were simply a way of going somewhere, of choosing or being in control. He surrounded himself with these objects, leaving and returning and leaving, and I lost him over and over again.

This loss was itself a way of teaching, a way of saying that fear would be the essential condition of my learning, as it was for him. I would be dropped into the fearsome place, into the school I hated or the church that enchained me or the storm that threatened to carry me away, and I would have no resources but my own. My life, my body, my instincts would teach me. If I learned what I had to learn, I would be parted from whatever old self lay crippled with fear; if I failed to learn, I would have to try again and again until I mastered the task and vanquished the fear. Since overcoming fear, oddly enough, was one of the main tenets of Christian Science, I felt as if my father and my religion were teaching me the same thing. "Be not afraid," Jesus said, and all would be well. But not to be afraid meant to be alone, as I was alone after learning to row; in fighting fear, one learned the love of parting, not the love of companionship. Except when I made it my business to please other people and earn their praise, I was alone. I knew that isolation too well.

And still do. I fold the map slowly, noticing the creases as one fold slips neatly into another. My son, Nathaniel, is not *my* father's son, but my son, and Lesley's, and somewhere in the transposition he seems—I think—to have come under a good sign, a sense of trust in people and himself that balances whatever fear he has. He is sweet and strong and kind, and though I see in him traces of the entire peaceable kingdom I see especially the hawk, his guardian, a sign of protection. He needs me, and yet he seems to feel something already that I have never felt—an instinctive right to be alive, to have a place in the world. Oddly enough, in a different way, my father too had this same instinctive confidence: Once he found machines they became his most powerful validations, and his need for love wrapped itself around them almost successfully. He made an instinctive choice to gamble away creatureliness: His spirit-animal became a spirit-machine, a great mechanical bird. He too knew something I have never known.

The red wall of the airport barn stands before me like a barrier, a monument to all I cannot do, to the man I cannot be or reach. I am too old to learn any more about life the way I learned to row, I tell myself, and anyway my father is far away, an old man living a life in which he has made it clear that I have no place. Besides, there are other ways to learn, compassionate ways: I do not have to wear myself down in the misery of fighting fear. And yet, in a way, my fear is my only real connection to my father. Backing out of the Marshfield parking lot, driving down the narrow lane to the main road, I am engulfed in a very clear mental blur, seeing the houses and trees and roads and yet thinking somehow I have never been here and will never leave.

III.

*T*he day before my scheduled flight with Steve, I call in sick. Maybe I *am* sick; my throat feels a little sore, and my muscles ache. It could be the flu. I'm doing the right thing, I tell myself as I call Marshfield. Steve answers the phone. Suddenly I'm deeply embarrassed. I make my voice sound scratchier than it really is. I tell him how bad I'm feeling; he sounds genuinely sympathetic, increasing my guilt. "How about, let's see, the twenty-first?" he asks. That's more than ten days away; it gives me plenty of time to think it over, and to cancel more than a day ahead if I finally come to my senses and realize I don't want to fly. "The twenty-first is fine," I say. The next day I'm flat in bed with a 102-degree fever, grateful at not having to feel guilty.

Once I recover, I throw myself into my work at MIT, teaching and correcting essays and talking to students with a practiced intensity; I seem to be hitting my stride, doing my job well. But the core of my thought is focused elsewhere. On the twentieth I pick up the phone once, then twice, to cancel the flight. Yet I cannot quite bring myself to call. That night, realizing that I will go ahead with what I do not want to do, I take one of the lower-dose Xanax tablets, feeling guilty because I know the FAA would never officially let me fly solo on tranquilizers. Why should I get away with it as a student, I ask myself? But I'm not a student, I tell myself. I'm just trying it out. I know

I won't really like it. Tomorrow I'll say no for sure.

But after eating breakfast late, eating no lunch, and downing a capful of Pepto-Bismol, I hook up with Steve in the early afternoon at Marshfield—and remember why I instantly liked him. He's so happy around airplanes, the question of confidence doesn't even arise: These machines are what he loves. Yet there's also something very unifying about Steve; he's genial, unaffected, interested in who I am and why I'm here.

"But I don't really know why I'm here," I tell him. "I mean, I had a lesson about twelve years ago, and it was terrible. And I went up with Larry last month, and that was okay, but to tell you the truth I still felt sick."

"That's okay," Steve says as we go through the preflight inspection and climb into the plane. "Either you'll figure out why you're here or you won't. Either way, this is a good day to fly."

And oddly enough, it is. Although the takeoff still frightens me, the air is almost monotonously smooth; there's no buffet, no turbulence at all. For once I have a vague inkling of what it might be like to ride on a magic carpet. Once we get above 1,000 feet, I can feel the smooth drone of the engine vibrating slightly through my seat, and the constancy calms me; I take my eyes off the instrument panel voluntarily and begin to look around. We climb high, over Cape Cod Bay, up to 5,500 feet— the highest I've ever flown in a small plane—and, looking down, I see Provincetown like a diorama from the Boston Museum of Science, perfect and clear and as manageably small as a Matchbox village of tiny cars and trucks and houses. A few gulls and terns ride the thermals below us; I can see our own small shadow far away on the gray expanse of ocean.

Steve watches me, waiting for my cues, pushing me a little but not too hard, showing me what the plane will do without ever quite drawing me away from the beauty below me. "Let's get a better look at Provincetown," he says, putting the plane into a left bank. "By the way, if you'll look back at the instrument panel you'll see the top outside line on the attitude indicator lined up with the third line on the inside. See?" He points to show me what he means. "That means we're in a thirty-degree bank. Why don't you try a thirty-degree bank to the right?"

I try, and flub it—we begin to lose altitude. I pull back on the control yoke, and suddenly my stomach begins to rise to my mouth as the g-forces kick in: I'm fighting gravity hard to keep the plane level, but Steve seems to know when to intervene, and in a second things are smooth and level again. I feel okay. We turn back toward Marshfield, descending below 3,000 feet so we don't accidentally break into the airspace near Logan Airport, and Steve talks a little about landings. He shows me how to slow the plane down to sixty-five knots, the final approach airspeed, and how to keep the plane flying straight and level at what's called minimum controllable airspeed.

"What do you think controls our altitude?" he asks as we buzz back and forth over Plymouth Harbor at about 65 knots.

"The control yoke," I say. "I mean, the stabilator. If I pull back, we go up."

"Try it," he says. I pull back, we rise slightly for a few seconds, then begin to sink as the airspeed drops below 50 knots and the stall warning begins its eerie "EEEEEEEEEE." Somehow, instinctively, I push the nose down, sweat beginning to form on my forehead.

"You've just had your first lesson in how pitch doesn't control altitude," Steve says cheerfully. "Actually, you control your altitude with the throttle. If you add more throttle, you'll go up; if you cut back, you'll go down."

This time, keeping the control yoke more or less in the same place, I push the throttle all the way forward and the plane begins to climb. It doesn't make sense to me, but that's what happens.

"Remember this: pitch for airspeed, throttle for altitude," he says. "Rule number one of flying—there're a bunch of 'rule number one's.'" He smiles. "If you want to increase your airspeed, lower your nose. If you want to increase your altitude, add throttle. This is really important when you're learning to land," he says seriously. I don't know why it's important, but I'm willing to take his word for it. It's still a beautiful day.

When we get down, everything has changed somehow: I'm happy, a little giddy at what I've done, and reluctant to be on the ground. These sensations are so astonishing that, for a few minutes, I feel as if I'm walking around outside of myself, a second person who's translucent, full of delight, though otherwise identical to me. What's strangest is that I can't explain it at all: Like any true happiness—or more truly, like love at first sight—it descends without reason, without the possibility of explanation.

"You seemed to have a pretty good time," Steve observes as we head into the airport. "We were up for more than an hour."

"We *were?*" I know an hour is a kind of dividing line in student lore: People who can't last an hour in a small plane have no hope of becoming pilots, while people who break the hour barrier at least stand a chance. I always assumed I was a half hour man at best.

"One point one, to be exact," he says. "Sixty-six minutes. Hope you can afford to pay me."

As I hand Steve a credit card—one of my lifelines to sanity

and hope—I crane my neck around to ponder the upside-down schedule book.

"Want to go up again on Friday?" I ask. Today is Wednesday; even Steve looks a little surprised.

"Sure," he says. "How about two o'clock?"

I leave feeling clean, as if a powerful wind had blown through me and torn away everything that was partial and weak and fearful; but all I did was fly a plane. Was that, I wondered, why people meditated—to achieve that effect, that cleanness? It felt wonderful.

The wonder tapered a little on Thursday, as I navigated through student essays and assigned readings and conversations with colleagues at MIT, but by Thursday evening I was looking forward to Friday at Marshfield. Then, around eight o'clock, I got a call from a particularly gifted student. I had first met her a year ago in a poetry-writing course I had taught. Now she was in my advanced essay workshop, a course for upper-class students whose prose writing earned them special distinction. The class met on Monday evenings from seven to ten; she virtually never missed a class. She had been absent this past Monday, I remembered, but she had been doing well, and I wasn't all that worried. I knew she had been coping with depression a year ago, brought on largely by the stresses of life at MIT, but I also knew she had sought treatment for it through the MIT medical department, and I trusted her to let me know if anything was wrong. Perhaps I was too trusting.

"Well, Tom," she said, "the good news is that I'm not dead. At least I think that's the good news."

My whole body seemed to grow silent. "What?" I said very quietly.

"I'm in McLean Hospital right now, calling from a pay

phone in a locked ward," she said quickly. "I tried to kill myself a couple of nights ago by taking a bunch of pills. They pumped my stomach at Mount Auburn Hospital, and now I'm here. They call it 'Club Head.' Pretty funny, huh?"

This couldn't be. How could I have missed the signs? I thought quickly; I was no idiot, and I had seen her regularly these past few weeks and talked to her extensively about her work and her life. But I couldn't think of any signs. There wasn't anything I had known to do. I felt powerless. We talked briefly, and I promised to go see her the next evening—she could have visitors—but before hanging up she got to her main point.

"I really need your help," she said. "I found out today that the dean wants to kick me out of MIT for this. If they kick me out this semester, I have nowhere to go. I have no money. I'll probably be out of McLean in a couple of weeks. MIT is driving me crazy, but the only thing keeping me sane are the two writing classes I'm taking. Well, and maybe the thought I might actually graduate from that hellhole someday. Tom, they can't kick me out. Can't you do something?"

After promising her that I would do everything I could to keep her enrolled, I hung up seething. I was angry at myself for not intervening, even though—or perhaps because—I'd had no idea any intervention was necessary. But mostly I was angry at MIT. I had taught for three years at Stanford and five years at UC Berkeley before coming east, but at neither of the other schools had I witnessed anything like the degree of pressure I saw among students at MIT. It was reasonable for my students at Stanford to stay up all night two or three times a term to finish, say, a long history paper or an engineering problem set; at MIT I had students pulling all-nighters three nights a week every week of the term. I had students who regularly showed up in morning classes with a can of Jolt or two cans of Coke to keep themselves awake a little longer; I had students coming to my office, frantic to talk to anyone who would listen about the impossibility of their workload. And these same students told a more ominous story: physics, geology, chemistry, or engineering professors who overloaded them with problem sets, who explained difficulties badly or not at all, who belittled them in class when they asked questions, who spoke in accents too difficult to understand.

There were, I knew, students with extraordinary natural talent who thrived at MIT, but many of the students in my classes were clearly suffering; I'd had students before who had mental breakdowns in the middle of the term, although until now I'd had none who attempted suicide. And while I knew that other colleges and universities in the country also had cases of student suicide, I sensed a level of desperation and self-destructiveness at MIT that seemed new to me. My student at McLean embodied it, but her power over my thought came from the fact that I knew she was not unique.

At first I had simply found MIT a fascinating place. The institute offered majors in most fields, including not only electrical engineering and physics but also literature, history, and writing; its catalog displayed a meaty collection of courses and degrees. Beyond the matter of course offerings was a larger question of intellectual liberty, controlled chaos. There was a Wild West quality to the institute: People came here because they relished the intellectual pioneering in the lab, the hot pursuits into the deserts of knowledge. At least among the scientists, it seemed that one's training in any individual discipline was less important than one's native creativity. As I came to know a few professors in programs beyond my own, I began to see more clearly the interweavings of disciplines, the interpenetrations of science. Yet, despite these remarkable people and their talents both as researchers and as teachers, I began to think that, given the purpose of the institute as a whole, education was a relatively minor function. There was no serious incentive, no form of professional praise or security, for professors who chose to take their teaching seriously. The main undergraduate teaching award on campus, the Everett Moore Baker Award, was known among students and faculty alike as the "kiss of death" because so many of the faculty who had received it had either been denied tenure or had gone elsewhere. What seemed to count even more at MIT than at other institutions was research.

In 1989, my first year at MIT, the Department of Defense alone spent almost $48 million on research grants at MIT, according to the MIT Planning Office. The Department of Health and Human Services spent over $52 million, the Department of Energy $54 million, and NASA over $15 million. These expenditures did not place MIT at the top of the federal chart, according to the National Science Foundation; MIT ranked number three, with $231,126,000 in total U.S. spending on academic science and engineering. Johns Hopkins, with $604,567,000, was first, while Stanford, with $265,282,000, was second; Harvard was fourteenth, UC Berkeley fifteenth.

It was true that, in some categories, MIT far outstripped the other institutions. The Department of Energy expenditures at MIT in 1989, for example, were more than three times those at Stanford. Even so, there were categories in which Stanford surpassed MIT, and in the funding race no one institution was utterly dominant. What most struck me was that I could not remember seeing, at Stanford, the preoccupation with research that seemed to grip MIT at all levels. The reasons for this were probably many: some had to do with Stanford's formation around a core of liberal values, while others had to do with

MIT's primary reputation as a source of technological innovation. But for a time I resisted exploring those reasons. I tried to talk myself out of the notion that MIT was really a research institute that happened to admit undergraduates. Surely it could educate them as well as Stanford or Berkeley. And yet, hearing the difficulties these gifted students faced—the nearly overwhelming problem sets, the exams that covered significantly different material from class lectures, the sink-or-swim attitude of some faculty who taught dozens of students in a single class, the widely varying quality of some recitations (MIT's word for sections), and the teaching assistants who often seemed too burdened or preoccupied to explain the material—I began to sense that whatever happened at MIT was based on a fundamentally different attitude about education.

The worst thing that could happen was for someone, anyone—a professor, a student—to admit weakness; to be strong, to endure, was to succeed. And while I knew of many pockets of compassion—attentive professors of physics, good souls and vivid teachers in geology and chemistry and psychology—I had also heard too many stories of teaching through punishment and humiliation, and only those who survived this onslaught could make it through to the bachelor of science degree. Indeed, the same method prevailed at the level of faculty: Although I had been extensively courted for my job, told that I was the best of 270 applicants, and assured that my prospects at MIT were bright if I accepted the position, it was not long before the opposite story began to take shape. Four months after I arrived, one faculty member in my program took me aside to tell me that MIT would "crucify" me if I didn't publish the kind of book they thought would enhance my reputation (and by extension the reputation of the program). Over the next several months, I began to hear from various sources that my writing was progressing too slowly, my publishing was too minor and various, my work was of dubious quality. I was a good teacher, but teaching was only tangentially relevant. My colleagues made it clear that a clock was ticking on me and I was falling behind in the race to bring distinction to myself and thus to the institute.

This was in some ways even more of an obsession in the humanities than in engineering and the sciences, because the humanities at MIT still seemed to labor under a sense of inferiority, as if because what they did was different it was therefore less socially valuable than what went on in the labs around campus. "You have to understand," the acting dean of humanities and social science told me during my second year at the institute, "in order to win the respect of the scientists we have to be better than the best." To be better than the best as a young professor you had to make a mold for yourself and your work and then fill it perfectly; if you were imperfect, or broke the mold for a new one, you triggered an avalanche of doubt among senior faculty. This was what I had done, but I was not alone; I knew other junior faculty who had left for other schools because they judged MIT to be essentially an insane place to work. "You should write a book about this place," my MIT physician told me one day when I came in with my third possible strep throat in as many months. "This is a great place, in some ways the greatest place in the world. But it's also very cruel."

And now one of my students was in despair, on the verge of a forced leave of absence, having come back from the verge of death. Perhaps ironically, I was determined to keep her in school. MIT might be a crazy place, but at least it gave her a context, and while I was no psychiatrist I well understood her fear of being cut loose—of having choice taken from her. I barely slept that night, and in the morning I called the dean's office as soon as it opened.

What happened might have been comical under different circumstances. I spoke with one of the dean's assistants. "I'm a professor in the writing program," I said, "and I got a call from a student who's out at McLean. She's having some medical difficulties, and I understand that the dean is planning to arrange a leave of absence for her today. I think that would be a mistake, and I need to talk to him right away."

"He's not in yet," said the soothing voice. "May I take a message?"

I left a message, waited forty-five minutes, and called back again. "Oh, he's just stepped out," she said. "May I take your name and number?"

"Look, this is urgent," I said. "Please have him call as soon as he gets in."

After another half hour it was quarter after ten, and I thought a decision was coming down soon. I called again.

"Listen," I said, "I have a brief message. Tell the dean I'm hand-delivering him a letter about this student, and that it would be extremely unwise of him to take any action on her behalf before receiving it."

"I'll give him the message," the soothing person said. I slammed down the receiver.

But I wrote the letter, the most passionate defense I could muster for a student who had felt so wounded and had needed to make such a large statement just to be heard, and I drove over to the dean's office, where I handed it to the receptionist. The dean's office door was ajar; I could see he was in. "I'm Professor Simmons," I said softly, "and I'm asking you to take this letter in to the dean right now. I don't care if he's busy. I want you to hand this to him *now*, please." She vanished into his office with my letter. "I know he'll read it," she said reassuringly when she returned. Aside from lurching into his office and demanding an audience, there was nothing more for me to do. At this point, as infuriated as I was, I would be less convincing in person than on paper. I walked out of the office into the so-called Infinite Corridor at the heart of MIT. I was fleeing now to Marshfield, and I knew it. At least flying might calm me down, I thought, or scare me in a different way, and I could make sense of what was happening.

During the hour it took me to get from MIT to Marshfield, I tried to figure out how I had come to MIT. All of the standard reasons, the good reasons, made sense: I had come because the writing program looked interesting, because the job asked for someone who could teach and write poetry, essays, and literary criticism, because the faculty seemed like an interesting group of people. I had come because I knew Boston from my days as an intern on the *Christian Science Monitor*, and because Lesley needed to do research for her dissertation on nineteenth-century American art. But now I began to think I had come here because, at some strange level, I wanted to be punished and knew that MIT would punish me. To be punished meant, not that I was bad, but that I was good: I was good because I was not free, I had followed the expected route, done the right things, assumed the right obligations. I was not running from the serious responsibilities of life; I was facing them head-on, and the more they abused me the more I demonstrated my strength and virtue. I realized I had been thinking this way for so long that I could not remember when it started, or even what was the matter with it. In some way it made perfect sense. And yet I was fleeing.

Steve was waiting for me when I walked through the door.

"I just got down a few minutes ago," he said. "It's pretty bumpy up there. You still want to go?"

I was too distracted to say no, and anyway I wanted an exit. And I wanted to prove that I was strong. I could take the punishment of MIT; I could even take the punishment of a rough day in a small airplane.

I realized my mistake the minute the wheels squeaked off the runway and the plane yawed hard to the right in a gust of wind. We seesawed up to 2,000 feet, clawing our way into the air, dropping 3 or 5 feet all of a sudden, climbing back again, as my stomach became an elastic pendulum, bouncing and swinging closer to my throat.

"Let's go out over the water," Steve shouted. "It might be smoother there." I nodded, staring at the instruments. It seemed louder in the cockpit than before. The overcast sky descended around us, as if in climbing we were actually falling *up*; I felt vaguely dizzy. We leveled off, more or less, at 2,000 feet. Although the air was smoother over the Atlantic, it was still choppy, and the constant washboard effect made me grit my teeth.

"Let's do some slow flight," Steve said, and I obediently brought the throttle back until the engine tachometer showed 1,500 RPM; we slowed to 65 knots and began to drop like a stone. I added throttle; we climbed, but the airspeed also went up. I put the nose down, the airspeed climbed further, we were still ascending, and I suddenly began to feel sick. Steve was watching the instruments.

"Gently, gently," he said. "Small corrections. Remember, once you've regained altitude, reduce the throttle and pull the nose up to bleed off the airspeed. Look, you're chasing the airspeed all over the place."

It was true; now we were at 65 knots, now 60, now 70, now 80; the altitude was fluctuating wildly. The plane bumped and shook in the choppy air.

"Try to nail one of the numbers before going for the other," Steve said. I was thinking of my student in her locked ward at McLean, about the dean, about my life. "Try to get the altitude." We were at 2,300 feet; I cut the throttle, lowered the nose, and in a few seconds we were more or less at 2,000.

"Good," said Steve. "Now slowly reduce the throttle, pull the nose up, and trim the aircraft to keep that pitch." The Warrior had a metal wheel about eight inches in diameter on the floor in between the two front seats; it controlled a trim tab on the back of the stabilator, which made it easier to hold the plane at a certain pitch or attitude. I pulled back on the throttle, pulled the nose up, trimmed the plane, and began to fall through the sky once again. Furious, I rammed the throttle forward to get back to the assigned altitude. The plane revved and reared like a wild stallion. Steve looked at me.

"Let me demonstrate again," he said.

"No," I said suddenly. "Let's just go back. I don't feel too great. Let's just bag it."

It was hard to interpret Steve's look, and I wasn't much in the mood anyway, but I felt disappointment and self-reproach: "I shouldn't have brought him up," I could hear him saying to himself. We bounced back down to 1,000 feet as we approached the airport and I realized how sick I felt. This was it, the end; flying was as bad as everything else. It wasn't an escape, it wasn't a way of being strong; I was as ordinary in the air as anywhere else, and that was pretty ordinary. I wasn't going anywhere by small plane, I wasn't going to be a bush pilot, I wasn't going to learn whatever it was my father knew about life and love in the air. I was just going to be me, an average professor in a pressure cooker that couldn't wait to spit me out.

We were parallel with the runway now, on the downwind leg of our approach to the airport, and as Steve turned perpendicular to the runway for the base leg the turbulence increased. I felt as if I were inside a washing machine. A strong crosswind was blowing us south of the runway, and Steve banked the plane fairly steeply to keep us on course; a gust made the plane yaw hard to the left. We were on final approach now, roller-coastering, the plane yawing back and forth in the gusts, Steve crabbing it almost sideways to keep it pointed into the wind and on course with the runway. Incredibly, he held the course, but although some part of me was impressed I was mostly just scared. "If we get down," I told myself, "I'm going to buy that Narco radio, take it home, and listen to it all night." I focused on the radio—how beautiful it was, how I could hear all the flights coming in and out of Logan, how I could listen to the air traffic controllers as they guided each plane precisely to its destination. This would be my consolation prize, my reward for being weak. As we hovered over the runway, Steve eased the control yoke back and forward and around to keep the plane level and the nose up, but a downdraft caught us a second before the stall warning went on and we dropped a foot or two onto the dark pavement.

"Damn!" said Steve. He looked over at me for a response. I didn't care.

All of a sudden it was as if a whirlwind romance had ended. I wanted to be out of the plane, away from Marshfield, away from Steve. I never wanted to fly again. And Steve seemed to know it. We hardly exchanged words as we taxied back to the barn. Inside, I paid quickly without looking at the schedule book, and when I said "See ya" to Steve he said "You bet" almost automatically. Neither one of us believed it. Something had gotten lost, something inside of me, and all I wanted to do was crawl back into my car and be the same person I used to be. At least I could have some comfort in retreat. I didn't even glance at the Narco radio in the display case.

When I got home, I found a message from the dean asking me to call him at his home as soon as possible. He was apologetic, conciliatory. He was sorry not to have gotten back to me immediately, he said, and found my letter compelling: My student could stay at MIT as long as she remained under the care of a psychiatrist. I thanked him, breathing a sigh of relief. At least I wasn't totally ineffective. A couple of hours later, after getting a permission slip from the main desk at McLean Hospital, I entered a locked psychiatric ward for the first time in my life.

Although the metal door seemed unnaturally heavy, and the staff worked behind an enclosure fortified with Plexiglas, the ward didn't seem that odd. The central corridor was wide and spacious; it led down to a sitting room with slightly out-of-date Naugahyde lounge chairs and a TV. The carpet was a soothing, pale gray-maroon, complex as only carpet colors can be, and the walls were a delicate off-white. I could have been in the antechamber to the boardroom of a major corporation. Yet, having been buzzed in through a locked door and knowing I could not leave without being escorted out, I was prone to look for oddities, and noticed immediately that none of the patients' rooms had closed doors: Everyone was required to keep his or her door at least slightly ajar. The place looked peaceful, but fear and ominousness seemed to hang in the air. There was nothing potentially sharp anywhere—no flower vases, no glasses for water, no mirrors.

An attendant took me down to my student's room, a monastic chamber with a bed and a desk. She was sitting on her bed, smiling with a slightly wan, slightly comical smile. We hugged each other. "Bet you never thought you'd see me in a place like this," she said. "I'm glad you're here and not somewhere else," I said too awkwardly.

Someone shrieked behind us. I jumped, turned around. A profoundly anorexic woman, a walking skeleton in a blue-and-purple sweat suit, was walking rather peacefully down the hall, screaming. An attendant came by, talked to her quietly, tried to help her to her room. I didn't see any of the other patients. I looked back at my student.

She sighed. "I didn't know what crazy was until I got here," she said. "I think this place may drive me crazy. Let's go out to the sitting room."

Down the hall, in the comparative quiet of the always-on TV, she told me what had happened, how isolated and aimless she felt at MIT, how much smarter everyone else seemed to be, how she couldn't work as well as she used to, how she didn't know what she wanted to do, how she had to make sure no one knew she was suffering. Her facade got stronger and more polished the more desperate she became, even though she was giving clues to close friends—at one point she scratched geometric patterns on her wrists with razor blades. And now, having survived, she was in limbo.

"I don't know when I'll be out," she said sadly. "I'm supposed to be 'voluntarily' committed, but I can't get the doctor here to agree to release me. I think I've convinced my doctor at MIT that it's safe to let me out, but I don't know what's going to happen. What do I have to do to convince them I'm sane? I really am," she added, sweeping her arm out toward the rest of the ward. "You can tell just by looking around. I'm deeply depressed. But believe me, that's different."

We talked a little about calling lawyers, about the more

sympathetic doctor at MIT, and about ways of convincing him to intervene on her behalf. Periodically the blue-and-purple woman came out of her room, shrieked, and walked back in. She was a human being, a harpy, a creature I had never seen before. I felt sad and appalled; I could see how she frightened my student.

"You know," she said, "when things get bad here I keep telling myself that I'm going to have a *lot* of material for stories." It was a good joke. But after I left, a few minutes later, waiting for the attendant to open the heavy metal door, walking down the cold concrete staircase to the ground floor and the entryway, I stood outside in the clear winter night and looked at the stars. They were beautiful, crystalline; they sank down into the urban glow above the treetops, a canopy wider and older than anything I could imagine, an expanding adventure vaster than anything I would ever undertake. I was outside; my student was inside. I was not physically incarcerated. And so I had a kind of freedom. Yet it was precarious, and I did not know what to do with it. I wondered, as I drove back to my small apartment and my family in Belmont, whether my student was slowly beginning an adventure that would be in some ways more cohesive than my own. And then I caught myself: What adventure was I on? My adventure had ended earlier that day, with a bumpy flight and a hard crosswind landing. I forgot: I was ordinary again. I went back home to the roles, the husband and father and professor, I had played for so long.

Chapter Four

WHAT WE PRAY FOR

"*W*e always get what we pray for," Richard Bach writes in *A Gift of Wings*, "like it or not, no excuses accepted. Every day our prayers turn more into fact; whom we most want to be, we are."

It has been more than six months since I last stopped in at the Marshfield airport. Nevertheless I have come down to the town beach from time to time to walk, to follow the flight paths of the planes as they come in to land on runway two-four, and to think. Today, in early November 1990, a light, cool shower signals winter more than autumn; as I walk along the pebbly sand the rain feels salty, like a hard spray in an ocean wind. Ocean and sky, my two lifelong loves, the first always companionable, the second threatening. Richard Bach's words, which used to float in and out of mind like simple, interesting ideas, now take up the room I ordinarily reserve for specific riddles or answers to riddles: *What are you praying for?* I hear in my head, over and over. *Where is your love?*

A few days ago I was walking around Walden Pond in an

97

early snowfall. At one point I stopped on the far side of the lake among a small grove of pine trees—young, skinny trees around me like a tower with an oculus, so that, in looking up, I could see only the sky; the rest of the pond, the rest of Thoreau's precious forest, was off-limits to my sight. And somehow I knew this was my own sense of choice or need, my own prayer, thrown outward into the realities of the world. The route to the sky was straight up; there was no intermediate step, no way of easing into the air or easing away from my comfortable patch of earth. If I wanted the sky, I would have to leap for it.

But I didn't want the sky, or anything associated with it; at least I didn't think so. I had changed. Something about seeing my student at McLean, so wounded and yet so in need of my help, reminded me of who I was, *really*; it was time for fantasy to cease. If I prayed with my life, then my prayer was one of purposefulness and responsibility. I was happiest when I was needed, when I was helping other people. That was one of the reasons I had become a professor, and perhaps—though this was harder to admit to myself—one of the reasons I had become a father. And I was needed: My children loved to have me around on those mornings and afternoons when Lesley was working on her dissertation, and I felt lucky to be able to devote far more hours than most working parents to their care, even if for some reason that luck had a sour taste to it. My students needed me; I had already helped many of them with academic and personal problems, although none perhaps so vividly as my student at McLean. As the spring wore on, she moved beyond tragedy to a brighter, more idiosyncratic promise. She flourished in her writing classes, and by summer was planning a trip to New Zealand, an adventure she had long denied herself. She was more than alive, and I knew that in some way I had contributed to her rescue. And then, on the other side, there was a warning:

Step too far out of the bounds of your purposeful and responsible life, I told myself, take too many risks, and your prayer will fracture—*you* will fracture; you yourself will wind up in McLean in a locked ward, and for you there will be no rescuer.

I stayed out of small airplanes. And yet something had been set in motion, some hatch had opened in my life and cold air was rushing in; I seemed to be waking up in spite of myself. And I tried to close the hatch, tried to keep things warm and dark, but I could not.

This spring at MIT I did what I thought was expected; I devoted myself to a book—a book on Christian Science, as it turned out. Because the manuscript grew so clearly out of work that I had already done, I could not imagine it being a liability. The book could only enhance the mold I had already made for myself. Yet the more I tried to fit that mold, the more things kept going wrong. In late May, the chairman called me into his office to ask whether it were still possible to cancel the book contract with my publisher. He had read the first third of the book, he said, and had determined that it "lacked intellectual stature." It was not the kind of book that would clarify my standing at MIT, he explained charitably. He pressed me again to publish my dissertation, and left me with a warning about my other work: "We know you're a good teacher," he said, but teaching wouldn't cut it at MIT.

My book had already been judged a detriment to my career; I was wasting my time even finishing it. My good behavior had turned sour once again. I went home that evening, drank a great deal of cheap California cabernet sauvignon, and attempted to call the parents of my first girlfriend at shortly after midnight (fortunately they lived in California, so it was only a little after nine, and they were out). I left an elaborate message on their answering machine, repeating a few words to get them right. I then went back into the living room, my book manu-script in my hand. I flipped through the pages. So much thought, so much life lived. Could this truly lack "intellectual stature"? What the hell did that mean anyway? A drunken anger came over me, and as I paced the room I vowed to finish the book even if it cost me my job. At least I would have one thing I could call my own.

I went back to writing the next morning. A few days later I received a letter from the chairman officially outlining my "dim" prospects at MIT. It was early June now, and the aca-demic year was coming to a close. I received a different kind of letter from the MIT awards committee, urging me to attend the awards convocation a few days later. When it came time to announce the Everett Moore Baker Award for teaching—the "kiss of death"—I was one of three recipients. What was most astonishing, aside from the wonder of the award itself, was the reaction of the faculty outside my program. "Congratulations and condolences," said several professors as they came up to—to what? To share my happiness? To console me? The award went unacknowledged in my program for two days, until I finally called one of the senior professors just to ask whether anyone had heard about it.

I was doing badly at MIT by doing well; but even that seemed unclear to me. What did "doing well" mean? I had thought it meant doing what I always did—being good, filling the mold. Yet somehow I seemed to keep fracturing the mold, and my "goodness" was a source of trouble. The prayer of my life seemed to be, not to fit in, but to stumble and stand out and help people and cause difficulty. Was that what I wanted?

The questions haven't changed over the past few months, although the book on religion is done and settled with its publisher and I have gone back to another semester of teaching—this time with packed classes, since so many students want to see what another "kiss of death" winner is like. I have come down to the Marshfield beach to get away from all that, and to get away from mounting worries about all the things my salary won't do for my family.

Yet there is really nothing for me in Marshfield beside the beach and the airport, and I haven't been to the airport in months. The rain falls around me like a refuge, but it's cold, and the water is running into the pockets of my Gore-Tex jacket. My hands are beginning to freeze. I trudge back to the car, climb in, and sit for a few minutes, listening to a tape a friend gave me.

It's an album by Rickie Lee Jones called *The Magazine*, and somehow it's gotten to the third song on side two without my even noticing. The light rain thrums on the roof and windshield, oddly resonant, waking me up. Jones's voice is a little harsh, defiant. A burst of wind turns the houses near me into a blur of water. The song quiets into a final refrain—"take a deep breath and break that chain," she sings as the wind picks up and the car rocks slightly. "Take a deep breath and break that chain," she sings, and now I am listening, more than listening, looking somehow, although there is nowhere to look and nothing to see. The song fades into silence.

A few minutes later I have pulled into the airport parking lot. The low cloud ceiling has kept the pilots away; there are only a couple of other cars around. I recognize the red Toyota Supra, which belongs to Keith Douglass, who runs the place; the rusting Volkswagen Scirocco, attractively camouflaged with red Rustoleum, belongs to Rod. I wander inside.

It's quiet here, almost like a museum, and as usual when I come here after a long absence, little seems to have changed. The bathrooms are finally in, and someone bought the Narco 830 radio I wanted, but other than that it looks just the way it looked back in March. Through the lounge windows in the far side of the barn I can see the planes tied down, wet, gleaming. Keith is sitting behind the counter, studying a manual for instrument flight.

"Mind if I go take a look at the planes?" I ask.

Keith, whom I've seen before in sullen or preoccupied moods, now looks up with a warmth in his eyes, a look I don't know. He's glad to see me, even though we've only said hello a couple of times before. I wonder briefly what I've done to deserve this welcome.

"No problem," he says. "Not the best day for walking around outside, though."

"I kind of like days like these."

"You won't when you're a pilot," he says, smiling. Nodding a good-bye, I head out the back door toward the ramp and the planes.

"*When* you're a pilot." He said that. But I haven't given any signs of being one. I walk out onto the ramp, past the gasoline pump with 100-octane low-lead fuel, past the hangar that used to house celebrated trial lawyer F. Lee Bailey's Learjet when he ran the airport and hoped to turn it into a miniature Logan for business air traffic. The lore around Marshfield is pretty extensive, and even people like me who just pass through pick it up quickly, in part because the place is such a classic piece of Americana. Like many small airports, it started in the 1930s as a farm with a grass landing strip; the red barn really was a barn then, and what are now pilots' and flight instructors' offices were stalls for horses and cows. Once, going upstairs to the old bathroom, I came across the block and tackle the farmhands had used to haul hay up to the loft. By the late 1930s, the farm had become an airport in earnest. An early photograph shows Stinsons and Taylorcrafts and Piper Cubs lined up in front of the barn, where someone has painted MARSHFIELD in eight-foot-high letters on the roof. It was, as I think about it, much like Summerton, the airport where my father learned to fly. He would have liked it here; he would have felt comfortable.

The Marshfield grass strip dozed through three decades of takeoffs and landings until 1965, when the town bought the 150-acre site and its three buildings for $20,000. It was Harold Scott, a math teacher in town, who swung opinion in favor of a public airport; his figures showed that an airport would cost homeowners fewer tax dollars than a 120-house development. Bailey, who had formed a partnership to run the operation (known as an FBO, a fixed-base operator), won the first lease. Three years later, the town installed a 3,000-foot paved runway that took the airport out of amateur status and offered enough room for larger planes—twin-engine prop planes, like the Beechcraft Travelair or the Cessna 310, or even a small jet—to get in and out. Yet the place never really became a business aviation mecca, and Bailey bailed out after a few years, having turned the FBO over to Charlie Hancock.

In the 1970s two brothers, Dave and Lars Riggs, worked out an arrangement with Hancock to offer flight instruction, teaching students in a Cessna 172 and an old Piper Cherokee 140—one high-wing plane and one low-wing plane, one with a radio and one without. It was a shoestring operation, done, as so much of general aviation was done, out of love and habit. After Hancock sold the FBO in the late '70s, it went through a couple of owners—one who saw a good chance to make a profit, another who mostly wanted to be closer to the world of flying—until 1988, when Keith and his mechanic partner, Ed Novak, bought the place. In the meantime the town, with federal and state aid, had made a number of improvements, including new taxiways and a parking ramp, and an NDB—a non-directional beacon—to give Marshfield a basic instrument approach for instrument-rated pilots. About sixty pilots currently keep their planes at the airport, either outdoors in tie-down spots near the barn or in fancy metal hangars that go for about $50,000 in condominiumlike deals. A tie-down spot costs $40 a month—more in my price range, if I had a plane.

Passing the blue maintenance hangar, I walk down the taxiway to the far tie-down spots, where old-timers and late-comers and people who for some reason or another just don't want to be up near the barn leave their planes. This is a more idiosyncratic assortment—not the Piper Archer with its metallic red-and-blue paint, or the Piper Cherokee Cruiser fully equipped for instrument flying, but the aging Cessna 150 with faded maroon-and-white paint, and the even older Cessna 140, and the Grumman Tiger painted to look like a Spitfire from World War II. Strange old planes, some well loved, some not. I stop beside the plane farthest from the hangars—an older Piper Cherokee 140, white with black and red stripes, number N9666J, as in "Juliet."

It's hard to tell how old six-six-Juliet is just from looking at it; the old-style engine cowling with its small air vents reminds me of the first Cherokees, which came off the Piper assembly line in Vero Beach, Florida, in 1961. They were a revelation in the aircraft industry then: low-wing, all-metal airplanes, priced at $9,995, with wide landing gear and oleo gear struts to make landings smooth (or smoother than they might otherwise have been). They cruised at about 104 knots on about eight gallons of 96-octane gasoline an hour, and they were relatively inexpensive to maintain and repair. Simplicity of design was a central motive behind the airplane, and the Cherokee came with four hundred fewer parts than its nearest Piper competitor, the Comanche (evidently none of those four hundred parts was essential to a safe flight). The first Cherokee had a strange control yoke, a kind of swollen black metal half-moon, like a David Lynch vision of a steering wheel for a diabolical 1961 Chevrolet Bel Air. Later versions had a more conventional yoke, an elongated metal U that the pilot could easily grasp with either one or both hands, and later planes shifted to a heavy plastic yoke. This one, oddly enough, has the plastic yoke, but it also has old-style instruments—a gray-and-black attitude indicator, rather than a blue-and-black one. The seats are all torn up, the damage somewhat clumsily covered with sheepskins, and the glass is scratched and needs replacing. The vinyl interior trim is cracked and torn in various places, and in general the plane looks as if it could use a good interior teardown and rebuild. Yet I like this plane. The paint is good, and I can tell from the smoothness of the propeller that it's been recently overhauled. I could have a lot of fun in a plane like this.

I stare at the instruments, thinking about what they do, what they mean. Suddenly I realize water's dripping down my nose. I've been here a long time. The rain is falling harder, with a harsh wind. I look up to see a maroon Jeep driving down the taxiway toward me.

It's Steve. He pulls up beside six-six-Juliet, popping open the passenger door on his Jeep.

"I was just about to leave for the day," he says, "but I saw your car in the lot. Figured you'd be out here somewhere. Want a ride back?"

It's a big 2,500 feet from where I stand to the barn, but I'm flattered that Steve would remember my old Subaru and would bother to drive down the taxiway to find me. Again, something I feel I haven't earned—friendship.

"Sure," I say. I start to hop in—I've always wanted a Jeep, though I've never ridden in one—but first I have to clear a couple of books from the seat. I scoop them up, sit down, and look at them: Richard Bach's *Jonathan Livingston Seagull* and *A Gift of Wings*. One of them has a leather bookmark with an Indian design etched into it.

"You read Bach?"

"A new student gave those to me," Steve says as he turns around on the taxiway. We begin to drive back slowly, the barn alternately clear and blurred in the wind-driven rain. "She wanted me to read them—said they were why she decided to start flying. I've never heard of him. You ever read any of his stuff?"

I laugh, thinking about how I spent hours in the fall of 1972 with my first girlfriend, Janet, talking about *Jonathan Livingston Seagull*, about being an outcast and trying things no one else was willing to try, about seeking perfection. That book brought us together. A long time ago.

"Yeah, I've read Bach. There's some stuff there you might like. What's your student's name?"

"Priscilla."

I want to tell Steve about the part of Bach that's been on my mind lately, the part from *A Gift of Wings* about praying with your whole life, but can't do it. Besides, I'm interested in this new student and her gift of books. In the past year Steve and I have had a couple of hours of cockpit time to talk, and I know he's engaged. I also know a gift of books can be a funny thing, magical—meaning almost nothing at all, and everything.

"So—you gonna do some more flying?" Steve asks as we approach the barn.

"I don't know, Steve. I don't think I'll ever be a pilot. I really don't."

"You know what?" he says. "I've spent a lot of time at airports. I've taught a lot of people to fly. And I've never seen

106

anyone come down to the airport in the rain and look at planes who doesn't sooner or later become a pilot. That's just the way it is. You'll get that license."

I stare at him for a moment, seeing his complete sincerity. "This is a nice Jeep," I say.

"Yeah, it is," he says. "My parents told me to get something practical, and they nearly hit the roof when I came home with this. But it's been wonderful." He drives me around to the front of the barn where my car, as old as it is, looks new in the rain. I do like the Jeep: It's simple, small on the outside, big inside—a machine for the outdoors. I think briefly of Alaska, of the De Havilland Beaver, of my father.

"I'll see you around," I say, remembering the last time I said good-bye to Steve. Then something had gone wrong, something had ended; but now there seemed to be some understanding between us.

"Yeah, take it easy," he says. "Remember what I said."

"Let me know what you think of Bach," I say. "And that student."

He smiles. "Okay," he says as I shut the door. Then he's off, past the birch and alder lining Old Colony Lane, and I'm back in my car, listening to Rickie Lee Jones, getting what I prayed for.

II.

*T*he physical world is full of secrets. For so many years I simply never knew that, or never let myself realize it. "Spirit is the real and eternal," said Mary Baker Eddy, the discoverer and founder of Christian Science, and "matter is the unreal and temporal." I did not want to live in an unreal world of time, but in a real world of eternity; I had the choice. My mother, for whom the "unreal and temporal" world was a frightening place of possibilities and temptations that she could not bring herself to embrace, was perhaps more strict with me than most Christian Science mothers in emphasizing the value of the spiritual gift I had been given. The world into which I seemed to have been born could not help or harm me, she explained, because it was not part of God's creation; it was a kind of fiction, a human misperception of the spiritual universe all around us. Because we did not go to doctors, relying on Christian Science to heal us of whatever illusion of illness or injury we might experience, it was essential for me to believe what my mother and her church taught me. I hung close to the language and spirit of the religion, which itself nurtured my interest in words and ways of seeing the unseen even as it truncated my interest in the physical world.

Yet I could never quite extricate myself from that world, for it was the world of my father: It was where fast cars moved freely across the highway, where motorboats pulled water-skiers in precise formations through buoyant salty water, where metal objects weighing tons lifted themselves into the air and flew thousands of miles without a mishap. This, I knew in my heart, was physical; yet whatever made my father's world work was, I thought, lodged in a knowledge of physical science that was simply inaccessible to me. I was bad at math and science in grade school and high school, not because I was not talented but because I could not see the point: To be faithful to my primary beliefs, I had to leave my father's science behind. For him science was a matter of physical laws (he always wanted to put a bumper sticker saying "Repeal the Ohms Law" on our car), while for me Science—that is, Christian Science—was a matter of faith and spiritual understanding. The two lines of thought crossed at no point, and although my father came regularly to church with my mother he never lost his primary allegiance to what he had learned as a boy in Summerton: that a wing worked in a certain way, a piston inside a cylinder worked in a certain way, a carburetor worked in a certain way, and the combination could lift you into the air in a way wholly different from the kind of prayer my mother practiced. I could not find a place in my life for my father's knowledge, because to accept it would have been to admit that my unrealities were realities—that medicine was a reality and could, in fact, heal, that the body and its pleasures were realities, that the study of fluid dynamics as it related to wing design was a reality, that technological advances were important in themselves and not signs or symbols of some spiritual knowledge. I stayed close to my father, or as close as I could, by rejecting what he loved, as he seemed to reject what I loved or thought I had to love; the tension between us had a strange balance that, while making us unavailable to each other, never quite drove us apart. But if there were many details of the physical world that I felt compelled to deny even though their existence fascinated me, the one underlying fact of my father—his occasional, instinctive sense of humanity—always threw me off. He made me wonder if the knowledge I resisted was rooted, not in facts and equations, but in a heartfelt conviction that the world worked in a particular way and could be loved for itself.

I saw this in him once when I was a child and our cat, Siddhartha, had disappeared. I knew that the cat had injured himself a few days earlier when he tried to leap from a tree branch to my parents' third-story bedroom window. I did not see him fall to the ground, but I did see him shortly afterward, running sideways with an odd and slightly horrible awkwardness. He stayed near the house for several days, more or less eating, more or less all right. Then he vanished.

In an unusual moment of candor, my father explained to

me that Siddhartha had probably gone away to die. Something inside him told him he couldn't survive, my father said, and he wanted to go where people wouldn't pester him by trying to help. The explanation astonished me. It had never occurred to me that a living being, a cat or even a person, might sense that it was time to die. By the time I was four or five, my mother had already made it clear that when people left the earth, they didn't really die; it just seemed that way to us, although we could learn to know better.

I remember, for example, when my grandfather—my father's father—died. I was about six. My father cried during and after the funeral, although he tried not to. My mother remained impassive—though slightly solicitous toward me—and reminded me that death was something that only *seemed* real. In reality, she said, the perfect identity of my grandfather was eternal. What that meant, she explained, was that he was still alive, although we couldn't see or hear him. As I talked with my mother about this, I glanced frequently toward my father, whose tears awed me. I had no idea what to say to him. Yet I felt the greatest sympathy for him as he clearly summoned all his husbandly devotion to support, with his silence, my mother's authority.

When, a couple of years later, my father explained to me about our cat, I again felt a rush of sympathy for him—and, oddly, of gratitude. There was something unexpectedly comforting about the view of the world that his explanation implied. Somewhere in himself, despite his large-scale fears, he knew that no tricks were being played: Creatures did what they did from an instinct deeper than fear, from a kind of intelligence at once simpler and more profound than the Mind I had been introduced to in Sunday school. His words soothed my sense of loss; I was almost happy. A day or two later he came into the yard with Siddhartha's matted body, which he had found by a hedge while walking the dog. He buried him right then. My mother came out later and, in line with some superstitions that she admitted to having and refused to relinquish, did a little ritual of Christian burial that she herself had created.

Siddhartha's instinct to die alone came back to mind about twenty years later, in 1980, when my mother had grown incurably ill. We were, of course, not supposed to admit her incurability. She had spent so much of her life denying the reality of whatever was animal or material that my father, brother, sister and I were all supposed to be ready to witness her own great realization of her spiritual being, which would also restore her "temple," her body. But we were not to be preached to. We knew we were witnessing the ravages of cancer, and before that solemn pain we held to our sense of the real—real pain, real love, a depth of feeling that moved from my mother's shrunken body to the blessed fact of our own corporeal existence.

What astonished us, however, was my mother's slowly increasing, unmistakable desire to die alone. At first she would tell us what ideas and encouragement the Christian Science practitioners were giving to heal her. Then she began, so gradually, to complain: how these practitioners rarely visited her, preferring to pray with her over the telephone; how their ideas were trite or simpleminded, their prayers ineffectual. Then she refused to discuss her faith at all. Finally, when it had become difficult for her to speak, and to lift the telephone receiver, she announced without a trace of either pride or sadness that she now refused to talk to the practitioners when they telephoned. After that, she said very little. For a couple of months I sat regularly in her room, occasionally speaking, earning silence in return. On my next-to-last visit with her, as I was leaving, she suddenly pointed, in an act of almost scorching clarity, to the full moon outside the window. I saw her in a silent anticlimax the next afternoon; she died two days later.

But I have never gotten over how this woman and this cat should die the same death. My mother was a crusader for the spirit; in her healthy years, had someone suggested that she would want to die the way her animals died, she would certainly have scoffed. Yet there was a time when we could say, with the full authority of the heart, this death was not illusion; this communion between the dying and death was not some metaphysical sleight of hand. There was no room for euphemism or clever jargon; this death guaranteed at least one taste of what was real. Though our whole intelligence resisted it, it was there. It was the fundamental instinct resolving itself into a kind of pure presence—cat and prey, cat leaping, sheer experience that no external portrait can capture.

Animals crawl toward the privacy of their death from this instinct. I believe my mother, too, was finally in the hands of this fundamental directive, so much more powerful and straightforward than the spirituality she preached to us, and had had preached to her. But it was my father—the failed engineering professor, the mechanic, the pilot who lived in a realm of aerial love and knowledge and who gave up his wings to raise a family—it was my father who taught me this. And this, I realize suddenly, was the evidence of his gentleness, rare as it was; this was what he meant by being gentle. The heresy he once confided to me, regarding the seemingly small matter of a cat, became at last my mother's faith.

The secret that made it possible for my father to be so instinctive and yet so frightened of instinct, so committed to scientific knowledge that I could not reach him, was a secret I could never unlock. Yet now, veering toward the sky because of some need I can hardly identify, I begin to get the faintest whiff of joy that comes with new knowledge, and begin to realize the pleasure my father must have taken in what he knew.

Steve and I go up on November 20, a few days before Thanksgiving. It's a brilliantly clear, calm day.

"Why don't you do the takeoff this time," he says after we've done the engine run-up to make sure everything's operating smoothly.

"No thanks." Things still happen too quickly for me in small planes, especially on takeoffs (I try not to think about landings). Suddenly you're rolling down the runway, surrounded by a half-deafening roar, and you're trying to keep the airplane headed straight down the centerline, but as you pick up speed you press a little too hard on the left rudder pedal and the plane begins to veer left, then right as you overcorrect with the right rudder pedal, and suddenly you're all over the runway at 50 knots and a second away from crashing into a hangar—no thanks.

"Come on," Steve says nudgingly as we roll out onto the end of runway six. He's got the plane headed precisely on the runway centerline; I can see 3,000 feet to the far end, where the alders and ground shrubs make a minor wilderness. "You're never going to get this if you don't try it. What could go wrong?"

"Plenty," I say aloud, but I push the throttle forward—when in doubt, go, I tell myself, my old motorcycling motto—and I'm suddenly alone in a cocoon of thunder as the 160-horsepower Lycoming engine roars up to its maximum takeoff RPM and we begin to roll, rather slowly it seems to me, down the runway. Thirty-five knots, and I'm doing pretty well; we've passed the barn and the blue maintenance hangar. I shift my eyes back to the centerline, then back to the airspeed indicator at the upper left of the instrument panel. Forty-three

113

knots. All of a sudden the plane begins to veer left, which makes sense because I'm looking left, but the runway is only 37 feet wide on either side of the centerline and we've already chewed up 10 feet of that while I've spent a couple of microseconds fixated on the airspeed. In another second we'll be off the runway. I push down on the right pedal, too hard, just as I feared, and suddenly the centerline rushes off to the left in a blur as we reach fifty-five knots and the plane begins to struggle into the air, its nosewheel up, its main gear not quite off the ground, its nose pointed the wrong way: We're half taking off into the bushes to the right of the runway. I freeze; at the same moment I hear a reassuring clunk from Steve's side of the plane, where he's planted his foot squarely on the left rudder pedal, and suddenly we're up, headed straight and true down the runway about 50 feet off the ground, then 100, wobbling slightly, then 200; we're passing over the houses along the Marshfield beach, and then we're out to sea. "It's all yours," Steve says, and I begin to fly.

"You've got to trust the airplane," he says to me as we make a right climbing turn toward Duxbury Harbor. "The airplane *will* do what you want it to do. It *will* run straight down the centerline. It *will* take off. You don't have to believe in the airplane. But you do have to believe that *you* can make it happen."

What a distinction, I think to myself. I've always tried to believe in what didn't require belief or faith; the only thing I haven't believed in was my own ability to be, to do. And I almost just killed myself by not believing—or would have if Steve hadn't been doing his job, which was about five-tenths flying and five-tenths sizing up the student. I was lucky. No— not lucky. I was in good hands.

But it was more excitement than I needed, and as we turn

southwest over the Gurnet Point Lighthouse toward Plymouth
my stomach begins to react. Sensing this may be a short flight,
I try to figure out what might distract me from the slight motion
of the plane and my recurrent fear of impending death. There's
one instrument on the panel that I've never seen in operation—
the VOR. I know it's a navigational device of some kind; my
pilot's manual has told me that VOR stands for "very-high-
frequency-omnidirectional-rangefinding" and that all those big
compass circles I saw on my aviation map, my sectional chart,
were actually centered around VOR ground stations. Each
ground station has a specific radio frequency, and on that frequency it sends out 360 radio beams or radials—one for each
degree of the compass. In theory, I seem to remember from my
reading, if you turn on your VOR receiver in the airplane you
ought to be able to pick up one of those radials, and then you
fly your airplane directly to the VOR station. If that's not exactly where you want to go, well—you can tune in the next
station closer to your destination. And so on.

"How does this thing work?" I tap the glass in front of the
VOR. Steve, who has sensed that I'm already fading, brightens.

"Oh, this thing's great," he says. "You can go anywhere
with it, almost. Let's look at it for a second." He explains it to
me simply, precisely. Around the outside of the VOR is a ring
of numbers—compass headings—that you can adjust with a
knob called an "omnibearing selector" ("Just think of it as the
knob you turn for now," he says helpfully). In the middle of the
instrument is a white vertical needle, with a series of white dots
running to the left and right of the needle. At the bottom are
the numbers you use to dial in the appropriate radio frequency.

"Let's say you want to go to Providence," he says, pulling
a sectional chart out of his bag and opening it. I look over at the
chart—Providence looks a long way away. It's a big airport; I

can't quite imagine taking this little plane there. We begin to lose altitude as I study the map. Steve pulls back gently on the yoke without commenting.

"See this little box above the airport that says 'Providence VORTAC'?" he asks. "A VORTAC is just like a VOR only it also has military uses. Anyway, there's a radio frequency off to the left—one-one-five-point-six. Go ahead and dial one-one-five-point-six into the VOR."

As I dial in the numbers, the needle—which until now has hewed to the center as if it were glued there—suddenly swings way off to the left. In a tiny window on the right side of the instrument, a little orange-and-yellow flag goes away and the word *to* appears. This makes no sense.

"Okay, good," Steve says. "Everything's fine. What it's telling you is that you're on some radial that's going *to* the station—that is, to Providence—but you're way off to the right. You have to think of the needle as the ground and the dots as the airplane. If the needle swings left, it's like the ground moving left, which means you're off to the right. Okay, now let's turn that knob to find out what compass numbers we need for a course to Providence."

I turn the omnibearing knob and the numbers pass—180, 190, 200—but nothing happens. I keep turning—250, 260, 270—and the needle swings suddenly to the right.

"Slowly, slowly," says Steve. "You went past your heading. The VOR is very sensitive. Turn the knob back, slowly."

I do, and as I approach 260 I see the needle begin to move slightly toward the center. Slowing way down, I turn the knob until 250 is showing at the top of the VOR, and amazingly enough, the needle falls smack into the center of the instrument.

"Great," says Steve. "That means we need a course of two hundred fifty degrees, or slightly west of southwest, to get to

Providence. Now, what course are we actually flying?"

Looking at the directional gyro, I discover I'm flying west-northwest, about 320 degrees.

"All you have to do now is turn left seventy degrees," Steve explains, "and you'll be on course for Providence. It's as simple as that—well, almost."

I've come to recognize "well, almost" among pilots as a sign that there's more I'll need to learn about something that appears simple. Yet as I roar on toward Providence at 2,500 feet, keeping the plane more or less headed on a course of 250 degrees, I feel a strange kind of fascination, and a happiness much like what came over me when it suddenly dawned on me how a wing flew. If one of the secrets of the physical world for me was the low-pressure zone above a wing, another was the radio wave—a constant oscillation but also a straight line on a particular frequency that could snatch pilots from the terror of being lost and give them a route and a destination. Before this somehow I had imagined myself flying rather aimlessly through the air, hoping my course heading matched the landmarks I was supposed to see on the ground, expecting somehow that sooner or later I would get off course and lost, like the early transcontinental pilots I had read about in the adventure books of my childhood. Some of them found safe places to land, reoriented themselves, and arrived safely at their destinations; some crashed and died. It was a crapshoot, and if the wind blew you off course or darkness fell before you could get down you were done for; you had no backup systems, no technological version of mercy.

Modern airliners have complex satellite-based and ground-based navigation systems, and while I feared airliners for other reasons I never worried about them getting lost. But somehow I had never foreseen that a small plane, too, could rely on radio equipment to find its way, and that it could travel safely all across the country from VOR to VOR. There was a kind of ground-based prayer of life for the airplane I was in that said simply, "You will not be lost; or, if you are lost, you will always know how to find yourself."

I glance over at the map again: Blue lines, highways of the air, run from the Providence VOR southeast to Martha's Vineyard and Nantucket, and west on a route that ultimately crosses the Newark–LaGuardia–John F. Kennedy Terminal Control Area, on its way toward Philadelphia or Allentown or Williamsport, Pennsylvania, where the engine for this airplane was manufactured. And beyond that, I can see from looking at the far side of this chart, is the Detroit sectional chart, then the Chicago and Omaha and Cheyenne and Salt Lake City and finally the Klamath Falls sectional, where—if I followed the blue lines from VOR to VOR—I would wind up near my most-loved coast, perhaps somewhere near Eugene, Oregon, where I had friends and where I might once have lived before coming to MIT. Maybe Steve is right—maybe somehow I do have an instinct to fly—but beyond that is something more like a guided instinct, sustained and corrected by knowledge, the knowledge of radio beacons across the country drawing me on, helping me to learn by going where I have to go.

Back on earth a half hour later, Steve and I talk briefly as we tie down the plane.

"You were doing a lot all of a sudden there," he says with real enthusiasm. "That radio work, and the way you stayed with me all the way through the landing—that was the first time you've done that. You're catching on. How did you feel about it?"

"I don't know," I say. It still seems a little dreamlike. But for the first time I thought I liked it. No—that wasn't right—I thought it was something I could actually *do*, something I actually *was* doing.

Steve smiles. "Some people just freeze up. It's surprising how long it takes to learn that when you're flying the airplane, you're flying the airplane. You'd think people would be born with that, but not many are."

Was my father? My mind clicks back to him in an instant, thinking of how he seemed on those rare occasions when he really talked about flying—how fully engaged he was, as if he were reliving each precise moment of the flight. He had the instinct to aviate, and yet he was afraid; he had the instinct to teach through love, yet he mostly taught through fear. How had he been so harmed? What had ruined him? Christian Science, a religion that fought his instinctive faith, had come to him with his marriage to my mother, but his wounds had much earlier origins. Wounds of the soul can be healed slowly, given the right circumstances, or can be made chronically worse through the critical passages of life—religion, marriage, children. How much did these passages make him feel even more disconnected with the self he began to create in the air? Were marriage and family, supposedly the best kinds of behavior for him, actually the worst? Maybe he just shouldn't have had a family. But then—it's an awful thought.

"See that man over there?" Steve points to a tall, slightly portly, handsome older man standing near the barn, talking with one of the other flight instructors. "That's Lew Owen. He's the FAA's designated examiner for our students here—the guy who takes you up for your check-ride. He's a great guy, really wonderful. His whole life is flying."

Steve pauses for a moment. "You remember the Samantha Smith crash?" I nod; like the Sioux City crash and the earlier disasters in Chicago and San Diego, the crash of that Bar Harbor

Airlines flight in 1985 hovers in the back of my mind like a never-quite-familiar nightmare. Samantha Smith, the Maine schoolgirl who had written Soviet Premier Yuri Andropov asking him to stop the nuclear arms race, had won me over as she had won over millions of others. Her genuineness seemed immune to media hype, and I found myself happily following the news reports of her adventures in the Soviet Union. That she and her father and four other passengers and the pilot and first officer could die on a simple hop from Boston to the Auburn-Lewiston airport aboard a Beechcraft 99, a wonderfully reliable commuter airliner that I myself had taken several times in the late 1970s—it was horrible, inconceivable. Yet it had happened. I'm sorry all over again, and my face must show it, because Steve pauses even longer than usual before continuing.

"Lew, you see . . ." says Steve, "Well, his son David was the first officer on that flight."

I stare at Owen, and suddenly Marshfield seems very large and real and deeply connected to the rest of the world, to fathers and sons who lose each other. I want to help this man who stands across the ramp from me, whose life I know nothing about, whom I have not even met. I glance at Steve, who seems to know what I'm thinking.

"I'll introduce you," he says.

III.

*L*ew Owen has the kindest smile I've ever seen, even from a distance. He's talking with Rod as Steve and I approach; I don't quite catch the conversation because I'm so interested in Owen. His job, it seems to me, is one of the jobs my father might have held if things had turned out a little differently, if he had had more luck or more money or more faith in his dreams—the biggest "ifs" in life. I feel a sudden burst of anger at Richard Bach and his idea of always getting what you pray for. You don't always get what you pray for; you don't always pray with your life. Your life is woven into a web of other lives, and sometimes the web is so dense—so well tied with love and loss and care— that you can't get what you pray for even if all you pray for is more room within the web. Lew Owen didn't pray for his son's death; my father didn't pray for his mother's death, or his wife's. But death is one sure constrictor of the web, and what you get afterward is nothing like a blessing, a divine benefaction; it is a cold, hard, lonely ground, a living zero in which you find that some force of fate or chance has given you a shove in a way you hadn't expected and could not control. Your life is nothing so benignly courageous as a prayer. And yet I still believe in Bach's words, as if they were one version of matter in modern phys- ics—meaningless as waves, essential as particles. I hang on to the particles.

Steve introduces me to Lew. He's a big-featured man, big-boned, and his face is wide enough to accommodate a capa- cious smile without seeming the least bit compromised. He wears what I think of as an old navy flight instructor's uniform— black polished shoes, black pants, white shirt, white tie, and a time-tried A-2 leather jacket—the real thing, not some $300 knockoff from a specialty catalog—with wings and his name embroidered over the left breast pocket. The only variation on the uniform is his black V-necked sweater; as his unzipped jacket flaps slightly in the breeze, I can see "Eastern Express" embroidered on the sweater.

"How was it up there today?" Lew asks.

"It was great," I say. "We were doing some VOR work. That's really a neat instrument."

Lew looks a little distant, and I assume it's because he's

trying to figure out why I'm learning the VOR so early in my flight training: VOR use is part of the navigation instruction that comes a little later, after you learn to take off and land without scattering yourself all over the runway. I want to tell him that Steve's one of the smartest instructors I ever met—that he teaches by following my questions rather than following some rigid set of lesson tasks—but Lew's thinking about something else.

"You know, it's incredible what's happened in general aviation navigation in the past few years," he says, "just incredible. We didn't even have the VOR when I was learning to fly, and now there's Loran and global positioning systems, satellite systems for small planes—just amazing." What's striking is how amazed, how delighted, Lew looks, as if he were watching genuine miracles occur in his own profession. I feel a little jaded, even though I hardly know what he's talking about. But then I also notice something else—something about his eyes. They're as kind and generous as his smile when he's looking right at you, but there's also something inherently distant in them, and when he looks away—as he does now, looking toward the sky while talking about VORs and Lorans—his eyes seem small suddenly, and luminous, as if they had never finished with tears. I want to bring him back, but I'm clumsy.

"I was, ah, just noticing your sweater," I say. "Didn't Bar Harbor Airlines become Eastern Express when Eastern bought them out?"

I can feel Steve stiffen slightly at my question, and I realize what a land mine I might have stepped on. But after all, it's Lew who's wearing the sweater.

Lew looks down at his sweater, almost as if he'd forgotten it. "Yes, that's right," he says, with a smaller smile. "It was Bar Harbor."

122

"That was a wonderful airline," I say. "I used to love those Beechcraft ninety-nine's they flew. I took them a lot in the late seventies to visit my sister up in Maine."

"Where's she live?" he asks, a little unexpectedly.

"Swan's Island. I'd fly into Bar Harbor."

"Right, sure," he says. "Beautiful country there. Acadia National Park. My son flew for Bar Harbor, you know."

"Yes," I say awkwardly. I don't know what else to say; I don't know if I've done any damage. There's silence until Steve eases us into the next moment. "Well, I guess we'll wrap things up inside," he says, motioning to me to head toward the door. "It's a good day to fly if you're going up, Lew."

Lew's smile grows wide again. "Any day like this is a good day to fly."

"Did I blow it with Lew?" I ask Steve after we get inside.

"You mean about Bar Harbor?" he says. "No, I don't think so. Lew actually talks about his son pretty often. He'll probably talk to you more about it if you're down here more. He's really a good guy who's been through a lot. You should get to know him."

"I'd like to," I say as I pay my bill—1.4 hours of flying (how could I have stayed in the air that long?) at $62 an hour, plus $23 an hour for the flight instructor. It's cheaper than psychotherapy, I tell myself jokingly, but since money is one of my problems I don't know how I'm going to afford this if I decide to keep going.

"Want to book another time now?" Steve asks.

"I'll call in," I say, unable to explain why. Steve doesn't ask.

"No problem," he says. "You did well today. Hope I'll see you soon."

Pulling out of the Marshfield parking lot, I feel like a man who's been given a second chance at romance. Yes, things ended badly six months ago; the plane pulled me too hard from my ordinary life. If I flew I might be free, I might escape. But how would I be free? What would I escape? Flying was all passion and confusion, and my old fear of being bad quickly overcame my urge to widen the web, to gain some kind of breathing room. I pulled back. Yet even that retreat was useful, although I came away from flying full of self-loathing, as if I had failed somehow. I had not failed; maybe I had merely moved too fast. I did not realize how much I had acquired, as Sara Ruddick writes about mothers, the "authority of care": Staying at home with my children, teaching and advising students, encouraging my sad spouse, I had helped weave a web of care that seemed to go practically around the world. And yet I felt like a soulless person, a shadow. I had descended into shadowland.

But there were no shadows in Marshfield; it was a place of light and lift and aluminum and gyroscopic balance, and its people, whatever faults they may have had, knew something about being themselves. They were knowers, but not in any abstract, intellectual sense, and their knowledge seemed to come to me as a slightly exasperated invitation. This place and the planes and all of us know that you love it here, they seemed to say; why can't you act on your love? The only way you'll come into yourself is if you love.

But I do love, I say: I love my family, my students, my career. And I'm still afraid of flying.

Then why are you here?

"Dad," I say to myself in the car as I drive home, "was this what you meant? Did it all come back to knowledge? Love without knowledge was chaos—it was your mother dying, my mother dying. And knowledge without love—well, that was the university, the professorship you never got. But knowledge with love—was that the air, the airplane, your old Taylorcraft and your Waco and the planes you flew in the war? You loved the planes the way you loved yourself, and I'm not sure you loved yourself or knew yourself when you weren't around planes."

"But why were you afraid of so much?" I ask the air as Rickie Lee Jones's keen voice fills the silence. "Was love always too much like chaos? Was that why we were always fighting fear—the whole family? Did Mom and her Christian Science make that fight harder? How could you have given up the air?"

I sigh. How will I answer these questions? What good does it do even to ask them? I flick off the tape player and drive home in an old silence.

When I get home, there's a new *Flying* magazine in the mail; also an invitation from Signet, some credit card company I haven't heard of, to accept a card with a credit limit of $3,500. Because Lesley is in the worst possible academic bind—laboring at her dissertation but not getting paid for it, still looking for jobs that don't turn up—we're trying to live on my salary alone, which is effectively impossible in Boston. Each month we sink a little deeper in debt, and now our bank account is below the credit limit for this card. Usually I just throw these unsolicited offers away, taking my usual minute to fume at the tightening web of financial disaster around us, but for some reason this time I hang on to the Signet offer. It's the amount that catches my attention. As it turns out, $3,500 is almost exactly what it costs to get a private pilot's license.

"Don't think this way, Tom," I say to myself. "Hey, Tom! If you can't afford flying, don't fly. *Don't* get a credit card for flying, for God's sake."

I don't sleep much that night. Love and knowledge, love and knowledge. What is it I love, and what do I know? Lesley sleeps soundly beside me; my restlessness seems not to disturb her. Nathaniel, four years old, and baby Georgia, six months, sleep unusually well in their own beds; no nightmares or bursts of wakeful energy have descended on them so far. I am alone with my thoughts. But these become more intense, not less, as the night wears on, until I remember the tale of Jacob wrestling with the angel, refusing to let go until he receives a blessing. What were angels but love and knowledge? "I will not let thee go until thou bless me," I say, pacing the dining room at four in the morning. Then suddenly I notice the silence. My mind is silent. Is this a blessing, or simply a departure? I feel nothing in particular, nothing I would call clarity or peace, only a kind of space. I flick on the light, sit down at the table, and fill out the Signet application.

I sleep after that, and in the morning, when I return from mailing the application, I call a pilot supply shop that advertises in *Flying* and order the John and Martha King video course for private pilot ground school. The credit card arrives almost as quickly as the videos. I seem to have set things in motion in spite of myself; I still cannot say exactly what I am doing. But it is the first time I can remember, the first time in years, that I am following an instinct, as strange as it might appear, and what arises from it is no longer fear so much as a sense of deliberate possibility—like rowing, I tell myself, like rowing back to shore through a storm.

Chapter Five

SOLO

*T*he man approaching me on the ramp is wearing running shoes, shorts, a Hawaiian T-shirt, a coral necklace, and sunglasses. It is March 16, 1991, a sunny day in Marshfield, but the season hasn't yet given in to spring. I'm wearing running shoes, long underwear, long pants, a long-sleeved shirt, a sweater, and a windbreaker, and I'm still cold. Every now and then some oddball shows up at Marshfield—one of the aircraft owners who never flies, or just some beachcomber who wanders in to see what an airport looks like—and this is probably one of those guys. He couldn't be a flight instructor. I hope.

"I don't suppose you know who Donnie Whittle is?" I ask him, a little too loudly, since he's now practically standing in front of me.

"Sure do," he says, smiling broadly. "You're looking at him."

"Oh, God," I say without thinking.

The month or so that brought me, a sometime student pilot with exactly 6.3 total hours of flight time, from Steve Grable to Donald Whittle, a genuine imitation beach bum but also a certified flight instructor capable of teaching instrument and multiengine flight, with over 7,000 hours of flight time to his name, was an odd combination of my own actions and actions over which I had no control. As it turned out, my flight with Steve in November was pivotal, though I did not quite realize it then. I was still backing into flying, leaving myself an out, as Chuck Yeager once said, figuring that I had no real commitment to airplanes if I couldn't even explain to myself why I was flying. But somehow, with Steve, I began to picture myself in the air in a way that before had been impossible.

Steve was quiet, nonjudgmental, and intensely patient; he seemed to understand, as I did not, that flying was part of a larger picture of myself that I had not yet sketched in, and that I could not be rushed into flight in the same way I could not be rushed into acknowledging that I was changing radically, becoming much more the person I never thought I would be. So much of my life had been given over to the pressures of fear disguised as love—disguised as God's love, my parents' love, my love of school and of being good—that I could not recognize the person I was becoming under the pressure of love disguised as fear. But an odd ease descended after November, even though I only flew with Steve twice after that, and although I still told myself I was never going to get a pilot's license and would never even get to the stage of solo flight, things began to happen and I made things happen. The Signet credit card became my airplane card, and although it was a minor detail, it occupied a special place in my wallet—cradled within my folded eyeglass prescription—so that I knew, each time I pulled out a dollar for a subway token or for a Coke at the MIT cafeteria, I had a way to fly. Evenings that before had been devoted to scholarly reading or class preparations now fell prey to the King private pilot videos, which I watched until I began to have nightmares of John and Martha

King flying into my bedroom and saying, in far-too-cheerful voices, "Crosswind engine-out complete-power-failure emergency landings at tower-controlled airports below the Los Angeles Terminal Control Area? Nothing to it! Piece of cake!"

When the videos became unendurable, I switched over to the study guide, which had sample questions from the FAA written exam and forced me to reconsider my loathing of math. Why should I hate something that allowed me to figure, for example, whether an airplane was carrying too much weight for a safe takeoff? The King private pilot study series did not cure my math hatred, but it reminded me that some kinds of knowledge work the same way, over and over again, like weight-and-balance calculations and course-plotting procedures, and that these could be relied on with a confidence beyond faith. After a couple of weeks of study I suddenly realized that I probably knew enough to pass the private pilot written test. I took it a few days later at the Diamond Air charter service at Hanscom Field, an authorized FAA test facility right next door to the local FAA office, and did—well, okay: 86 out of 100. The less-than-great results (many students manage to get perfect scores, at least according to various flight instructors I spoke with) actually cheered me: They confirmed something that had begun to take shape in my mind as an essential experiment. For so many years I had equated learning with excellence according to other people's standards, and had endured considerable punishment to achieve that level of success. What if I refused to learn that way anymore? What if I simply did the best I could, refusing to spend long hours in study, taking note of wrong answers and seeking the right ones but refusing to suffer from wrongness or failure? It was a heretical notion, but it fascinated me, and I felt released to learn what interested me. Flying was *mine*, and although I did not know exactly who that "I" was, I knew he was more attentive to the world and more forgiving of risk than anyone I had called by that name before.

And then, one evening in early January, Steve called. He had just landed a job with American Eagle, the commuter wing of American Airlines. He'd be leaving to begin flight training in less than a week. He sounded ecstatic, and I envied his happiness. He had leaped squarely across the threshold of a career that would ultimately enable him to pilot 747s across the Atlantic, if that was what he chose to do. But his departure also jarred me more than I had expected. I was still fiddling, even though I had picked up the pace a little; I was still hardly flying at all. And I was not flying because part of me still thought that I could wait forever, that I could avoid the person I was becoming, the person I needed to be. Who needs change anyway? It's uncomfortable and frightening. The status quo is almost always preferable: You always get to sleep with yourself, the same self you woke up with. But the change Steve had sought had finally come to him, and I realized that I would have to declare myself. Was I going to do this, or not? Private pilots could go on to become instrument-rated pilots, capable of flying in bad weather, and then commercial pilots, capable of flying for hire, and then flight instructors and air transport pilots, and then— if they were gifted and lucky—they could land jobs with the major airlines; they could make their living in the air. But first they had to engage, to say yes. My favorite old maybe wouldn't do.

Now I had a way to cover the cost of flying, and I had my private pilot written exam behind me. I even had my medical certificate, required of all pilots, for which I went to an FAA-designated physician who gave me the most thorough physical I had ever had. I had stopped taking tranquilizers, and so did not have to face that medical hurdle; and my eyesight was fine for the level of certification I needed. All that stood between me and a pilot's license were 40 or 50 more hours of flight time—a mere eight times what I already had.

I called Shoreline to sign on with Larry, the instructor I had first flown with. But for some reason, on the cold sunny morning of March 16, when I showed up with my usual nausea and my usual supply of self-doubt, I found a snafu in the schedule book: Larry had to do a charter flight that morning, bringing someone into Marshfield in the big twin-engine Cessna 310 that Shoreline used for such purposes, and I would have someone named Donnie.

"Whoo-hoo," says Donnie as I stand before him. My shock doesn't seem to register at all; he shakes my hand warmly, the only warm thing that has happened to me so far that morning. "Beautiful morning for flying, ain't it? What're we doin' this morning?"

"We're doing an intro flight," I say stonily.

For just a second Donnie looks confused. "But I thought you'd flown before," he says. He must have talked to Steve.

"I have," I say. "But, you know, it's been a couple of weeks, and I just wanted to, well, see . . ."

"No problem, piece of cake," he says. He doesn't look anything like John or Martha King. Where did he learn to talk like them? "We'll just go out and do some normal takeoffs and landings."

We're scheduled this morning in the plane I'm slowly beginning to like the most here—Warrior 44949, "niner-four-niner." Niner-four-niner is a barbarian plane, with gooey sun visors and a worn velour interior that looks like fake bearskin. Yet there's something comforting about it. It's a machine, and it makes no effort to hide its basic machineness. What it does best is fly, and it does that because it has a good engine and a certain number of instruments that allow someone like me to make some sense of all the crazy motions associated with moving a one-ton object through the air. Basic but not uncomplicated, it offers a kind of imperfection I can live with. I don't want to be perfect; I'm not Jonathan Livingston Seagull; I don't want to soar toward a greater reality. I want *this* reality, and in this one some seat covers look like bear fur and some visors get held up with tape and what matters most is whether you return in one piece from whatever adventure you attempt. Mr. Hawaii on the ground, Donnie has become Mr. Flight Instructor in the plane; he's meticulously attentive to every preflight check we do. But he's got this funny grin, too, almost a smirk, as if there were one key element missing from the checklist and only he knew what it was. I keep thinking he ought to be wearing a cowboy hat, but I don't know why. As we taxi out to runway six now, I announce our departure on the unicom frequency—122.8. Some of this is almost routine. I don't spot any other traffic, and no one else is calling in; we're ready to go. I pull the plane onto the runway, align the nosewheel more or less with the centerline, and stop. This is where I always want to get out.

"Whee-hoo!" The loud noise right next to me startles me so much I jerk my head back to the left, banging it on the side window. I look at Donnie. "Rock'n'roll, boy!" he yells, looking at me. Suddenly I know what's behind that funny grin, that smirk: He's having fun! He's having a good time! I look doubtfully down the runway.

He nudges me. "Come on, Cap'n," he says. "Let's go!" It's silly, but no one has ever called me "Captain" before. I push the throttle from idle to full open, counting one-thousand-one, one-thousand-two so I don't ram it forward and choke the engine, and we're wobbling down the runway, not too far from the centerline on either side, with Donnie yelling "Whee-hoo" and me wondering what I've gotten myself into. We're heading either for the Ponderosa or the starship *Enterprise.*

Donnie sparkles; he's happy, magical, good luck. It's a gorgeous day, and we're rocketing straight out from runway six, climbing at 800 feet per minute in calm air, rising steady and true to about 700 feet, where I begin a left-hand turn back toward the airport. We're supposed to level off at 1,000 feet, but I shoot through it as usual, climbing to 1,100 feet before I can push the nose down, pull back on the throttle, and fiddle with the trim. Donnie scarcely looks at what I'm doing, but reminds me, in a voice filled with happiness, that I should begin to push the nose over and cut back on the throttle about 50 feet below my intended altitude. "And re-*mem*-ber," he says, growling, as if he were experimenting with sternness just for the hell of it, "get your altitude first with the control yoke, *then* trim the plane so it'll almost fly by itself. You want just a touch of back pressure on the yoke—you want to be able to keep your altitude with your index finger, like this." He holds the yoke on his side with his right index finger; as if under a spell, knowing who's in control for these few seconds, the plane stops roller-coastering and levels off. "Don't chase your altitude with trim," he says. "You'll never get it right."

Okay, okay, I know this; I just never do it. That's part of the problem with flying: Knowledge doesn't count for much if it doesn't translate into action in the cockpit, and my whole professional career has been built largely on untranslatable knowledge. I'm not used to applying what I know. But we ease back down to 1,000 feet, then 900 feet as I look too long at the engine tachometer to see if it's where it's supposed to be— 2,300 RPM. Donnie frowns.

"Fly the plane, man," he says. "Stop looking at all the gauges. You can do that later. Get a feel for it. You don't need to look at the tach. What's the engine *sound* like at twenty-three hundred RPM? Listen." He adds throttle and pulls back on the yoke to get us up to 1,000 feet. The engine roar increases. Then, when we're level, he pulls the throttle back to 2,300. It's a smooth, high-pitched whine with an underlying, slightly ominous rumble. I know that sound.

"Got it?" Donnie asks. "Okay—that's your cruise sound. You don't need the tachometer for that. Let's concentrate on landing."

Every landing, as I've heard over and over by now from Steve and from John and Martha King, begins with a good approach pattern. You fly the downwind leg at a certain speed and a certain altitude, you fly the base leg at a certain speed with a standard rate of descent, you fly the final approach at a slightly lower speed with a standard rate of descent. The only variations from landing to landing are the last few seconds, when the plane enters that strange transition from bird to dead weight and falters to the ground a little differently each time. In general, a smooth, consistent pattern makes for smooth landings; weave and wobble through the downwind and base legs of your approach, and you're setting yourself up for trouble.

Donnie and I are now in the downwind leg, paralleling runway six at Marshfield, about a mile north of the airport.

"Okay, it's all yours again," he says. "What do you do?"

This time I know some of the routine: You turn on the second fuel pump so that, if the engine-driven fuel pump dies on final approach, you still have power; you use carburetor heat to melt whatever ice may have accumulated in the carburetor during your flight; you turn on your landing light.

"Good," says Donnie. "Notice you've gained a hundred feet of altitude while doing all that. We're now at eleven hundred feet—too high. You can *feel* that kind of climb, man—you can

134

feel almost anything in an airplane. Get your head out of the cockpit and let your body tell you what the plane's doing."

Body first, mind second—that's a switch. But right now there's too much else to think about. As we pull even with the far end of the runway, it's time to cut the power to 1,500 RPM and hold the nose up to bleed off the airspeed. We've been going at about 100 knots; we have to get it down to about 70 or 75. But as I hold the nose up the airspeed doesn't seem to decline much, and we're shooting well out beyond the airport. I start to lower the nose; I want to go down.

Donnie pulls back. "Slow down, slow down," he says. "See how your airspeed indicator shows the needle inside the white arc? What's that mean?"

Let's see, I say to myself rapidly, the green arc is the normal cruise speed range of the plane, the yellow arc is the caution zone, the red arc is no-no land, and the white arc is—what the hell is the white arc?

"Flaps," Donnie says as if he's been listening to me. He reaches down to pull up the handle between our seats. "You can add flaps once you get below a hundred and three knots. Flaps add lift but also drag, remember? You get a steeper descent, and you also get to *slow down*. See?"

It's true: we've gone from 100 knots to less than 80, and the airspeed indicator is still falling slowly.

"This is a pretty good descent attitude," Donnie says. "That means the plane is basically sinking at the right angle. Let's hold this and trim it so it stays this way. Look around outside you; look at the plane relative to the horizon. See how this feels? This is how you come in."

We turn onto the base leg, perpendicular to the runway, announcing our presence on the radio, and add another notch of flaps. This is where I get nervous. The plane takes its own sweet time, losing altitude, slowing down, closing slowly on the airport, but I want everything to be *over*: I want to be down. Glancing at the altimeter, I see we're about 500 feet up—500 feet—not much. We're low over a golf course—I've always hated golf—just past the brick police station, where I can see the police cars and the maintenance yard and even a couple of cops walking across the yard, not looking up at us. Everything looks a little too big to be toylike and unreal, but too small to be welcoming. I hate this transition. I want to be a bird or an earthling, not something in between. But my life depends on this in-between, and Donnie notices my distraction with something like happy alarm.

"Come on, guy, you've got to land this plane," he says as I turn onto final approach. "Look—how does it *look*? Runway's kind of climbing up the windshield, getting wilder? You're too low. Your nose is too high. See those trees? Doesn't look like it would be much fun to land in them. Put the nose down and add power *now*. Get back up to that glide slope. That's it. That's it. Okay, that's what the runway should look like on final. Hold it, hold it—"

We're less than 100 feet up, coming over the fence just beyond the runway threshold, and I don't know which of us is landing the plane. God, the runway is coming up fast—and our nose is still pointed down. We're going to ram right into the runway! I pull back on the yoke, but Donnie stops me.

"Wait!" he yells. Everything is staccato, imperative: hour-long microseconds. Jesus! The runway is all around us now, a wide solid asphalt strip whose painted lines leap at me like tea leaf warnings, threatening disaster and death, and we're still going down, we're going to bury ourselves in pavement—

"Ease it back now, ease it back," shouts Donnie, loosening his grip on the yoke. I pull back too hard, the nose flies up, and suddenly we're floating down the runway perhaps five feet off the ground, wasting the same precious asphalt I thought was going to kill me a few seconds ago, heading for the other end.

"Add a little power, put the nose down, then pull back again," Donnie commands, and as I do the airplane seems really to fly again for a second, rather than float, and as it flies it begins to sink until I ease back on the yoke, more slowly this time, and the nose comes up as the main gear touch down with something between a loud squeak and a bang, and we're rolling down the last third of the runway, our last 1,000 feet, as I push on the brakes with my toes and we come slowly to rest at the far end of the runway.

"We probably should have gone around," Donnie says as I sit there for a second, half impressed, half stunned. "Basically the rule is, if anything's happening on final approach that you don't like, go around. Fly away and try again. But I wanted you to see that you could land the plane. You *did* land the plane, pretty much. That's what it feels like. Let's go up one more time, do the same thing, and call it a day."

On the next attempt we touch down a little hard, with a sound I politely describe to myself as a muffled bang. Donnie explains about the oleo landing gear struts in this airplane, and how they'll take some pretty hard landings before complaining. "Anyway, remember," he says, "the airplane is insured. There's not much you can do to break it, but if you do break it, *c'est la vie.* The point here is for you to learn to fly, not worry about whether you're going to break the plane. Let me worry about that."

"Did you kind of get a sense of what it feels like to land?" he asks when we're back on the ground. I think so.

"Two things," Donnie says as he writes the lesson down in my logbook. "First, once you get over the runway threshold, stop staring down at the runway like you're going to crash. Steve must have told you that, too. If you keep staring at the threshold you'll pull back too late and whack the plane down on the nosewheel—bad move. Could rip the engine right off its mount. If you look *down* the runway, you'll give yourself more time, more perspective. Everything won't seem to be happening all at once. Right? And also—land with your butt. Don't just land with your eyes. You've got to know where the ground is with the seat of your pants. Where d'you think that expression came from anyway?"

I sit out in the car a few minutes later, trying to imagine what it feels like to land a plane by the seat of my pants. How could anyone feel the approaching ground right up through his or her body? I can feel the old seat springs—I've sat in this seat for most of the 189,000 miles on the car—and if I put my imagination to work, I can imagine feeling the aluminum seat frame and the bolts holding it to the chassis, and the chassis itself—but that's not what Donnie's talking about. I'm not supposed to imagine landing. I'm supposed to land. I'm supposed to feel the ground as if it were coming right up to my bottom. I've never listened to my body that well.

II.

*T*o go solo—to fly alone as a student pilot—you must, according to the FAA's Federal Aviation Regulations, already be able to demonstrate no fewer than fifteen specific tasks associated with flying, including "descents with and without turns using high and low drag configurations [i.e. flaps or no flaps]," "emergency procedures and equipment malfunctions," and "forced landing procedures initiated on takeoff, during initial climb, cruise, descent, and in the landing pattern." But what it really boils down to is this: You need to be able to take off and land without killing yourself. Better yet, you need to be able to take off and land without wrecking the plane. It seems strange to me that, somewhere over the last two weeks, I've shifted to wondering what it would be like to fly solo instead of announcing to myself that I will never fly solo. This is part of Donnie's magic, his happiness, I think, but it's also part of my own fascination with the fact that some part of learning to fly really *has* to be instinctive: I may be able to think myself into the air, more or less, but I can't think myself down. I need the good old body to tell me what the plane is doing. I wonder if that was what my first flight instructor meant, twelve years ago, when he described that wretched Cessna 150 as an extension of my body. Small planes don't look much like hawks or kestrels, but pilots may have more in common with those birds than they do with the machines around them. I think of my father, en route to instinct through a machine.

By the time April 13 rolls around, Donnie and I have done most of what the FAA requires for solo student pilots. It's about 7:15 A.M.; we've been around the field a couple of times. I've done a simulated emergency landing, with the engine idling as I glide down from about 1,000 feet to the runway, and a simulated emergency takeoff with partial power. The plane stutters and yaws its way into the sky at a scant 300 feet a minute, until, at about 700 feet, we begin a turn back to the airport, checking the fuel selector and the fuel pump switch, checking the magnetos, pretending nothing will work, pretending to shut down the engine for another power-off descent. Twelve years ago it would have terrified me even to attempt one of these maneuvers, and a week ago it made me anxious to think about them, but now—now is Donnie, and his magic and confidence, which has rubbed off on me, and now I'm in the half-fiction, half-fact land of aerial emergency, and I have room to live and breathe.

We get down again, pull off onto the taxiway, and stop. I retract the flaps, shut off the auxiliary fuel pump, shut off the landing light. We just sit there for a minute, engine running at 1,000 RPM, my feet on the brakes. Donnie's staring at me, sizing me up. I know what he's thinking. I want to say "No way, not today, not ever—this is not what I want, I'm no good at this," but even as I hear that voice in my head I know it's shouting against a solid wall of yes: "Yes, I do want to solo, I do want to take this airplane up alone on this bright April morning, I do want to land it by myself, I do want to do all of this without panicking or feeling hopeless." As I look at Donnie, he sees the yes has won. He smiles, but only slightly. In all honesty he looks a little worried.

"Got your medical certificate?" he says.

"Sure." Even though, as I student, I technically can fly without it as long as I'm with an instructor, it seems silly not to have it with me, since it also doubles as my student pilot's license. I pull it out of my wallet.

Donnie flips it over, where two boxes on the back provide room for instructors' signatures authorizing solo flight and solo cross-country flight. Staring at the first box for a second, pausing—is this always a ritual?—Donnie writes the date, the make and model of aircraft, his signature, his instructor's certificate number and its expiration date. He folds the medical certificate and hands it back to me.

"You ready to do this?" he asks, more serious than I have ever seen him.

"I think so," I say, emphasizing "so" without really thinking about it.

"Okay," he says, looking me straight in the eye, wanting me

140

to look back at him. "I'm gonna be right here on the ground, I'm gonna be watching you. Remember everything we've done, emergency procedures, looking down the runway, pulling back on the yoke, holding it back if you're a little high until the plane gets down on the runway. Most important thing—if you don't like something, *anything*, about your approach, go around and do another one. Remember, you never *have* to land. You have all the time in the world. It's a beautiful morning. Have fun."

He claps me on the shoulder, pops open the door, steps out, shuts and latches the door, steps off the wing and away from the airplane. Looking off to the right rear of the plane, I can see him salute, not quite informally, then smile and wave. I'm alone in the cockpit of a Piper Warrior, and sometime in the next couple of minutes I'm going to take off alone. I guess this is what I wanted. No—this *is* what I wanted.

Strangely enough, for the first few seconds everything feels ordinary. With the wind from the northwest, we're using runway 24 this morning; I turn right on the taxiway and begin the long journey to the end of the runway. The plane jounces along slowly, the tachometer showing 800 RPM, the engine gauges normal. I watch the pale spring grass slide beneath the outer edge of the wing, and beyond it the small scrub forest; the new leaves sparkle in the early sun. Every few seconds I glance back into the cockpit to take in another instrument—the airspeed indicator, the compass and directional gyro (both pointing to the same heading, as they should be), the attitude indicator, the vertical speed indicator. The more I glance at them, the more they begin to seem larger, brighter, almost as if they were looming at me from the instrument panel, and then I realize I am very nervous. I hear a sudden, strange sucking noise, followed by breaking glass. Damn! I must have run over something on the taxiway. Stopping the plane, setting the hand brake, I look all around outside through the window, craning my head to try to see behind me where the wheels have just passed; I don't see anything that looks like glass. Then I hear it again—*swooook, pop, brink brink brink brink*. It's the radio. For some reason it's making this awful sound, the sound of something crashing. I fiddle with the radio for a moment, switching back and forth between frequencies, adjusting the volume; nevertheless, in a few seconds, the sound returns. For a moment I consider bagging the flight. I don't want to go up in the air with a radio that makes crashing noises. Donnie is approaching the plane from the right rear, several yards away, gesturing, looking puzzled. Is everything okay? I think about myself for a moment. Actually, quite a lot would have to go wrong for things not to be okay—more than a diabolical radio. I *do* know what I'm doing, I know what it feels like to land an airplane. Right now is as good a time as any to see if I can translate that trust into action. I release the hand brake, give Donnie a confident-looking wave, and *swook* and *pop* my way along the taxiway.

Then the rabbit shows up. A gray bunny with long ears and a white tail, he hops out of the field between the taxiway and the runway to sit right in the middle of the taxiway. I stop the plane again, beginning to feel as if I'm in some medieval allegory where everything along the way to the main adventure has some deep symbolic meaning. What the hell is he doing? Is he just going to sit there in terror, and if so, will I run over him or shut down the plane and chase him off the taxiway? Does he want to go with me? I try to remember any FAA regulations about transporting animals in the cockpit. Would he be the first rabbit to fly in a Piper Warrior? He'd certainly be the first rabbit to fly with a student pilot on his first solo flight. But then it wouldn't exactly be a *solo* flight.

I stare at him through the windshield. He really doesn't

look terrified; in fact, he looks quite calm. He looks as if he owns the place. He probably does this all the time, I tell myself, and I just haven't had the pleasure before. The airport rabbit. I wonder if I can go around him. I'm just trying to gauge the degree to which I can ease the nosewheel behind him without squishing him under the main gear when, attentive to something in the brush or perhaps a hawk above us, he hops off the taxiway. In three quick leaps he's vanished from view, safe again in the brush. I sigh. *Swooook, pop, brink brink brink brink.* This could be a very strange flight.

By the time I follow the last turn of the taxiway to the edge of runway 24, my left leg is trembling uncontrollably. I really can't get it to stop. I try holding it with my left hand, which helps a little, but I can't do that on takeoff. "God," some part of me says to some other part that's not quite paying attention, "you must be really scared." The only refuge at this point is the checklist. I run through all the pretakeoff checks, touching each gauge and saying what it's supposed to do or show as I go through the list, making this as physical an experience as possible. If I crash, my fingerprints will be on every piece of glass in the cockpit, which for some reason I find comforting. The plane looks good; everything is normal. I pull my voice together and radio my departure, then pull onto the runway, backtaxiing down to the very end. I turn around, line the plane up with the centerline, and sit.

"Don't sit," a more powerful voice inside me says. "Don't wait. Everything okay? Yes, it's all okay. Push that throttle forward. *Get out of here.*"

And I do. My left leg is still trembling, but I've got to stay straight on the runway as I begin to roll, and this absolute necessity gives me the strength to keep my leg pressed firmly on the rudder pedals. No braking. I'm rolling now, past thirty-five knots, easing the control yoke back almost automatically, the ground beginning to blur, forty-five knots now, the nose getting light; I'm going up, I'm going up. Fifty-five knots going on sixty, pull back, pull back now on the control yoke—I'm talking to myself, giving myself instructions, my own flight instructor—pull back a little more, 63 knots, a slight clunk as the main gear leave the ground, I'm flying. Climb out at seventy-nine knots. Faster than I can keep up with it, the plane reaches eighty-five knots; I pull the nose up, the airspeed drops to seventy knots, I push the nose down again, then up, then down, until after a few seconds I nail eighty knots and leave it there. Below me the houses and harbors and marshes of Marshfield and Duxbury grow smaller and more precise, more real than they have ever seemed before. I feel a strange rush of delight.

At 700 feet I shut off the auxiliary fuel pump, pitch the nose down to make sure the air is clear of other traffic, then begin my turn back toward the airport as I climb to 1,000 feet. What am I supposed to do? Suddenly my mind blanks. I grab the printed checklist and look it over. "Preflight inspection"—damn! That's not what I want. Wrong side. I flip it over to the preland-ing section. Okay, fuel pump back on, carburetor heat, landing light. I radio my downwind position on the unicom frequency; the radio has stopped making its fatal noises. No one else is on the frequency this early in the morning; I'm alone up here. But that feels fine, much better than it does on the ground. I check the sky carefully anyway, then cut the throttle, pull on a notch of flaps, and begin my descent.

When I make my left turn to the base leg of my approach, about 800 feet above the ground, I glance at the airspeed indica-tor: It tells me I'm going about 75 knots. That's the last time I look at it. I don't look at the vertical speed indicator at all. This is an eyeball operation all the way; I'm going in by the seat of my pants, flying the plane down to the ground. My mind isn't cluttered, exactly, but recollections are passing through it like lightning: my first flight, when I couldn't even line the plane up with the runway; my father, the rowboat, learning through fear. I can see Donnie on the grass between the runway and the taxiway. He's walked me through all of this, he's done these landings with me several times, he's let me do them myself, he's cheered and encouraged me. He's been a good companion; he's taught by companionship. It's made a big difference. And I'm okay, I'm doing fine; this landing's going to be just fine, though part of me is completely shocked.

I'm coming in high. The runway is starting to look as if it might vanish beneath the plane. Cut power, full flaps. Still high. I shouldn't put the nose down, I know, shouldn't dive for the runway, because that will drive my airspeed way up, but I put the nose down anyway, until the panic moment hits and I look away from the runway threshold and down toward the last third of the runway, pulling back gently on the yoke. Argh! Too high! The plane is losing lift well above the runway. It's going to drop right out of the sky if I don't do something. I push the nose over, give it a shot of power; I'm gliding down again, not falling. I wait a second, then cut the power, pull back on the yoke, and suddenly the nose is coming up and a *poomph* right under my seat tells me the main gear have touched down. The nose drops down a second later; I'm back. I've even managed to land within the first 2,000 feet of the runway. Things could be worse. I pull onto the taxiway, retract the flaps, shut off the auxiliary fuel pump and the landing light, and wait for Donnie.

He hops right up on the wing, grinning as he opens the door. "Not bad, Cap'n," he says. "Not bad at all. How did it feel?"

What a question. How did it feel? It felt like breathing, like starting over, like leaving. "It was fine," I say, "just fine."

145

III.

Definitions are everything and nothing, as Miranda, one of my favorite characters in literature, discovers in Katherine Anne Porter's *Pale Horse, Pale Rider*. She needs to escape from all those who corner her by questioning: "Where are you going, What are you doing, What are you thinking, How do you feel, Why do you say such things, What do you mean?" But what does escape mean for her? It has no definition apart from her life; it becomes a series of actions taken in a fog of uncertainty; it becomes what it always is—part intention, part fate.

I am caught up now in an escape I can almost hold, but I cannot say what it is or where it will lead. Bound up with the sky, with defying gravity, with new knowledge, this escape makes me feel like a dark, heavy angel, but there is nowhere I particularly want to go and nothing I particularly want to do with this. I simply want to feel it, the way a man or woman who has been chronically ill wants to feel health as a phenomenon, as something identifiably distinct from past experience. "Distance is not to be found," writes Antoine de Saint-Exupéry in *Flight to Arras*; "It melts away. And escape has never led anywhere. . . . What we are worth when motionless, is the question." But sometimes distance is the only possibility, even when it ultimately leads back to the starting point, and motionlessness is the soul of a man or woman within the equilibrium of thrust and drag, lift and weight, the four fundamental forces of flight. Or it is the little airplane in the center of the attitude indicator, motionless against the rising and falling ocean that is the world. There is a kind of motionlessness that comes only with great upheaval. These days, when I wake, I feel tremors through myself like those I used to feel in California, between the great earthquakes.

Four months ago I began searching in earnest for another job. I thought of this step in tandem with my efforts to fly: My desire for flight was not reckless or self-destructive but, at some level, calculated and sure of itself. Sheldon Simmons, the Alaskan bush pilot who saved the crew of the *Patterson*, once commented on his public image: "They thought I was pretty reckless," he said. "Guess I did take a few chances. But I always had a plan. I always had a plan." I was banging around in the air, sometimes making myself sick, spending money I did not have, suppressing my fury at being treated like a cipher or a child at MIT, but I was also trying to let go of old fears and entrapments, expectations of goodness I could no longer afford, and as these began to evaporate in the thinner air of high altitude I began to get glimpses, as through heavy clouds, of what I might do to save myself. These glimpses began to form themselves into a kind of plan. "Get out of MIT," I saw in one glimpse; "Find a place that will give you room to run, room to breathe. Try to find it with Lesley, but don't assume you will. Don't die from your good intentions."

The first item in this coalition of plans and advice was hardly news; I simply had to act on it. Nor was the second much of a surprise. In California I had always let off steam by going on long hikes in the Pacific coastal range or in the Sierras. I had always had room, physical room, to let myself out of my caged life as a graduate student or a teacher. But the last two bits of advice sounded heretical and frightening. Lesley was as bound up in my life as anyone had ever been. She knew me at a level no one else shared, and I could not imagine moving somewhere without her. This was true despite our increasingly sullen silences and exhausted evenings when, after Nathaniel and Georgia were in bed, we sat in the living room, mute and wounded. We had lost touch with each other, and were both

147

too proud and stubborn to admit it. The pressure I felt at MIT made me an embittering companion, and Lesley's stalled dissertation and lack of job prospects made her not much more delightful. Scrambling to survive amid a ring of hostilities, we had become more hostile than we knew.

But that hostility might dissipate if the right changes could be made to work. In February I had flown out to the English department of the University of Iowa for a job interview. The job sounded appealing, and although I arrived exhausted—bad weather had delayed flights out of Boston and Chicago, and while I was expected in the early evening I did not arrive in Iowa City until the following morning—I was met by colleagues who seemed genuinely delighted with me and my work. For the first time in years, I caught a whiff of what it might be like to have room to explore what I loved. And there *was* space around me, physical space—lots of it. A professor of medieval studies at Iowa, Jon Wilcox, who was also a pilot, took me up in a Piper Warrior to scout the terrain around Iowa City. We stayed up for an hour, turning in ever-widening circles like Yeats's errant falcon, noting the vast rectangles of farmland and the hundreds of little red sheds for pigs, but also observing the way the land and sky seemed to be the only features here: no mountains, few hills, few rivers. It seemed almost too generous, too foreign. Could I make this experience my own?

I had applied, in part, because there was also a job available for Lesley in the art history department at Iowa; that job had not come through for her. If, then, Iowa was our destination, we would have to live again as we had been living—on one income with Lesley still struggling over her dissertation—or something else would have to break the logjam.

Then, as in a fated reprieve, Lesley became a finalist for a professorship at the University of California, Santa Barbara. We both knew Santa Barbara well, since my brother had spent almost a decade there as an undergraduate and a graduate student in religious studies. Lesley and I frequently made the six-hour drive from Palo Alto to Isla Vista, the town adjacent to the university, where he and his spouse lived. Santa Barbara seemed lovely and corrupted, with flames rising from the oil derricks in the Santa Barbara channel, and beach tar so thick you couldn't go out for a walk without ruining a pair of shoes. Yet I had always liked it. From the graduate student housing in Isla Vista, you could walk up a hill, across a road, and through the lush vegetable gardens of the student families, then on through eucalyptus and live oak past the new faculty housing—Mediterranean-styled villas, pale pink in the setting sun—and on to the lagoon, where biologists still ran experiments on natural habitats and joggers skirted the nature preserve on trails across the high bluffs by the ocean. It was a beautiful, magical place; it also had a major airport. It was ideal.

I had already been in touch with the writing program at Santa Barbara for my own reasons, and knew I had a job there. If Lesley were a professor, we would both be employed, I would have time to write and to take my kids on long walks around the beach, and we wouldn't feel as trapped and poor as we did now. This felt, I told myself, like good fortune; it had to go forward.

Lesley was scheduled to fly out to San Francisco on Saturday afternoon, April 20. She would take Georgia with her, leaving her with Lesley's mother in Palo Alto, then head down to Santa Barbara for the interview. I would stay with Nathaniel, teach, grade papers, do what I usually did.

By this time I had passed my second supervised solo with Donnie at Marshfield, and I was supposed to get solo number three out of the way on the morning of April 20. After that I would be legally free to fly by myself at any time between sunrise and sunset. I could come down to the airport, rent a plane, and go up and down to my heart's content—as long as the weather didn't go below VFR minimums and I didn't stray more than twenty-five nautical miles from Marshfield. It might have seemed like getting the keys to a car still connected to the garage by a long leash, but to me it felt like an absolute dividing line. Before, I was tentative, fumbling with past fears, unlikely to succeed as a pilot; after this, I was on my way, flying alone into a wide-open sky. It seemed right, somehow, that I should do this on the day Lesley left for Santa Barbara. Our lives were not spinning out of control; on the contrary, we had them in hand, and on this day we were each doing something to confirm both our independence and our faith in each other. We would get through this bad space.

When I got down to Marshfield, however, I didn't feel much like flying. I found I was thinking about Lesley, hoping ardently that things would go well and trying to imagine what she might face in her interview. Most of all I wanted to go with her: I was craving the West. But I had a job here, classes to teach; it made sense that Nathaniel and I should stay. At Marshfield I seemed fine, joking with Donnie and the other flight instructors before going out to the plane. The run-up and takeoff were both good. Yet I felt as if the plane were ahead of me somehow, making its own choices before I could decide on them, gaining airspeed before I had intended to, gaining or losing altitude more quickly than I could control. It was an odd sensation, not alarming, but new and strange. I didn't seem to have any intuition about the plane today.

"You've been doing great takeoffs and landings at Marshfield," Donnie said as we climbed to 2,000 feet, "but it'd be good practice to do them somewhere else. Let's go over to Plymouth and you can do some there. If it goes okay—and I'm sure it will"—he gives me a big, confident smile—"I'll sign you off so you can fly solo to Plymouth." I smiled back; this was a considerable compliment. Flight instructors were technically permitted to sign a solo student off in his or her logbook for flights to an airport within twenty-five miles of the student's home base. From what I had heard, however, it was a relatively rare practice.

We were over Plymouth in a few minutes. I called in for an airport advisory, notified the other traffic that I was entering the downwind leg, and went through the prelanding checklist. Then I reduced power and started to add a notch of flaps.

"Watcha doin'?" he asked. "Look at your airspeed."

I did, and saw that it was still hovering above 103 knots—maximum flap speed.

"Pull the nose up a little and wait till the airspeed bleeds off," he said. "Patience, my son, patience." He didn't seem worried.

In a second or two we were down to ninety-five knots. I added the flaps, then looked down at the airport. It was a beautiful day, sunny and windless, and we could have landed on any of the four runways, but the unicom had called for runway six. Although an extensive forest surrounded the airport, runway six had a grassy strip perhaps 300 feet long leading up to the threshold; consequently it didn't seem quite as intimidating as the other choices. But as I looked to the front, it seemed to me that we were shooting out well past the airport, and all I could see ahead of me was forest. The plane felt low. I began my turn to the base leg, adding another notch of flaps. Donnie watched me, glancing for other traffic, but said nothing.

As I turned onto my final approach, I knew that everything felt wrong. The plane still seemed low, and we seemed to be going too slowly. The nose seemed higher than usual, too. I pushed it down a little, but then I suddenly realized that if we kept up this approach we were going to land on the grass strip in front of the runway, not on the runway itself. What should I do? I froze for a second.

"Go around," said Donnie firmly, pushing the throttle forward himself at the same time. I radioed that we were going around, then took control of the plane. Out of the corner of my eye I could see Donnie looking at me pretty hard.

"So what was wrong with that?" he asked.

"Well, I almost landed short of the runway," I said, feeling strangely confused.

"Yeh, I know," said Donnie. "But what did you see happening? What told you it was wrong?"

"Well—" I couldn't explain. We had seemed high in the downwind leg, had lost a lot of altitude on base; maybe I should have added power on final approach? Maybe I should have—

"What was your airspeed on final?" Donnie asks.

"I don't know."

"Didn't you look?"

"No."

"Well, what did the vertical speed indicator say?"

"I don't know."

"You didn't look at that either?"

"I wanted to see what it *looked* like to land here," I said. "I didn't want to rely on the instruments. You know, I wanted the *feel* of it."

"Yeh, but it wasn't working," said Donnie. "Let's go around and do it again."

I set up another approach to Plymouth, but this time, trying to compensate for being too low, I turned too soon onto the base leg, and on final approach, having cut the power down

152

to idle, I was still too high. I glanced at the vertical speed indicator; we were dropping at close to 1,000 feet per minute. I started to glance over at the airspeed indicator, since somewhere in the back of my mind I remembered that I could stall the plane if I descended too fast at too low an airspeed. But then I noticed another plane, a blue-and-white Cessna, pulling onto the runway. We were only a few seconds from landing; I had radioed my positions all the way through the approach. The Cessna pilot *knew* I was coming in—unless he didn't have a radio, which technically at this field he didn't have to have. As the Cessna began slowly to roll down the runway, I realized that if I tried to land behind him I'd hit him. In an instant I gave the plane full throttle and, scarcely 50 feet over the runway, we began to climb. But now we were right on the Cessna's flight path, and so close I could see the gap between the horizontal stabilizer and the elevator on his tail. I banked to the right.

"Bank left, bank left," Donnie urged. Suddenly I remembered that over to the right, at Plymouth, was a grass field used for glider operations. Glider tow planes would be taking off and landing on the right. I swung the plane to the left.

"Son of a bitch," Donnie said, grabbing the mike and calling the Cessna. No response. "That bastard either doesn't have a radio or doesn't have it on," he said, "but man, he didn't even look before he pulled onto the runway. That was good work, going around. You did well there. But your approach still stank. Let's try again."

I thought of my first flight instructor's comment—"Everything happens"—and knew the relief of someone who makes more or less the right decision in a life-threatening situation. But I was still rattled, and I hadn't felt all that much like flying to begin with. My next approach was no better. I came in high, pushing the nose down and then pulling it back over the runway to bleed off airspeed, touching down more than halfway along the 3,500-foot stretch of asphalt. By this time Donnie looked baffled.

"Tell you what," he said. "Let's check with the unicom and see what the other traffic is doing. If no one's around, let's try landing on runway two-four. I think that grassy strip in front of runway six is messing up your depth perception or something."

That made sense, although somehow I didn't think it was the problem. Dutifully I set up an approach to runway 24; the same thing happened. This time I came in too low, gunning the engine at the last minute and ballooning over the threshold of the runway, only to sink suddenly and fly up again as I dumped in more throttle, until I seesawed my way over the asphalt, cut the throttle, and touched down hard on all three wheels. Donnie was looking out the window, thinking to himself.

"Let's go back to Marshfield," he said.

We made it back to home base with a landing much like the last one at Plymouth. Pulling the Warrior up to the fuel pumps, I shut down the engine. The silence in the cockpit lasted a few seconds too long.

"Well," Donnie said. "The only thing I can think is you were very, very preoccupied today. You were landing today like someone doing his first presolo landings. I couldn't sign you off for solo with landings like that. What's up with you?"

I told him about Lesley's interview and our job prospects in California, but then hesitated a moment and said, "Look, I thought this was supposed to be seat-of-the-pants stuff, okay? That's what I was trying to do. I've just been trying to get the feel of the plane. Today I didn't."

"Yeah, but you didn't know any of the numbers, either," Donnie said. "Flying's not just feeling. Look—you need to show about seventy to seventy-five knots on the downwind and base

legs. You need about sixty-five to seventy knots in final. You
need to lose between four hundred and six hundred feet per
minute. Airspeed indicator, vertical speed indicator. Look back
and forth and outside. *Know* what the plane is doing. You just
didn't know what the plane was doing today."

He was right. I didn't have anything to say. I simply nodded.
I didn't even think about how I must have looked to Donnie,
although his expression struck me as brotherly in a way I
couldn't quite remember seeing before.

"Listen," he said as we walked into the barn, "I know this
was a bad day. Try not to get too upset about it. You learned
a lot today. Remember—seventy knots, sixty-five knots on final.
Four hundred to six hundred feet on the vertical speed indicator. And that go-around when the Cessna pulled in front of
us—boy, you were cool on that! That was great emergency
work. You have good instincts, Tom. Put 'em together with
knowledge and you've got a pilot."

I went down to 1st Stop, the coffee-and-doughnut hangout
in Marshfield, ordered a big cup of black coffee and a jelly
doughnut, and stood by the side of the car, looking out at the
marshes beside the North River as it headed out to sea. And
then I slammed my fist on the top of the car, fighting back tears.
How could I have flown so badly? It all came out in a disorderly
rush—I wanted to go to California this afternoon, I wanted to
move there, to be there, I wanted to live again in my beloved
landscape. But more than that, I wanted to be whole. And I saw
today I was not whole; I still thought heavily in oppositions,
particularly mind and body. I was—even at this moment, banging my fist, spilling my coffee on the car roof—too intellectual;
I thought it all out, thought I could manage everything by
thinking. And then, when I discovered I could land an airplane
strictly by feeling, I thought I'd found a liberation: Flying really

was basically instinctive, a right-brained activity, and I could do it by touch and sight and by something deep within me I couldn't name. When I flew, I had a refuge from my mind. But no; that was false. Flying, Donnie was trying to tell me, was an act of integration more than anything else; mind and body and intuition had to be one, and although I had known this, I hadn't really seen what it meant. Now, suddenly, I saw. I had to be able to fly with every nerve ending of my fingers, with my eyes and the seat of my pants, but also with a calculating mind, one that could instantly interpret signals from the instruments before me. I had to make sense of radically different kinds of meaning, all of it essential to flight. There was no "material" and "spiritual," as there had been in my childhood; there was one experience, flying, and it drew on the body of mind, or the mind of body, more insistently than anything I had ever known. I had grown up with oppositions, and now I had to unlearn them. It was going to be a long journey—if I kept going. But I promised myself I would.

IV.

*L*esley returned from California three days later in a dulled, shocked repose. She had pulled so tightly into herself that I had a difficult time even finding a route to comfort her. Gradually the story came out. The trip, as stressful as it was, might as well not have been made. The chairman of the department never even met with her, she said; the same three professors ushered her around the whole time; her talk had gone well but had been only politely received; the graduate students were cordial but wary. She left with the distinct impression that she had never been a serious candidate for the job. We talked about what it meant to be an "affirmative action candidate," interviewed only for the sake of appearances, and whether we should take action against the department. "Can you imagine what would happen to my career if I did something like that?" she said.

"But they were playing with you," I said.

"I couldn't prove that," she said sadly. "Anyway, it's over."

More and more we were retreating into sadness and isolation. We had played the game by the rules for so long; now, repeatedly, our good behavior was flung back in our faces, but we had nothing else to turn to. We were beginning to fade into our private quests for strength, for badness, for energy that we could not find. What we shared was half-comforting routine—the routine of child care, of my job, of her academic research. But what we needed was something to make us feel whole again, and neither of us had the words even to say how much had been lost or how much was at stake.

Two days after Lesley returned, I went back to Marshfield. Despite my earlier promise to myself to keep on the journey, I was discouraged. What good would it do to learn to fly? Would spending money on flying help Lesley find a job, or make me feel more secure, or make it easier for me to travel in commercial airliners, or ease the pressures on either of us? It was true that, since starting flight training, I had been able to fly in jetliners once again with relative ease. On the other hand, I was beginning to have stress headaches, which I had never experienced before, and when I consulted my doctor at MIT he asked me what I was doing for recreation. "I fly airplanes," I said. "That's *not* recreation," he said. "Piloting is very stressful." I had simply found a way of adding more stress to my life—or had, I told myself, unless I could reconnect with whatever that old dream of mine had meant. But who was that young teenager in a car with his parents, dreaming of an Alaskan flight? Did his life parallel mine, and if so was it still there somehow, or had it simply faded into nothing?

Donnie was waiting for me in the lounge when I arrived; he had a large, soft-sided case with him. "I brought something for you," he said.

"What?"

"My video camera. I'm gonna tape you flying today. That way you'll have something to show Lesley and the kids, 'case they ever have doubts about what you're up to. *You* can even watch it," he said with a trace grin.

"It'll be pretty crowded in that cockpit if the camera's as big as that case," I said. "What are you going to do, put the lens right in my face?"

"Oh, yeah, the camera's a big old thing, but it won't matter. I'm not gonna be in the front seat," Donnie said. "I'm gonna be in the back. I'll be shooting over your shoulder. That way people can see you *and* what you're seeing."

"You're going to be in the back?"

"Uh-huh. Well, not right away. But when you're ready."

I considered this. I hadn't really made a successful landing in almost ten days. If I blew it this time, Donnie wouldn't be anywhere near the controls.

We went up in four-seven-hotel, setting up an approach and landing to Marshfield, which I actually did reasonably well with Donnie sitting in the seat next to me. Part of me was focused purely on the runway, part of me on the instruments, and whatever attention I was paying seemed enough: When the airspeed climbed, I raised the nose; when we began to sink too quickly, I lowered the nose a little and added power. Thinking, I began to feel again what the airplane needed, and it responded like a creature who trusted the touch of the master. Yet I was still sweating, not from concentrating on landings but from imagining a landing with Donnie in the back seat. What if we crashed? What if I killed him? Oddly enough, I didn't think much about what would happen to me. Donnie was the one gambling on my ability, and I didn't want him to pay for it.

"Let's go over to Plymouth," he said. I turned to the southwest, radioing for an airport advisory, and heard the runway in use—runway 33. The short runway—500 feet shorter than the one at Marshfield. Great.

We approached the airport from the north, descending to pattern altitude as I radioed our position and awaited a response from other traffic. No one else was up. We were paralleling runway 33 now, about a mile away from it, and Donnie gave me one of his searching looks.

"You feel okay about this?" he asked.

I thought for a second. I could feel the plane again today; I could also think it, think through what it was doing and what it needed. If anything went wrong with instinct, I had thought to back me up. I was okay.

Donnie didn't belabor the point. Smiling, he clapped me on the shoulder, then pulled himself around the edge of the front seat and clambered in back. I was alone in front. The right seat seemed larger than it had ever been. I could hear Donnie fiddling with the camera, getting it set.

"Okay, Mr. Simmons," Donnie said, his voice muffled in the roar of the plane, "the whole world is watching your landing at Plymouth Municipal Airport in Plymouth, Massachusetts. Don't get nervous." He leaned forward so I could see him. "Just kidding," he said.

"Well," I said as I turned onto the base leg, "if something goes wrong at least the FAA and the National Transportation Safety Board will have something to look at. Maybe they can even show it in ground school—'a real crash: what not to do with your instructor.' " All of a sudden it didn't sound so funny, but I could just hear the camera whirring above the noise of the plane, and I remembered I had work to do. I was about to turn onto my final approach when I felt that creeping sensation of wrongness: We were too low. The runway was beginning to rise up the windshield, too far away to reach in a glide. Damn! What do I do? Pitch and power, pitch and power—pitch controls airspeed, power controls altitude. I'm too low—add power. I eased the throttle forward, being careful to be gentle—my father's unexpected advice from so long ago—as the plane slid back up to a glide slope I recognized. This felt good.

I glanced at the instruments. We were descending at about 500 feet a minute at seventy knots, a little fast, with the altimeter showing 300 feet—150 feet above ground level. Everything looked fine. I was getting excited: This was going to be a good solo landing, I was going to pull it off, I was flying! Over the threshold I shifted my gaze down the runway, but suddenly I wanted to be down, wanted it to be over and fine, and wanting it too soon I pulled back on the yoke, flaring the plane a few feet above the asphalt. We banged down on the main gear, bouncing back into the air as I held the yoke back, then settling down again as I sighed and turned onto the nearest taxiway. A landing. Not a great landing, but one in which no one was killed or even particularly jarred. I was back on track.

"Not bad, Mr. Simmons," Donnie said from the rear. "Don't rush. Be patient. Now, I'll film a takeoff, and you can take us back to Marshfield."

That evening, back at home, I ask if anyone wants to see the tape Donnie made. No one does. Later, when everyone has gone to bed, I play it back to myself twice, watching my approach to 33, seeing the nose come up too soon over the runway, almost feeling again the plane bounce and then settle onto the pavement. I can see what I did right and what I did wrong, but mostly I can see that I *did* it: I brought the plane down safely. Donnie was with me, still my instructor, but he was also more obviously a man who trusted me with his life. It was a brilliant teaching ploy—in part because it was no ploy at all: Donnie's confidence, and his desire to see me fly, were uncalculated. He won my admiration, but perhaps more important, he succeeded at what he was trying to do, for as I watched the tape I won my admiration as well.

Two days later, April 27: The first couple of trips around the airport with Donnie are almost routine. I handle the plane with something like confidence, and as I talk myself through the landings it seems clear, both to me and to Donnie, that this plane and I are companions, partners. After the third successful takeoff and landing, Donnie hops out on the taxiway. "See ya in a half hour or so," he says. "Have fun." He gives my shoulder a companionable shove, waves, and is gone. I'm alone again, alone as I taxi out to runway 24, alone as I give the Warrior full throttle and roll down the runway into the air, alone as I fly out over Duxbury Beach for a few minutes before coming back in for a landing. It's a happy, strong aloneness, the kind I haven't felt for years. I think again of California and the places I loved there; they keep me company as I see them in tandem with Duxbury Harbor in the early morning sun.

When I get back down, after a reasonably smooth landing, Donnie has added an endorsement to my logbook. "I have instructed and checked Mr. Thomas Simmons in the areas prescribed in Part 61 of the FARs," he's written, "and find him competent to make solo flights in a PA28-161." PA28-161 is the Piper code for the Warrior. He's signed it, adding his flight instructor's number and the expiration date of my solo permit—three months from today.

"There you go, Cap'n," he says. "You're free." I can't help laughing, laughing with pride and relief and pleasure, with the knowledge of how wrong he is—and how right.

Chapter Six

CROSSWINDS

*T*he cockpit of a Piper Warrior II smells of hard, sunfried plastic and hot circuit boards. Its air carries traces of gasoline swept into cylinders a few feet away at the rate of 4,800 shots a minute, an occasional whiff of exhaust, the cooked odor of old navcoms and old vinyl seats. These mingle with all the evidence of human inhabitants—four thousand hours' worth of students' and flight instructors' deodorants, perfume, cologne, fading over the ten- or twelve- or fourteen-year life of the airplane, refined by time to something slightly more physical than a memory. A finely tuned pilot's nose can detect subtler fragrances—years of the celebrated "pilot's lunch," a Coke and a Snickers bar; coffee spilled on the indestructible carpet; Pepto-Bismol and Trident gum for the passengers in the rear. It is an odd combination of smells, not at all like the canned-air-and-cocktails of jetliners, and although it may not be the first thing a prospective student notices about an airplane, it can cause its own kind of dislocation: It contributes to the general sense of strangeness, like the initial scent of some ancestor's finally opened hope chest. Like the hope chest, however, it ultimately becomes companionable because of its strangeness. A pilot may never get used to the scent, but will come to look forward to it simply because it is like nothing else in the world.

On this early Saturday morning in early May, I am sitting in the cockpit of Warrior 44949, staring at the instruments, thinking about the plane and the day. The day is gorgeous. A cold front, with its attendant high pressure and blue skies, is passing through southern New England, and although I'm still on the ground I know that, once I'm in the air, I'll easily be able to see Provincetown and possibly Nantucket as well. I'm cut loose now, free to solo.

But there's a slight hitch in my plan for a smooth, easy flight. The cold front has brought with it a solid 15-knot cross-wind—a wind blowing from the northwest, almost at right angles to runway 24. I had wondered about the wind on my drive down to Marshfield, my car rocking and wandering slightly in gusts along Route 3. I wondered still more when I walked into the airport: Usually crowded on Saturday mornings, it was virtually deserted. The only person there, in fact, was Ann Pollard, a witty and alarmingly self-possessed student pilot who helped run the place on weekends. Since I usually flew weekday mornings, I didn't often see her; in the few times I'd met her before, she was enviably imposing, giving airport advisories on the radio and pumping fuel and handling bills and generally ordering people around with a sense of humor that can only come from absolute authority. I'd taken her to be at least twenty-five until Donnie asked me casually as we were taxiing out one morning how old I thought she was. He just laughed when I told him. "She's still a month away from graduating from Marshfield High," he said. "No way," I said. "Ask her yourself," he said. I didn't ask.

This morning I felt a little embarrassed, as if I had come to a party on the wrong day. Where was everyone? Ann flashed a cryptic smile. "Going up, Mr. Simmons?" she asked. She tended, I noticed, to use people's last names when something needed to be discussed.

"I was planning on it," I said. I wanted to sound professional. What should I ask? "What's the wind doing?"

Ann glanced over to the wind speed and direction indicators on the wall above the computer terminal. "Looks like three-twenty at . . . oh, pretty steady at fifteen knots. Some gusts." Three hundred twenty degrees—80 degrees to the right of the runway. The maximum crosswind for a Piper Warrior is 17 knots. No wonder no one was flying.

Ann glanced back at me. She had a disarming way of sizing people up while trying to reassure them. " 'Course, it all depends on how good you are at crosswind landings. You *could* fly in this. I'm sure we'll have a few people coming through all day."

I noticed that the radio, normally squealing and screeching with weekend pilots' position reports, was silent: Even though Marshfield shares a frequency with Provincetown and Chatham and several other airports within an eighty-mile radius, no one was talking. No one was flying. Yet.

Donnie had often emphasized the importance of "good judgment," a concept so pervasive in the cockpit that, despite its ambiguous definition, it might as well have been an official test category for pilots. The phrase meant much to the FAA, whose examiners could fail a prospective pilot for "bad judgment," which might mean anything from landing after a poor approach (instead of going around) to continuing an instrument approach slightly below minimum altitudes to bringing along an outdated navigation chart or tuning one of the aircraft radios to an AM baseball broadcast. Most commonly it meant flying into a "situation" beyond the abilities of the pilot. One such situation, clearly, was gusty weather. I knew this. On the other hand, Donnie and I had done a number of crosswind landings; all of my landings on my second supervised solo flight had a ten-knot crosswind 45 degrees to the left of the runway. Admittedly, there was a considerable difference between ten knots and fifteen, especially when the fifteen were coming almost perpendicular to the runway. But—perhaps as a psychic reward for my earlier fear of crosswinds—I had learned to be relatively adept at landing an airplane almost sideways, keeping its nose into the wind as I glided over the runway, straightening it out at the last second and dropping it onto the asphalt.

"There're really two kinds of pilots," Donnie said after the second supervised solo. "First there're the hangar jocks. They hang around the airport trading stories but only fly when it's calm. Then there're the pilots. They may not tell as many stories, but they always know how to get down in a crosswind. And they fly in 'em. It's up to you when you fly, but I think you could be a good *pilot*."

"I think I'll give it a shot," I said to Ann. "If I can't get down I'll just land over at Plymouth and get someone here to come pick me up."

"Ooo-kaaay," said Ann, somewhat ominously. She handed me a blue plastic binder with the operating handbook and weight-and-balance information, along with the keys. Then she smiled her most confident smile. I wondered if she reserved it for days like this, or simply for people like me?

"By the way," I said as I was headed out the door, "Donnie said you were about to graduate from high school. Is that true?"

"Amazing as it may seem, yes," said Ann. I had a feeling Ann and I were being amazed at two different things, but at the moment it seemed better to fly than to talk.

166

Now, in the cockpit, I reconsider. The plane rocks notice-ably in gusts; the windsock on the big blue hangar rides the air with uncharacteristic firmness. "You never have to land," Don-nie once said, but what if you want to land and can't? You never have to take off, either. On the other hand, if you don't take off . . . I flip back suddenly to Sheldon Simmons, flying beneath the clouds in wild air to reach the *Patterson*, seeking a patch of water just long enough to land on. Bleah. I'm not interested in heroics. They just get you killed. But do I think of Shell Sim-mons as a hero? I don't. Interesting—I'd never realized that before. What I liked most about Simmons was his awareness of the difference between other people's perceptions of him and his own perceptions: *They* thought he was reckless, but *he* knew he always had a plan. He was a smart man, hard-driving, com-passionate, a risk taker, and a careful pilot. He was also a master of the crosswind landing.

Firing up the engine of 44949, I taxi out to the run-up area, rev the engine to 2,000 RPM, run through the checklist, call Ann for a radio check, then idle down to the end of runway 24. With a strong wind off my left tail as I taxi, I keep the left aileron down to prevent a gust from lifting the wing and flipping the plane over. I've read some less-than-amusing accident reports from the National Transportation Safety Board about just such incidents. The Warrior shivers in the gusty air. As I line the plane up with the centerline of the runway, I pause for a moment to look around. Everything is crisp, sharp; the newly green alders on either side of the runway seem almost prismatic as they scatter the sunlight among themselves, and the red barn and the planes on the ramp hold down the sun with a hard-edged brilliance. It is beautiful—not a place or a time for any-thing to go wrong. I push the throttle forward, keep an eye on the centerline, watch the airspeed needle climb and the oil pressure needle hold steady, and wait to feel the plane.

The feeling comes fast. Suddenly, as I roll along at about 45 knots, the wheels seem to tremble under me, the nose comes up and begins to yaw to the right as I bank toward the wind, but the plane is not yet off the ground and the wheels *thunk-bump* a little as they ease off the asphalt. The plane is banking right but now nosing left, the nose coming up too fast—more right rudder, lower the nose, ignore the hard air as it whips around me, keep the plane aligned with the centerline of the runway, aim into the wind, climb, climb. Seventy-nine knots on climb-out; I'm at 150 feet, tossed around as if I were back in my small rowboat in New Jersey, but it's different now. With only a couple of wrong moves I can destroy the plane and kill myself. Airspeed is still low, seventy knots; now suddenly it's eighty-five, heading for ninety. Pull up the nose. A gust from the right lifts the right wing faster than I can respond; I bank left, recover, bank a little to the right. Around 700 feet I reach for the fuel pump switch to shut off the auxiliary pump, but a gust jams the plane down through the air as I slam my finger into the radio panel above the switch. I have to get the plane stabilized. Keep the wings level, accept minor variations in altitude, keep trying for seventy-nine knots.

Above 1,000 feet the air, freed from the worst of the ground friction, smooths out, and suddenly, after fighting my way up, I have time to breathe, to look around. Heading south over Duxbury Harbor, I can see more of Cape Cod than ever before. Provincetown is clearer than my best imagining, a child's toy of a town in crystal, jasper, jade; the thin line near the horizon to the south is not a layer of cloud but Nantucket, forty miles away. If I were to fly west for a few minutes, I could see the eastern tip of Long Island. The joy of sight comes back to me, a sensual, spiritual pleasure.

"Play a little," says the joyous voice; "Stay in the air. Do turns, slow flight, scenic tours. Pay a visit to the *Mayflower*. This is where you wanted to be, so *stay here*."

I stay. Breaking my usual routine of several takeoffs and landings in a row, I climb to 2,000 feet over Duxbury Harbor and settle into the cocoon of the Warrior—its vibrations, its slight dips and skids, its fragrances. I pull back on the control yoke; the plane climbs. I feel the slight disorientation of change, the easing back, as the real horizon sinks below the windshield and my body registers a climb. But I also see the artificial horizon sinking in the attitude indicator, see the airspeed falling slightly and the altimeter needle climbing as the vertical speed indicator needle rises, and I know that each one of these is confirming something to the airplane, a thing without consciousness: If I keep pulling back, cutting the power and raising the nose, the airspeed will drop even faster, the vertical speed indicator needle will start to stutter and then fall, the nose will fill my whole view as the stall warning lights up the cockpit with its aural phosphorescence—and suddenly the plane will pitch forward like a roller coaster going over the top, the nose vanishing as the ground fills my field of view, airspeed gathering suddenly, my stomach heading for my mouth. This is the stall.

As I make it happen this time, looking down at the ground while shoving the throttle forward and getting the plane to climb, trying not to lose more than 100 feet of altitude, I taste the cockpit air in my mouth and grip the hard black plastic of the throttle and know this plane to be a body, enmeshed in its own rhythms and methods, sensual, potentially an enemy. I come out of a life on the ground, where I don't have to worry about falling accidentally out of the sky or turning too sharply or landing hard. The Warrior comes out of a factory in Vero Beach, Florida, where it is designed to conform to physical principles of lift and thrust, drag and weight, and where those are its primary ancestry and guidance. It moves through the air according to them. We have almost nothing in common. But put us together and the effect is almost—almost—like love.

I put the plane into a steep left turn, 45 degrees, looking almost directly down now at the frigid Atlantic Ocean. Remembering what I'm supposed to be doing, I break that momentary trance and glance up. To keep the plane level in such a steep bank, I want to keep the farthest right engine cowling rivet level with the horizon. Already I'm too late. The whole nose is low. The vertical speed indicator shows a drop of more than 500 feet a minute; the altimeter is sliding smoothly counterclockwise. I pull back hard on the control yoke, but as the nose rises I'm squished in my seat by the double g-forces. I have the illusion of becoming tiny in relation to this other body, which even now is heading toward danger: If I keep the control yoke back without leveling the wings I'll quickly run out of airspeed, stall the low wing before the high wing, and put the plane in a potentially deadly spin. Ease up on the control yoke, level the wings. The g-forces subside. I've lost 200 feet, but I'm listening to the plane, feeling it, knowing it. We are each of us potential killers, but the combined possibilities of a greater life exceed the danger each of us represents. Recovery, in flying as in love, is sweet: Sometimes we have the power to save ourselves.

It is time to turn back to Marshfield. Flying over Plymouth, doing stalls and steep turns and shallow turns over Duxbury Harbor, I have consumed an hour of flight time almost without noticing. Six months ago I would never have believed I could do such a thing. The air is a fine place for changes, but it is no refuge, and as I descend the turbulence picks up, reminding me of the nature of the landing I have been avoiding. Back in the Marshfield traffic pattern, more or less at 1,000 feet, I bounce around like a life raft, angling the plane toward the runway to keep from being blown down to Green Harbor. Focusing on the landing checklist, transmitting my location on the radio, I wait too long to turn from the downwind leg to the base leg. The wind pushes me out over the Atlantic as I aim the plane north-west, castigating myself for careless planning: If the engine quits now the wind will keep me from making an emergency landing at the airport. I'd have to try to land on the beach or in the wildlife preserve south of the airport.

The engine doesn't quit, however, and in a few seconds I'm more or less lined up with runway 24. The wind is so stiff from the northwest that I'm crabbed heavily to the right. To see the runway I have to look out my side window instead of the windshield. It's gusty; all of a sudden a powerful wind whips over the plane, and despite all I can do to hold the control yoke forward I rise from 300 feet to 500 feet—way high for final approach. Then the bottom drops out. The plane falls like a dead weight as I hold the nose down and add power. Although I climb back more or less to the glide slope, I've forgotten to keep the plane aimed to the right, and now I've drifted south of the runway. "Save the landing," some instinctive voice tells me; warning voices of various kinds are beginning to go off in my head. I'm about 200 feet up, a few seconds from touchdown. "You can save it!" I bank the plane to the right, keeping the nose down and adding power, but the power increases my altitude too much. I'm almost back over the runway centerline now, at least 50 feet too high and almost over the threshold. I'll have to dive for the runway, but the airspeed indicator already shows seventy knots; it will show eighty by the time I get the plane on the runway. I won't have the wheels down for at least 500 feet. Bad, bad. "You never have to land," says Donnie. I'm fighting the control yoke, keeping the plane angled into the wind and easing down, watching too much runway go by. The first taxiway is coming up and I'm still not down. . . . Full power. Full power. Get the hell out of here.

Slowly, about halfway down the runway, the Warrior begins to climb, bouncing in the gusty air as I wait until the vertical speed indicator confirms a positive rate of climb and then begin to retract the flaps. I don't need either their lift or their drag now. I need a smooth, clean ascent with the maximum rate of climb. My stomach is doing gymnastics again, a sensation that throws me back to the first hours of flight time, and I begin to panic until I remember that, for now, this is my airplane; there's no one else to help, no one else to land, and my stomach can just damn well settle down and wait until we're back on the ground. Back in the downwind leg, I set up another landing, hugging the shore more tightly on the base leg, adding flaps a little earlier, losing a little more altitude than before, keeping the plane angled firmly into the wind. It's still bumpy, but I know now what the ride will be like, and I'm prepared. At the first hint of a gust I shove the throttle forward, then quickly pull it halfway back; the plane and I stay on the glide slope. Airspeed hovers around 70 knots, 65, 70. Anger at my earlier performance makes me more attentive to the slightest motions of the wings and ailerons, until I feel as if the skin of the airplane is somehow connected to my own: I sense a gust before I actually feel it through the motion of the plane, correcting for it just as it happens rather than afterward. I feel my life at the edge of the wing as we come up on the threshold, a few feet above the ground, crabbed right, the wind blowing steadily at 15 knots, until I spin the plane parallel to the centerline, dipping the upwind wing so the wind won't catch it and flip me off the runway, pulling back on the yoke to flare out the glide. We begin to drift to the left, but not much, and the firm touch of the main gear on the pavement tells me all I want to know.

"How was it up there?" asks Ann casually after I park the Warrior on the ramp and tie it down.

"Bumpy," I say, grimacing.

"Ah-ha," she says. Somehow it seems like a much longer conversation.

A few evenings later, Lesley answers the phone at home, then calls me. "It's Donnie," she says. I feel a burst of confusion. Donnie's going to want to know why I haven't scheduled any cross-country flights. What will I say? I pick up the phone with fake cheerfulness in my voice, but Donnie doesn't notice. His voice rings with authentic delight.

"Guess what?" he says. "I just got a job with Nantucket Airlines."

II.

*F*or many airline transport pilots (and some student pilots), Nantucket Airlines is a world unto itself, a species of success all too rare in the air. Its route structure is simple. It makes multiple daily flights from Hyannis to Nantucket and Nantucket to Hyannis. That's it. The airline uses Cessna 402s, six- or eight-seat planes powered by two big Continental piston engines. Pilot qualifications are unusually stringent for what is basically a commuter airline. Nantucket Air usually won't look at pilots with fewer than 3,500 hours' total time and fewer than 2,500 hours specifically in 402s. They're picky: They want pilots with lots of experience who love twin-engine Cessnas. They also expect considerable loyalty—or perhaps their pilots just bring it along, happy to show gratitude to an airline that cares about their unusual skills. Pilot turnover at Nantucket Air is low, and the airline rewards its fliers with salaries noticeably higher than those of other commuter airlines.

But then, it's not really fair to call Nantucket Air a commuter line. For those who fly it—and those who fly for it—it's more of an addiction, a fascination, a delight. It has almost the same kind of following as U2 or the Grateful Dead; the Nantucket Airlines sweatshirt is a collector's item, with a picture of a 402 on the back and a little slogan underneath—"The ACK and Back Attack!" (ACK is the three-letter airport identifier for Nantucket). Each trip from Hyannis to Nantucket lasts about six minutes, not including taxi, takeoff, and approach time; the whole flight consumes perhaps a half hour. En route, the pilots and passengers are treated to some of the most beautiful scenery on the Atlantic coast. It's really the only way to get to the island—unless you fly yourself in a Piper Warrior.

It wasn't hard to understand what a big deal this was for Donnie. Like most teachers, flight instructors make comparatively little money—not enough to sustain a life, really—and Donnie needed a break. He was between airline jobs, I knew, but the economic climate was bad, and it didn't seem likely that he'd find something in a hurry. We used to commiserate about finances in the cockpit while taxiing out to the runway. Now— in one of those true stories that ought to be called "When Good Things Happen to Good People"—Donnie had gotten the break he needed. I brought him a bottle of champagne on my next trip down to Marshfield, but he had already left for airline training in Hyannis.

As much as I missed him, his departure was a break for me as well. Suddenly I was without an instructor—any instructor. Although technically I was responsible to Larry, the chief flight instructor, Donnie had signed me off for the usual ninety days of solo flight. I didn't have to check in with anyone until July 26, more than two months from now. Two months was a long time to fly on my own terms. I could go back and forth to Plymouth, I could invent a multileg pseudo-cross-country flight, I could try to get comfortable with navigation before having to demonstrate my ability or klutziness to a teacher. I could set a plan in motion.

Those unsupervised days in Marshfield took on a special magic for me, a magic as powerful as my earlier anxiety and frustration had been. By this time I was a regular, and though none of the other flight instructors had flown with me recently, they knew me as one of Donnie's students. They trusted me. Larry seemed to reserve a special smile or nod of recognition for me. Every now and then he'd say something just odd enough to break my stereotype of him.

After the bottle of champagne for Donnie had sat in an odd corner of the airport for a couple of weeks, Larry waved me over to discuss it.

"I called Donnie to come pick it up," he said, "but he never came by. What do you want to do with it?"

"Why don't you guys go ahead and drink it?" I told him, trying to build up points now for any bad moment that might befall me in the distant future with an instructor.

Larry looked at me in horror. "Drinking at an airport? God, no! You know the rules—no drinking within eight feet of an airplane, no smoking eight hours before a flight."

"Isn't it the other way around?"

Larry looked at me critically. "You're even more gullible than I thought," he said. "What's the last thing that goes through a bug's mind when it hits the windshield?"

I grabbed the manual for the Warrior I was about to fly and headed for the door. "I've heard that one before," I said.

175

"Go ahead, ruin my day," Larry called after me. There was some chance, I told myself, that I might wind up liking this man someday.

Meanwhile a new plane had shown up on the Marshfield flight line. Actually it was an old plane, or at least older than the other two trainers—Warrior N44847, "847" for short. It had arrived in early May, when it spent a good deal of time on the ground or in the shop; its idiosyncrasies initially earned it a less-than-stellar reputation. I came in one day to hear Rod describing the end of a first lesson in which, while reassuring the student about the reliability of Warriors, he turned off the electrical instruments and pulled the mixture control all the way to lean—the usual way of shutting down a Warrior engine. "I told the student, 'It'll just stop now,' " he said. "Know what it did? It *revved*." Some of the instructors specifically asked not to be assigned to 847, even though—after several sessions with Ed Novak in the maintenance hangar—it had received more than its share of TLC.

I fell under the sway of 847 almost immediately because outcasts always appealed to me. But 847 also came recommended, after a fashion, by a tiny group of admirers, including Bob Pearson, an affable, holy-smoke kind of guy who had just begun his instrument training ("Bob makes you the second-nicest guy at Marshfield," Larry once told me as if I'd just lost the lottery). I hardly knew Bob, but something about his attitude toward flight reminded me of my own: He was so mellow that it was possible to mistake his mellowness for carelessness, but in fact he was a calculating risk taker, well briefed and sensitive to slight variations in aircraft performance and weather. He also had a good-luck air about him—an essential trait for a pilot. If 847 was okay with Bob, I reasoned, then maybe I ought to take it up for a flight. But this was really a way of justifying a decision I had already made.

One Tuesday morning in late May I stopped in at the barn to pick up the operating handbook and weight-and-balance information for 847, then wandered out to the flight line to inspect it. As careful as I usually was on the preflight inspection, I was even more careful this time—checking the engine mounts and cylinder heads for cracks, looking for oil leaks or signs of exhaust leaks, checking the fuel several times for sediment, examining the bolts in the stabilator fastening with a flashlight. The plane looked good, or rather, tough; whatever it had been through, it was clearly a survivor.

"Okay, plane," I say aloud as I roll into position for takeoff a few minutes later. "You are in the hands of a pilot with a total of nine, count 'em, nine hours of solo flight time. You spent more time than that this month in the maintenance hangar. Let's see if we can get into the air without killing each other." I open the throttle wide and watch what happens next.

It's all normal, utterly normal. The engine climbs smoothly to maximum power as the oil pressure needle stays just in the upper portion of its green range. In a few seconds we reach rotation speed, or takeoff speed, and the plane lifts uncomplainingly into the air. Somehow it feels a little heavier than the other Warriors, which might make sense, because it is; but I shouldn't be able to feel the slight difference. Yet I can tell immediately that this is not 47 Hotel or 949. I feel a difference, some of it real, some of it imaginary, but the combination gives me confidence.

I shoot out over Duxbury Harbor, tune in the automatic direction finder (ADF) to the Marshfield NDB station, practice turning to the station from different compass headings, then head toward Plymouth. Among some pilots Plymouth has the reputation of a "cowboy airport," where unorthodox and occasionally dangerous things happen; Donnie warned me about this after signing me off to go there, and other instructors have mentioned that they prefer not to have their students do solo flights to Plymouth. It's true that most of my approaches to Plymouth have involved other aircraft in the pattern, but—aside from the Cessna that pulled onto the runway in front of me a few weeks ago—I've never had any trouble there. It's a good way to ease into the idea of cross-country flight.

Switching the radio to the Plymouth frequency, 123.0, I call the unicom for an airport advisory and learn that runway 24 is not in use. Good—a nice, long patch of asphalt. It's barely nine o'clock, and the unicom reports no other traffic in the pattern. I swing south of the airport about four miles, then turn right to make a 45-degree approach to the downwind leg, known simply as a forty-five. Everything is normal. There's a kind of clunky ruggedness to the way 847 flies. Its controls feel a little heavier than in the other Warriors, yet not sluggish; the engine seems a little louder, and the windshield and side glass bear the slightly distorting scratches of years of outdoor winters. The windshield also has a slight crack in it. I don't know what people mean when they talk about an "honest" airplane, but if it means a plane that bears witness to its past while flying reliably, 847 may be the epitome of honesty.

Fuel pump on, carburetor heat—everything checks out okay. I pull back on the throttle, keeping the nose up to slow the plane down, and add 10 degrees of flaps. After a few seconds the plane is down to about seventy knots and beginning to descend. I broadcast my turn to base on the unicom frequency, turn, add another notch of flaps. This is a great approach. The plane sinks quietly at 500 feet a minute, almost a glider, stable and just above the flight path. I announce my turn to final, make the turn, add another notch of flaps. The frequency is quiet. I'm all alone up here.

Suddenly, out from under my nose, another plane appears—a Piper Warrior or Archer with a late-model paint scheme. It can't be more than 50 feet below me. Where in hell did it come from? I fumble with the microphone switch in the cockpit, but can't think what to say. The bastard's going to land right in front of me. We're both low now, he at about 200 feet and a quarter mile out, I at 250 feet and just behind him. He's almost filling my windshield—the closest I've ever been to another plane. No time for talk; I thrust the throttle forward and climb out. I'm trembling. He never made a single position report on the radio—probably never even saw me, or if he did thought he could just cut me off.

"Plymouth Traffic," I say as I climb, knowing that "Plymouth Traffic" consists only of my plane and that of the cretin below me, "Warrior 44847 is going around. Some guy just cut me off." No response from anyone. The idiot probably isn't even tuned in to the Plymouth frequency.

As I ease back into another downwind leg, I figure out what must have happened. The other plane arrived on what's called a "straight-in" approach—a patternless arrival, acceptable when approved by the tower at tower-controlled airports but highly unorthodox at uncontrolled fields. The other pilot had executed this approach without contacting anyone. If he had the wrong frequency tuned in to his radio, he may have simply assumed that everyone in the Plymouth pattern had heard him—or he might not have bothered using the radio at all. He wasn't watching for other traffic, or he would have seen me just above him as I turned onto my final approach. It was craziness, and I was glad I'd flown my final approach a little high: To have him come over my head rather than underneath me would have been even more frightening, and this way at least I had a chance to pull up and away. I looked for the culprit when I got down on the ground, but he had either vanished into a hangar or taken off again without telling anyone.

Back at Marshfield a few minutes later, I talked to Keith, the owner of the airport, about what had happened. He just shook his head.

"That place," he said. "I was landing there once when a guy came over my head and landed in front of me. I don't know what it is about Plymouth—I've just heard more people having trouble there than anywhere else." He tells a few more Plymouth stories.

"Listen," he says. "You take it easy over there. You did well going around, but you don't have to practice over there. Use your judgment."

I thank him with less gratitude than I actually feel. One thing I'm beginning to learn about Marshfield—one thing that keeps me coming back—is that I thrive on trust; I learn well and work well when people trust my judgment and my abilities. I almost never feel that trust at MIT except from my students. Here, by contrast, people rarely tell me not to do something unless it is forbidden by FAA directive. "Good judgment," which Donnie had drawn out of me in progressive steps like a form of training all its own, is the operative concept here. Since Donnie had signed me off for Plymouth, Keith wasn't going to interfere; he simply wanted me to think carefully about what I was doing. And he trusted me.

Trust carries its own risk. Someone—a flight instructor and, at some point, an FAA examiner—evidently trusted the skills of the idiot who nearly ran into me at Plymouth. The alternative to trust, however, is a situation like mine at MIT, where nothing is ever quite good enough and people are rarely brave enough to say what they really mean. The opposite of trust is not distrust, really, but furtive fear and doubt; no one can successfully operate in such an atmosphere. Keith's trust thus means even more to me than the risk I just faced at Plymouth. I also know vaguely that there are FAA enforcement procedures one might initiate against pilots like the one at Plymouth. Perhaps I should pursue this, but I just don't want to. Right now I'm mostly glad to know that, in a tight spot, I reacted well; I didn't panic; and I won the trust of the people whose planes I fly. And 847, despite its earlier reputation as a troublemaker, has won my trust.

A few days later the school year ends at MIT. Even apart from my credit card flying debt, Lesley and I have shot through our savings trying to make up the difference between our living expenses—rent, day care, utilities, groceries—and my MIT salary. We have $200 left in our savings account. It's hard to remember a time when things looked bleaker. In theory I have a job more desirable than most in the academic world; in fact the job has led us to the brink of financial disaster.

In mid-winter I knocked on various doors at universities and colleges in the Boston area, trying to find a position teaching summer school. Ironically, only MIT came to my rescue. The summer expository writing course will begin in just a couple of weeks. Although the course will chew up much of the time I'm supposed to spend revising my dissertation for publication, it may buy us some financial time. I may be able to pay down a couple of the credit cards, and Lesley can keep working on her dissertation without having to find another job. The money from summer school won't be enough to build up our bank account or get us even remotely out of debt, but it will be a stopgap, a finger in the dike.

It's hard to know how much longer we can live this way. Lesley and I move past each other, speaking the words of help and comfort, feeling angry and resentful and exhausted. Like people who, consumed with thirst, no longer feel thirsty, we have gotten beyond the point of seeking answers: There is nothing to be fixed, no change worth making. Everything is fine. This is just the way life is.

Does Lesley have a refuge? I don't know. Four years ago, if things had gotten this bad in California, I would have asked, but now something in me shuts off even the desire to ask. I feel the question breeding an anger stronger than any I have ever known. Too much is coming down on me, on *me*, God damn it, I hear myself beginning to say, and I don't know what to do. When Lesley's parents call from California, we have the usual cheerful conversations about the usual subjects. In moments of desperation we drop hints about how bad things are, but my flying is an obvious stumbling block: Things can't be that bad if Tom has the money to fly. Am I shafting everything? Is this failure—this failed job, this relationship—my fault?

Almost miraculously, the University of Iowa checks in with a loud yes—they want me. But there's a catch: They can't hire me until the fall of 1992, more than a year away. We've got another year to weather in Boston.

A S E A S O N
I N   T H E   A I R

*J*uly 2 dawns with pale sunlight through a high overcast—a classic Massachusetts summer day, as if New England had been granted a special dispensation to import meteorological scenes from the paintings of John Ruskin. Barometric pressure is steady, a bit lower than the standard 29.92 inches of mercury. A cold front may sweep through in a day or two, clearing all this out, but for now there's a stale stillness to the air.

Larry is waiting outside the red barn, smoking a cigarette, when I arrive. I think back on my first encounters with him, when he seemed gruff and somewhat unapproachable. Now, watching him smoke, I begin to wonder if the gruffness is a facade. He stands beside the door, absorbed in his own thoughts, glancing at the sky, sweeping the cigarette from his mouth with an instinctive grace. No one describes smokers as graceful anymore; it's not politically correct. But Larry's smoking is stylish and austere, somewhere between Humphrey Bogart's and Fred Astaire's. There's a shyness to his motions, as if he had not quite made peace with whatever had wounded him. I begin to feel a little like a voyeur, sitting in my car watching him.

He waves at me as I get out of the car—a small, gruff wave. "Ready to go?" he asks. He flicks the cigarette onto the pavement, taps it with his foot, stretches.

"Let me take a look at your course before we go," he says. "Did you get the weather and file a flight plan yet?"

I nod, showing him the weather notes I'd made on the back of my flight-planning sheet.

While Larry looks over the course I've plotted to Southbridge, I call the Bridgeport Flight Service Station again for a weather update. Most regions of the country have their own Flight Service Stations (FSS). Open twenty-four hours a day, the FSS has briefers who record pilots' flight plans, including the aircraft ID number, time and place of departure, expected time en route, and other essential information. If a pilot fails to call the FSS within a half hour of his or her expected arrival time, the FSS starts a search—calling the pilot's home base, the destination airport, and any airports along the way, until the plane is found or a wider search becomes necessary. The FSS also provides current weather reports, including cloud ceilings, visibility, barometric pressure, wind direction and speed, and the difference between the temperature and the dewpoint (important in summer as a measure of the potential for fog, or in winter as a measure of the potential for ice). Included in these reports are AIRMETS—warnings of hazards to general aviation aircraft—and SIGMETS—warnings of hazards to all aircraft, such as thunderstorms, tornadoes, or low-level wind shear.

The Bridgeport briefer reports a high overcast, winds aloft from the northwest at less than six knots, no turbulence. There's not much to say. "Looks good," he concludes after I file my flight plan. "Have a good trip."

"Everything's fine," I say halfheartedly as I walk back into the main lounge in the barn.

Larry looks up gruffly. "What's that mean?"

"Uh—high overcast, winds at three thousand from the northwest at less than six, no turbulence."

"Okay," he says, examining my flight plan. "You've done something a little funny here. Would you mind explaining it to me?"

I lean over to see what he means. It looks fine to me. I've drawn two alternative departures from Marshfield, depending on which runway we use. Each of these connects about three miles southwest of Marshfield with the main course to Southbridge. My landmark for turning onto the Southbridge course is Route 3; including the time to take off and climb, we should need about four minutes to get there. Larry looks at the sectional chart, then back at me. I detect some disbelief.

"That's way too complicated, man," he says. He draws a straight line from Marshfield to Southbridge. "If you start trying to fly this shit you'll get lost right away. All you have to do is climb to cruising altitude directly above Marshfield, then turn on course when we're right over the runway. Make it simple," he says, handing the sectional back to me.

Abashed, I take a few minutes to refigure my course. A straight flight from here to Southbridge requires a true course of 270 degrees—due west—with a 2-degree wind correction angle and 16 degrees of correction for magnetic deviation—the difference at this point on earth between magnetic north and true north. The course heading comes out to 288 degrees. It seems too simple.

Larry glances at the corrections, nods, and motions toward the plane. Feeling slightly like a zombie, I follow him outside to do the preflight.

Somehow 847 cheers me up. Its utilitarian funkiness brings San Francisco to mind, and its strange interior reminds me that life is really no fun without a sense of humor. Everything checks out okay. I climb in, pulling my headset and intercom from my flight bag; my Walkman also falls onto the seat.

Larry, who's standing on the wing waiting to get in, looks surprised. "What's all that stuff?" he asks.

Several years ago, when I first started to show anxiety about flying in commercial jetliners, a friend suggested that I take a Walkman and a few of my favorite tapes along with me. "I measure flight time now in numbers of tapes," he said. "Most of my flights are six tapes or less. It's pretty wonderful, holding six of your favorite tapes in your hand and knowing you'll be in California by the time you listen to all of them." He was right; it helped me, at least for a while. I couldn't quite break the habit of stuffing the Walkman and a couple of tapes into my flight bag, even though now I was the pilot and presumably too busy to listen to music. It helped me to know that, if I wanted to, I could plug the Walkman into my aircraft intercom and listen to music between radio transmissions. But I hadn't really intended to use it.

Explaining this to Larry, I was expecting him to glower and mention something about "good judgment," but instead he just looked happy.

"What a great idea," he said. "You can plug music into your intercom? No shit!"

I set up the Walkman and intercom as Larry runs out to his car to get a tape. I've never actually used this before. Figuring that the intercom must function more or less as an amplifier, I run a plug from the "line out" on the Walkman to the intercom receptacle. Larry comes back with a tape, pops it into the Walkman, presses Start. Because the intercom has its own power supply, we ought to be able to test it without turning on the master switch on the plane. What comes through, in a few seconds, is disheartening—a pale, distant complex of music, like someone performing something fascinating three floors up. Larry fiddles with the volume adjustment on the intercom, then on the Walkman; no change. We look at each other.

"Must be something wrong with it," I say mournfully.

"Ah, well, electronics are a pain in the butt," says Larry philosophically. "You can play with it later."

Starting the plane, doing the run-up, taxiing out to runway 24, we don't have much to say to each other. We're both disappointed, but I'm also suffering a little from what academics like to call "cognitive dissonance." Every time I talk to Larry, he's different from the person I imagined. I can't get a handle on him.

"All set?" His voice comes through loud and clear on my intercom. We've got voice but no music.

"I guess," I say. Larry glances at me with something approaching annoyance.

"Well, let's go then," he says, whacking the padded top of the instrument panel with his palm. I ease the throttle forward, and we're off.

At Larry's suggestion I make a left downwind turn, climbing through pattern altitude in a minute or so, circling the airport as I climb to 2,000 feet. We're over the departure end of runway 24 again, but it and all its planes look like one of Nathaniel's Galoob Micro-Machines setups, and I'm having a little trouble remembering that the world down there is real. Swinging out to the south, we begin to cross the midpoint of the runway at exactly 2,400 feet.

"Okay, turn on course now," says Larry. "Start your timer. What's the course again?"

"Two-eight-eight," I say, pushing the little red button on

my West Bend stopwatch: 00:01, 00:02—we're off. In about eleven minutes we ought to be over the city of Brockton, between railroad tracks and a major highway.

"What's the next thing you're supposed to do?" Larry asks. I blank. He taps the radio. It looks okay to me; we're tuned to 122.8, the Marshfield frequency, but it's also the Southbridge frequency, so we might as well stay on it. Larry looks at me; he's now drumming his fingers on the front of the radio, looking up innocently to the sky, saying to himself, "Hmm, now what am I supposed to do with this? Who else needs to know about this flight?"

Bridgeport! The FSS won't activate my flight plan until I call them from the plane and request it. Giving Larry a somewhat dim stare, I dial in 122.2. "You could have just told me," I say to him.

"Why?" he says. "You're the pilot."

"Bridgeport Radio, this is Warrior four-four-eight-four-seven," I say into my microphone. Silence. Larry is drumming his fingers on the radio again, just below the frequency setting.

"How many radio channels is Bridgeport monitoring?" he asks. "Just one? Just one-two-two-point-two?"

"Well, no, several . . ." I begin. Suddenly the problem dawns on me.

"Bridgeport Radio, this is Warrior four-four-eight-four-seven, with you on one-two-two-point-two," I say into the microphone.

"Warrior four-four-eight-four-seven, this is Bridgeport Radio." Larry smiles.

It only takes a few seconds to open the flight plan; when I'm done I glance at the timer, then turn my attention to the ground. About six minutes have passed since takeoff.

"Where are we?" Larry asks.

"What?"

"Where are we?" he asks again. "You were supposed to be flying a heading of two-eight-eight. You're actually flying two-eight-zero, heading I think toward two-seven-five, and I just thought you might have some other place you wanted to go."

As I look down again, I remember the relatively small number of things you can never prepare for, or warn someone about, ahead of time. You can never tell someone who hasn't experienced it what it's like to fall in love. You can never warn someone what it's like to fall out of love. You can't really anticipate the experience of jumping out of an airplane with a parachute, or guiding a motorcycle through a turn at high speed on a banked track. And you cannot, I now realize, really know beforehand what it's like to try to navigate over real, live terrain in a small airplane using only a sectional chart, your directional gyro, a pocket calculator, and a stopwatch.

Below me, to my left, are trees. *Lots* of trees. A long, narrow strip runs through them, but it's not paved—railroad tracks? Power lines? A few tiny ponds and marshes interrupt the dark green expanse. There's a city, with tiny brick buildings downtown and streets running every which way, disorderly as most cities are, and houses stretching out to the edge of the forests; but which city is this? It juts down south a little, with a kind of crooked finger at the eastern edge—is this part of Rockland? Whitman? Part of Brockton? Looking out, desperate for perspective, I can see the skyscrapers of Boston, but they're too far away to be much good. Ahead of me is what looks like an unbroken urban mass, urban sprawl, a reddish tan ground-based haze of buildings running almost to the horizon.

I glance down at the sectional in my lap. It's so neat, so clear. Over here is Marshfield; here is Brockton, just east of the highway; a few minutes west is another major highway, a large pond, and a smaller highway. So many landmarks! It ought to be so easy. But the people on the ground don't know I'm looking for these landmarks; they don't know there aren't supposed to be any houses or buildings or trees near these roads and railroad tracks. They don't know that their cities are supposed to be neatly contained in boundaries, with labels like "Brockton" and "Rockland" on the top for easy viewing. Damn this map, anyway. It doesn't look anything like what's on the ground.

"You're losing altitude," Larry says.

We're down to 2,200 feet and dropping at almost 500 feet per minute. I yank back on the yoke. My stomach rises as the airspeed drops. As I glance at the airspeed indicator, I notice the directional gyro pointing to 270. Almost 20 degrees off course! I bank 30 degrees to the right to compensate. How can I figure out where I am if the damned plane won't fly itself?

"Okay, okay, easy," Larry says. I glare at him. "What's over there, over my right shoulder?"

It looks like a large airport. Logan! No—that doesn't make sense; Larry would be freaking out. It must be Weymouth Naval Air Station. That's a big airport about fifteen miles northwest of Marshfield. A quick look at the sectional tells me we ought to be passing just south of it.

"Must be Weymouth," I say.

"Good," says Larry. "Watch your altitude. Now, look around you, right to left, from Weymouth. What do you see?"

"Well, there's a big city just off to the right, and a freeway, and a forest off to the left."

"So what does that correspond to, more or less, on the sectional?"

I look down again. As I do I ease the yoke forward, and the plane begins to drop again; I glance up, pull back on the yoke. Although the air is calm, I'm turning this flight into a roller

190

coaster ride. If I don't smooth it out soon, I'm going to have to answer to my stomach.

"It looks a little bit like the southern tip of Brockton."

"Does that make sense?" Larry asks. "How much time has gone by?"

The stopwatch shows ten minutes, fifty-five seconds—about the right amount of time to be over Brockton. And we've been 10 to 20 degrees south of the course, so we ought to be somewhere between the city and the forest.

"Yes, it makes sense," I say.

"Okay," says Larry. "Now you know where you are. See how simple that is? Now, how're you gonna get back on course?"

There's a procedure for getting back on course, I know, but my mind feels like a kaleidoscope and I can't think how to do it. A helpful article in one of the flying magazines several months ago pointed out that the average adult thumb represents about five nautical miles on a sectional chart. Placing one edge of my thumb a little south of Brockton, I find I'm about six nautical miles south of the course. It looks as if a 30-degree addition to the original course—318 or 320 degrees—would bring us back on course in, say, four minutes.

"Sounds good to me," Larry says. Resetting the stopwatch, reminding myself to set it again for the remainder of the second leg after four minutes are up, I realize why navigation was art, science, and religion for the early pilots: With no radio beacons, no VORs or NDBs, it took more vigilance than I can imagine to avoid becoming hopelessly lost.

We're down to 2,100 feet. Larry sighs.

"Look, Tom, you're really going to have to control the airplane better than this if you want to master cross-country. The test standards say you can only gain or lose a hundred feet of altitude. You're all over the map up here. Hey—I made a joke," he says, chuckling.

"I'm in hysterics," I say. It sounds less critical through the intercom.

"Oh, come on," he says. "The real problem is you never trimmed the plane properly over Marshfield. Remember? Trim it for a certain airspeed and it will more or less fly itself. Let's do it now. Throttle full forward."

The plane begins to climb as I push the throttle to the firewall. When we reach cruising altitude I hold the yoke forward, watching the airspeed climb to 100 knots, 105, 110 . . .

"Okay, now trim it," Larry says. I roll the trim wheel forward until the yoke needs just a touch from my fingers. The airspeed holds steady at 110 knots.

"Let go," Larry says. I do. The plane stays at 2,400 feet.

"You're working too hard," he says. "Four minutes are up. Let's get to Southbridge."

As if there were some astral compensation for my earlier screwups, the rest of the flight is almost serene. In eight more minutes we pass over a freeway and a major highway; Hopedale Industrial Airport is just to the north, and a large city—Milford —is just north of that. Everything is where it should be. The sectional and the ground don't look anything like each other, but at least they technically coincide.

For the next ten minutes we're over heavy forest, with only a pond here and there to confirm a course. I begin to sweat. Larry stretches, yawns.

"Okay," he says. "Time for the big picture. Not much in the way of landmarks below you. What's off to the right?"

I realize I haven't looked that way in several minutes. Not too far away is a big city—really big. The freeway running underneath us heads directly for it. My sectional shows Worcester more or less where this big city is. If that's true, then Southbridge ought to be straight ahead, barely five minutes away.

"You got it," Larry says. "Time to announce your arrival on one-two-two-point-eight."

"But I can't see the airport yet."

"You will in a second," he says. "Look a little to your left, in that valley down there."

It's a beautiful sight: an airport, with a paved runway running more or less north-south, just east of a long, tree-laden ridge. Southbridge. Would I have flown right past it if Larry hadn't known where it was? It's sobering to realize how new I am at this, and there's nothing I can do on the ground to improve. I can plot courses and draw wind triangles and calculate fuel burn all I want, but the only way to find my way across the country is to fly. And cross-country flight (which the FAA defines as any trip more than fifty nautical miles from the departure point) is detective work—learning your position from insignificant clues, trusting the passage of time and the accuracy of your directional gyro. It's faith and science—two of the oldest companions and antagonists in my life. But the faith feels different now, more truly humbling because the possibility of getting lost is so clear. And the science—well, the science is numbers rather than language, and in that sense almost diametrically opposed to the science I knew as part of my religion. I wonder, as we set up a landing at Southbridge, if I'll ever be more than a beginner.

II.

Later in the day, jubilant over a successful flight back from Southbridge, I decide to give my father a call. We haven't talked in almost a year. It seems to take each of us, or at least me, that long to recover from our conversations. The annual (or, occasionally, semiannual) event goes something like this: We greet each other happily, there's a pause, I ask how he is, he asks how I am. He's always completely fine; his impenetrable wellness, which I know is a deceit, deflates my own attempts to tell him how I'm actually doing. I make a few comments about good things and bad things, about Nathaniel and Georgia, about MIT. He wishes me all the best. We compare weather in Massachusetts and Florida. He tells me he's proud of me, I thank him, and we sign off.

Part of the difficulty is that, at some level, I don't begrudge him his reticence and cheerful facade. If he pushes me away this way, he has his reasons. As difficult as his life was within the family, it grew more difficult after my mother died. Her death haunted him with loneliness, a demon he had met before and had kept at bay with his airplanes, his friends, and his role as a flight instructor in World War II. But demons cannot be kept at bay indefinitely; eventually they must be faced and destroyed, or converted into part of oneself, or their invasions become lethally insidious. Had my father had some adequate way of preparing for my mother's death—friends and a church to comfort him, to prepare him to go back into himself with the knowledge that they would not abandon him—he might have confronted that primal terror successfully. But, even as he watched my mother's cancerous tumor grow and her body fade into a shadow, he understood that he had to continue to declare the unreality of the disease and the perfect spiritual reality of his wife. That was the only way, in Christian Science, that she could possibly recover. He had to deny her death, and thus the possibility of loneliness and grief. At some instinctive level, he could not deny this. Yet that consoling voice, which he had shown me when I was a child, was now too muffled, shoved too deeply down inside him. When, at last, she died, it was as if he had been launched into stormy seas in a small rowboat, but for him there were no oars. He would awaken at night in the terror of a storm-wracked man.

The woman who rescued him, Patti, was an old friend from high school—someone who knew him from his earliest flying days. Checking the grapevine of old friends, he found her in a neighboring town in California where she had, by coincidence, moved the year before. It seemed miraculous: From his shipwreck he had been washed onto an island refuge with wide strands of luxury and the soothing clarity of clear water. The whole family took a collective sigh of relief. Our father, who had so much mourning to do, would at least have someone to begin it with, someone who clearly treasured him. They were married within a few months.

But neither my father nor anyone else in the family knew that Patti had had two serious heart attacks in the past several years. Almost exactly a year after my mother died, my father heard the sound of a body crumpling to the floor and, racing into the bathroom, found Patti unconscious. This time he did what reason dictated: He called the paramedics. They arrived in less than five minutes, taking over the CPR that he had been applying from his old Navy training, and a few minutes later she was in the Intensive Care Unit of El Camino Hospital in Mountain View. But the damage to her heart was severe. "Critical condition" was in her case a euphemism.

Lesley and I went to see her that evening, dashing down from Berkeley to rendezvous with my father in Los Altos for the trip to the hospital. At first the shock was almost unmanageable. A year ago, I had watched my mother fade into a nightmare of unrelieved pain, crying out in a small room in a Christian Science care home in San Francisco as the nurses came in, not to administer medication but to tell her they were going to telephone her practitioner. Now, in an ICU, I saw a once-vigorous woman lying on her side, curled almost fetally with a pillow between her legs, IVs in her arms, a tube in her throat, the respirator breathing for her in its jerky, mechanical way. Here it seemed that everything that could be done had been done; ironically, perhaps, only prayer was left. Was this any better than what my mother had gone through?

I did not know how to answer that question, and yet something struck me quite distinctly about the El Camino ICU. The nurses and doctors there, who attended to Patti and to us, were full of love and compassion—exactly what I had been taught to expect in Christian Science but had so rarely found. They comforted my father, they explained what was going on and what was likely to happen, and they hovered over Patti with an attentiveness more generous than I had ever seen in any facility dedicated to health. It struck me then—as it had struck me only a few times before in my life—that love was not an intellectual abstraction or idea, or even necessarily a yearning, a desire to help. It was an act of intimate attentiveness to someone else. When you loved, you paid attention; you gave yourself to the reality of someone else's life without losing your own. What I had received when my mother died were the words of love from people who—sure they knew the meaning of God as love—wanted to tell me how to think and how to feel. What I received at El Camino Hospital was the attentiveness of people who knew what it meant to give attention. Perhaps I was unusually lucky there—I have had less successful encounters with medical practitioners since then—but I could take comfort in what I was given at El Camino, despite my grief. My father, however, was a different story.

Patti died after three days in the ICU. In two years my father had lost two wives, two precious souls. The only explanation, from his point of view, was cosmic: God had decided to punish him. He had not been a good-enough husband to my mother; he had been too angry, too distant; he had quit college in a fit of anger and given up a lucrative career as an engineer— he had done, he said, too much to harm too many people. And now God was punishing him.

Lesley and I, half astonished, half terrified, tried to talk him out of this the next evening as we sat around the intensely silent Los Altos house. God did not punish, I said; God was love. I stepped on a land mine, invoking the very language of the religion that had wounded us. The look my father gave me was one of simple revulsion. If this was love, he, like Job, needed none of it. "But you've been a good father," I said; instantly a fog descended upon us. What did I mean? Did I mean that he had been a good soul before becoming a father? Did I mean that he deserved praise for hanging in there despite everything he had suffered? Did I mean I forgave him for his departures and silences, his inability or refusal to connect?

Words can be demonic; they spin around crises like a ghostly whirlpool, creating such pure confusion that the only blessing is silence. My father and I ran out of things to say that night. After that, although Lesley and I saw him regularly for dinner, a different, larger distance set in: Our conversations with him became safe, tame. He married again; he and his wife became seminomadic. They moved to the Napa Valley, where another, terrible catastrophe befell them; they moved back near San Francisco, then moved to the north of Canada, where I lost touch with them for almost a year. They moved to Toronto, then to Florida. No place was good enough, safe enough. When the pain of the past is too great, sometimes the only recourse is flight. My father, who had known that recourse literally in his youth, now lived it in a slightly less literal way, staying on the ground but on the move, trying not to let the demons assemble too great a force. His life is an ongoing guerrilla action against the past, in which the sign of a bad ambush is a new address and phone number.

Tonight, as he answers in his quiet, hopeful voice, I beam with news he can hardly ever have expected to hear. "Guess what, Dad?" I say, a breathless thirty-five-year-old. "I did my first dual cross-country flight today! I'm flying!"

The pause at the end of the line is rich, everything I hoped. "Airplanes? Small planes?" he asks, with wonderful incredulity.

I laugh. "Yes, Dad—Piper Warriors. I got my solo permit a couple of months ago. Do you know where Marshfield is— south of Boston? I'm flying out of a small airport there."

"Well, how about that?" His words of astonishment sound almost as old as I am. I sit down on the bed, settling in for what I hope is a long conversation. And it is—longer than most, anyway. He begins to talk about Summerton; I ask him to wait a second so I can get my sectional chart to look it up. Another slight pause. "My son has a sectional?" I think I hear him saying to himself. "Great," he says out loud. "Oh, wait a minute—I don't think Summerton exists anymore. You see Northeast Philadelphia? Isn't there a highway right next to the airport? Summerton used to be on the other side of the highway, I think. Boy, that was a long time ago."

We talk about the airport, and about Ernest Buehl, the owner, who was one of the first hundred licensed commercial pilots in the United States and who gave introductory lessons for two dollars in a Piper Cub. His slogan was, "We dare you to try it." I describe what it's like to fly along Duxbury Beach; my dad tells of flying to Avalon, New Jersey, on early Sunday mornings.

For the first time in our lives, we meet in the air. A luminousness surrounds us across a two-thousand-mile divide.

"So how are you?" I finally ask. It's like shattering crystal. "Oh, fine, just fine," he says warily. "Everyone's fine here. Your work going okay?"

"Oh, not really," I say.

"That's too bad," he says. "Well, give it your best shot. You can do it if anyone can."

A pause.

"Dad, it's been good talking to you, you know, about the flying."

"Yeah—well, you be careful up there." He means this, I know, but he's also been watching too many "Hill Street Blues" reruns. We've left the live zone now; we're back on tape. And both of our tapes are coming to an end.

When I hang up, I notice how quiet the house is. Lesley and the kids have gone to the park with the neighbors for a late-evening swing in the beautiful summer light. I finger the sectional map. It crinkles with a sound I've heard before, not from a map but from something else—something at once sharp and muffled, like the sound of bare feet on a wooden boardwalk or the sound of waves breaking down the beach: summer sounds, sounds of the season. I think again of Avalon.

In Avalon, when I wasn't bodysurfing or taking long walks on the beach or rowing, I was reading. The town library was an old, high-ceilinged, white-and-green-shingled secular monastery, and its book collection was untamed and idiosyncratic. I thought you could find anything there. I read whatever there was, whatever cover or first page caught my eye, fifty books in a summer—Steven W. Meader adventures (*The Fish Hawk's Nest*, *The Muddy Road to Glory*), Hardy Boys, John Steinbeck's *Travels with Charley* and *Cannery Row*. But my favorite book, which I returned to a couple of times a summer for several years, was Arthur C. Clarke's *Dolphin Island.*

Although Johnny Clinton, the main character, is sixteen years old in the book, I always thought of him as my age—ten or eleven or twelve; being a teenager didn't seem that interesting to me, and what I liked most about Clinton was not his young adulthood but his willingness to ask almost any question and to take a seemingly insane risk when something inside him told him to. At least that was what I told myself I liked most; he was a very bright, sort of reckless kid. But he was also an orphan. His parents had died in a plane crash when he was four. At night, in Avalon, I would lie in the top bunk, looking toward the dark ceiling and imagining myself in the opening chapters of the book.

Clinton and I were asleep when one of the hovership freighters that crisscrossed the country in the early twenty-first century zoomed past on Transcontinental Thruway 21. We lived near a small midwestern town with our Aunt Martha, a widow who had children of her own. She had no qualms about reminding us how hard it had been for her to take us in after our parents died. We were fed, and clothed, and delivered to school and church, but otherwise we were pretty much on our own. Did we have a home? We had a place to go.

But now, suddenly, the noise that helped ease us from dream to dream stopped suddenly; the silence woke us. Slipping out of bed, creeping along the hallway to the balcony, we heard the muffled snoring of Aunt Martha and her kin and knew we were safe. When we opened the door we saw, perhaps a hundred yards away, a medium-sized freighter, fifteen or twenty thousand tons, resting on the grass near the side of the thruway.

"I've never seen one up close before," said Clinton, looking at me.

200

"Me either," I said, and within a few minutes we were dressed and out the back door, racing through the darkness to the ship.

Recessed into the hull were several access ladders; we paused in front of one of them, then began to climb. Fifteen feet up, Clinton looked down at me doubtfully. Just then, the whole ship began to vibrate, and clouds of dust and rocks and weeds flew up around my feet.

"Go! Go!" I yelled. We might already be doomed. But when I looked up again, Clinton was already inside the hatch, beckoning to me. Fighting the trembling ladder, I climbed until he could haul me in. We were stowaways.

We thought, at first, that we would try to find the bridge and report ourselves to the captain. But why tell anyone? Why not wait to see where we'd end up? What was there, *really*, to go back to? When Clinton found the lifeboat with its store of emergency food and water, we realized we were set for at least a couple of days. We carved out a place for ourselves in a storage locker and fell asleep.

What happened next was—everything: I woke as if I were in midair a second before Clinton crashed into me, something exploded far away, ropes and rain gear and assorted junk fell on top of us, the lights went out. Then we were pitching and rolling in the total blackness. We fell against the door and jerked it open. The corridor outside was bathed in the pale glow of an emergency light. It was also listing sharply, and when we rounded a corner where a hatch was supposed to be, we found instead a bulkhead already glowing hot. Sweating, retracing our steps, we found another corridor, and then another that looked vaguely familiar. Within minutes we had made it to the lifeboat, only to discover an empty space: The crew had already abandoned ship. Even as we stood there, silent in our confusion, the ship heaved itself upward and began to roll. We came up in a warm, oily sea, awash in debris from the wreck. As we rose on each wave we could see the lights of the lifeboat, too far away to hail.

Though we tried to stay together, Clinton and I were swept farther apart as the sea drew us into itself. And then something bumped me hard; I turned to find a large packing crate next to me, wide enough to support two boys. Screaming to Clinton, giving him at least a voice to track, I gradually led him to where I was.

With the morning came a ragged row of fins, slicing the water from the west. But as they drew nearer, we saw not sharks but dolphins, who came to play with the packing crate. They bumped it back and forth a couple of times until we almost slid off, and when we yelled they stopped suddenly, drawing back for several moments to look at us, whistling among themselves with excitement. Then, as the rest drew back a little more, four of them came up to the back and sides of the crate, nudging it slowly but firmly in one direction. Gradually they built up speed, pushing us westward at a steady pace. When they tired, they dropped back and another four took their places. By this time the sun had scorched our skin, and we prayed the dolphins had some kind of plan. When the island came into sight, our lips were so swollen that we could not open our mouths. I saw before me waterfalls, crystal springs, ice-cream sodas, milk shakes. Clinton and I slipped off the crate as the dolphins nudged it into water too shallow for them to swim; it seemed to me that a large number of people were running down the beach toward us. Then the sand rose to my face, and I lost consciousness.

In Avalon I lay in bed for hours, not so much waiting for sleep as retelling and embellishing the story, seeing the color of oil on the sea and the dappling of the dolphins' skin, then working backward to the mechanical darkness of the hovership, the wide thruway near the yard of Aunt Martha's small house, the days and days of needing to feel like a small creature, as innocuous as possible. Nothing I could do would please her; I was not like her; I was the child of another man and woman. And they had died. Being an orphan . . . I would set the story in forward motion again, slowing it down in my mind when the sun rose and the dolphins arrived, feeling the sun like a wide red welt on my back, seeing the island, knowing that I had been brought here. Then I would fade to black, awakening hours later to the pale Jersey sun.

But if I fell asleep to visions of disintegration and rescue, I lived during the day with a different part of the book. Clinton, I knew, had been brought to an island with a research station whose scientists studied dolphins. Professor Kazan, the head of the station (and the only scientist I ever idolized as a child), was scholarly but also playful and adventurous. He studied dolphins, not because some school required him to but because he loved them; they were creatures almost wholly unlike him and yet complementary, living in an adjacent reality. It interested me that Dr. Kazan had a wife who spent most of her time in Russia, venturing to Dolphin Island only two or three times a year. As odd as it was, their relationship seemed to work, although I couldn't explain it to myself; married people lived together, and togetherness was a sign of a perfect marriage—like my parents' marriage. The personal freedom of Dr. Kazan and his wife seemed to me not only unimaginable but also unjustifiable. My own parents were unhappy, I knew, but they were doing things the right way, and that was what counted. It bothered me somewhat that Dr. Kazan and his wife, who were clearly doing things the wrong way, actually seemed relatively content.

Fatherless for so long, Clinton thrived under Kazan's guidance. There was much to be learned, and Clinton was obliged to study biology, chemistry, mathematics. But Kazan made it clear that study alone was worse than ignorance, and Clinton had equal hours to explore the reef around the island, to play with the dolphins, and to join in the scientists' experiments to learn dolphin language and to teach them English.

What always struck me as odd about *Dolphin Island*, as I thought about it while walking along the beach or playing in the sand dunes of Avalon, was that it seemed as if Clinton got to choose his father. This was wrong, I knew, since the book made it clear, not only that Clinton's parents had died, but that Clinton had been brought to Dr. Kazan, rather than the other way around. Yet I was still envious of Clinton, who had risked his life more out of desperation to leave "home" than for any other reason, and who wound up with a man who saw more deeply into him than anyone had seen before—a man who offered him the first physical and spiritual home he had ever really known.

When a hurricane strikes Dolphin Island, destroying its boats and generator and medical supplies, Dr. Kazan is one of the casualties: He lies in a half-ruined island hospital, mortally ill with pneumonia. The only hope is for Clinton to ride his dolphin-towed surfboard over a hundred miles to the coast of Australia. The ocean wilderness he travels, in the wake of the hurricane, is as potentially deadly as the wilderness he left behind in the Midwest, but here his two closest friends, two dolphins, keep him company, and he has within him the knowledge that he is Dr. Kazan's lifeline.

Even as I read the first four chapters over and over, savoring the disastrous crash of the hovership and Clinton's rescue, I read the last four chapters repeatedly, knowing how easy it would be for Clinton to get lost, how much he had to trust the dolphins and his own instincts, and how finally—when he cut away the last traces of webbing around the surfboard and rode an avalanche of a wave to the Queensland beach—he lived every nerve of his body through the board itself into the wave rising around him, riding a power he could not control. Entering the pipeline, the curl of the wave, he was, in my mind, no longer an orphan. He had a guardian and a guide, and a home in the wild world. In risking his life to save the professor, he set the seal on his own new life.

Books from childhood often work the deepest magic on the heart. Now, coming out of a tandem dream of Avalon and *Dolphin Island*, I wonder if ultimately a man has to invent his own father. Sometimes that is the only way to have the kind of choice I once ascribed, as a boy, to Clinton. To be my father was to be enmeshed in the burdens of debt and unrewarding labor, to try to raise a family knowing that something precious lay elsewhere, still calling, unfulfilled—and necessary; it was to sacrifice virtually everything for duty, to muffle that summoning voice with every psychological device possible, and still to hear it. What followed, then, was rage and loneliness, despite the moments of joy. My father seemed to feel unworthy of life the longer he lived it. Would a son invent such a father? Only a sadist would do so, and yet that model of fatherhood still exists. I myself have felt the pull of its undertow. Knowing what my father has been through, knowing how far away he journeyed, I can grant him the distance but not without a prayer of deep regret and even revulsion for the world in which he had to live. Regret and revulsion are oddly seductive, like fire to a frostbitten adventurer; not until the skin is already burned beyond saving does the flame become painful. I need something, or someone, to draw me away from this fire. If, for me, there is no Dr. Kazan, there is nevertheless Clinton's wild world, secrets

205

still to be learned, and the danger of getting lost—a danger to be stared down again and again.

III.

*T*ime in this summer season has begun to feel expansive and strangely placid, like a calm before a hurricane. At MIT I teach two two-hour classes each week; in between I take care of Nathaniel and Georgia, and fly. Instead of my usual fifty or sixty students, I have only eight, and they are an appealingly idiosyncratic bunch, even for MIT. One, who is my age, is a secretary at MIT; she's taking classes part-time on her way to an undergraduate degree. I've never had a student my own age before, and at first I'm embarrassingly anxious. What if I have nothing to teach her? But after the first couple of weeks I come to look forward to her comments in class, and her writing improves. After a while I forget to ask myself whether or not the improvement is due to my teaching. Three of the other people in the class are graduate students in various schools around the institute, and the remaining undergraduates have equally varied backgrounds. Although this is an expository writing class, which always carries an implicit threat of deadly boredom, only one student seems miserable. After reading the first round of essays, I realize she may be one of the best writers I have ever had.

Stubbornly unexpository, her first essay is a two-page prose poem in which her love of the landscape spills out into an implicit faith that the human presence in nature may not be entirely destructive. It's an amazing piece of work; I read it over and over. Who the hell cares if it's not expository? I'll work on more analytic or argumentative writing with this student at some point, I tell myself, but for now it's clearly important for her to have a forum for her own voice. My suspicions about her past as a writer are confirmed when I speak to her briefly after class a few days later. She's never liked writing much, no one has ever much praised her for her work, and writing in high school was painful. Her story is one I've encountered often at MIT. Many students come here with natural talent in more than one field, but concentrate on science because it's what they like most or it's what their parents like most or it's what will guarantee them a job after graduation. When, finally, they give themselves a chance to write about what preoccupies them—world events or private events, matters of public policy or matters of the heart—their words seem tipped with fire: They come back into possession of lives they had left behind. Despite the often-maddening rigors of balancing teaching and writing—and the feeling that, too often, I'm simply going through the motions, playing a role—the teaching is what makes me want to stay at MIT. Teaching here is like being a talent scout for a major record label, and I sometimes think of myself as traveling the basements and out-of-the-way labs of this Cambridge research station, looking for people who are writing to themselves in the silence of notebooks and journals. When, in the relatively ideal setting of a small class, they have a chance to discuss what they've written and what they plan to write, the surge of energy is something I can feel; it keeps them going, keeps me going.

When the second round of essays comes in, I plan to read first the essay from the person I've thought of as particularly gifted, but I keep moving it to the bottom of the pile. What if I'm wrong? What if the first essay was a fluke? Bad writing is what I labor over; good writing cheers me up; great writing reminds me why I became a teacher. I hate to be wrong about these things. But finally, after having read the other seven essays, I read hers. It is even better than the first. She describes a place she knew as a girl where, among the cornfields of her native

Ohio, a small mound of rocks rose out of the earth. Because the corn shielded it from view in summer, only she, she thought, knew where it was. The rocks themselves offered a refuge and solace from ordinary life, yet did not keep the girl in solitude; their solace seemed driven by a mothering earth that wove a protective web among all women. It is an intensely vivid piece of mysticism, written as a reverie surrounding an MIT professor's scientific explanation of some geologic formation on Cape Cod. The contrast between the professor's monologue and the mystical vision would have been powerful enough, but the intensity of the vision strikes me more powerfully than anything I've read recently except for works I've sometimes taught in other classes—the essays of Gretel Ehrlich, for example, or Annie Dillard. I also find myself thrown back to *Dolphin Island*, whose imagined refuge was to me what the island of rocks was to her. But this student still seems to have no idea that what she's writing is exceptional. In the summer session there's time to give long responses to every student, but I take particular care with this one, explaining what strikes me as remarkable about the writing and pointing out that this talent really belongs to her; it's not something in my imagination. After a long dry spell, I'm beginning to feel as if I'm making a difference again.

Teaching distracts me from home, where nothing has really changed and nothing seems capable of changing. Lesley and I move smoothly in our own orbits, so heavily charged that one or the other of us will explode at the slightest mention of debt, of child-care obligations, of dissertations, of job searches. For comfort's sake we stay among friends with children, going over to each other's houses for lunch and dinner, watching our kids play in the long New England summer days. Sometimes, at night, I lie in bed thinking of times when Lesley and I used to backpack in the Sierras or at Point Reyes, or even when we took long walks on Friday afternoons in the foothills of the Pacific coastal range, just to catch up on the week. Our years together had a history of tensions, of comings and goings, yet there had been times when we had been able to keep track of each other. They seem like a dream now.

Another distraction comes from my first book, whose focus on Christian Science causes a ripple of attention in the media. I take the old Subaru on the road again, traveling to New York for television and radio interviews, talking with offended and irate Christian Scientists on talk shows back in Boston. As with my father, I begin again to see how words can be perilous. What I had wanted to do with my book was to show how one person carved out a route toward freedom from the worst habits of a potentially abusive religion. I wanted to show how things could go wrong, and had gone wrong, in a religion that, perhaps even more than most, prided itself on being right. But as time passes, I increasingly acquire the role of the expert apostate, the media source for criticism of the religion. The role anguishes me, despite my anguished past: Do I want to become a crusader against the church? I have, I remind myself, better things to do.

Somehow flying forms a comforting backdrop to these disparate events: I may be "distracted from distraction by distraction," as T. S. Eliot says, but flying is not a distraction. It has become the anchor of my life, and I go back to it as a source of discipline and progress and meaning. For the first time in many years, I am not on the giving end of teaching, but on the receiving end, and what I have learned here seems, in retrospect, enormous: basic aerodynamics that would have made no sense to me two years ago, basic meteorology, complex airspace regulations, the actual methods of flight. Despite so many years at the head of the classroom, I had forgotten what it feels like really to learn—what it feels like to be given back a part of one's life, a gift I had wanted to offer my own students. For years I had been hearing Larry's biblical invitation, "Ask and ye shall receive," as "Ask and more shall be asked of you." Now that one thing in my life, at least, was in its right relation to the world, I heard through Larry's words that it was all right for me to receive; that was why I went to Marshfield. The more we flew, the more grateful I was to him.

Having completed a flight to Manchester, New Hampshire, without incident, I had one more dual cross-country flight to do before Larry signed me off for solo cross-country. Once I got to that point, I was—I told myself—barely a hop, skip, and a short-field landing away from a private pilot's license. Although the end was some distance away, I thought I could see it; Steve had been right, so many months ago, when he came to rescue me from a day of rain on the ramp at Marshfield. I *would* get a license. But before I did, I quickly reminded myself, a few of my abilities still had to be tested, and some of these were involved in the final dual cross-country.

For this flight I was scheduled to go to Bradley International Airport in Windsor Locks, Connecticut. Bradley was a major regional airport, even larger than Manchester, and it had a different kind of airspace—more complex than the airport traffic area surrounding Manchester (although Manchester was scheduled to be upgraded in a few months), and only marginally less complex than the Boston Terminal Control Area (TCA). The Bradley airspace was known as an Airport Radar Service Area—an ARSA. Within ten nautical miles of the airport, and within 4,000 feet of the surface, all aircraft not only had to be in touch with Bradley approach controllers, they also had to have an altitude-encoding transponder, which would tell controllers their exact position on radar. Within twenty nautical miles of the airport, a pilot would radio the Bradley approach controllers of his intention to land at Bradley or to cross Bradley airspace. The controllers would then assign him a four-digit frequency which he would dial into his transponder. From then on, the controllers would track him by radar until he either landed at Bradley or departed the airspace. The required use of transponders within an ARSA gave controllers an additional measure of safety as they guided their planes, but it also added another level of complexity to my flight instruction. On the trip to Bradley I would effectively be communicating to the controllers both by voice and by radar; I would have to listen, not only for their authorizations to land, to go around, or to take off, but also for specific vectors and altitudes they would assign me in order to keep me out of the path of other planes. Since the requirements for flying within an ARSA were almost the same as those for flying within a TCA, I was basically flying into an airspace as challenging as any in the country (except for New York and Los Angeles, which gave *challenging* a new meaning).

For the first time, Larry didn't frown when he reviewed my flight plan on August 6. Everything looked good except the weather; we had a 4,500 cloud ceiling with reports of scattered clouds down to 3,000; a northwest wind was blowing at 17 knots. Visibility was twenty-five miles, but the storm forecast for that evening pushed a good measure of turbulence ahead of it: The flight would be bumpy. The news didn't phase me much. I had been flying small planes long enough to find reports of light to moderate turbulence less than alarming. We'd keep an eye on the weather and call Bridgeport Flight Watch for an update if it seemed necessary.

About twenty minutes into the flight, however, I began to regret my somewhat cavalier attitude about turbulence. The flight was nonstop chop. I recalled reading a NASA study that said that motion sickness had more to do with yawing motion than with up-and-down motion. I began to wonder if I should have offered to participate in the NASA study. Clearly I would have been one of their most useful subjects. Trying to get my mind off this, I concentrated on keeping the plane lined up with the signal from the Putnam VOR, about fifty miles west of Marshfield. We were closing in on Putnam now, and in a few minutes the "to" indicator in the little window on the right of my VOR would shift over to "from." Turning the omnibearing selector knob, I ought to get a course heading of 283 degrees at the top of the VOR; this would place us on the 283-degree radial from the Putnam station, which would guide us directly to Bradley, about forty miles away.

In some ways what was supposed to be most complicated about the flight to Bradley—the radio work—turned out to be easiest. Shortly after leaving Marshfield, I radioed the departure controllers in Boston, who watched over the airspace on my route until the Bradley approach controllers took over. The Boston controllers assigned me a transponder frequency and promised to hand me off to Bradley controllers at the appropriate time. Assuming there were no oversights, all I had to do was fly, listen for Boston's traffic reports, if any, and wait for Boston to hand me off. The Bradley controllers would already know my transponder frequency, and although they might ask me to change it they probably wouldn't; Boston had fixed me up to head right into Bradley. Either it was amazingly easy—even easier than flying to Southbridge—or I was finally settling into the electronic life of the modern pilot.

The Boston controllers handed me off to Bradley near the Putnam VOR, as promised. A little while later I asked the approach controllers for permission to leave the frequency for a minute to pick up the Bradley ATIS (Automated Terminal

Information Service) broadcast. Identified as information Victor, the ATIS reported pretty much what we had already heard about cloud ceilings and winds; runway 24 was in use. If we stayed on our current heading of 288 (adding 5 degrees for wind correction), we'd be approaching the active runway on what was effectively the base leg. The controllers might vector us in any number of ways to avoid other traffic, but if they didn't we could count on a left turn from base to final on runway 24. I tried to visualize this, but realized I was beginning to have trouble thinking about anything except the instruments, the world immediately outside the cockpit, and my stomach. Larry didn't look as if he felt all that wonderful, either.

Just as I was beginning to wonder if setting out for Bradley had been a terrible mistake, the approach controllers came on with a position update: We were about ten miles out, and they wanted to tell us to continue our approach and report any altitude changes. Their call distracted me from my nausea. It was time to get to work. Peering ahead at what looked like a standard-issue New England forest, I suddenly saw—as I had seen before at Manchester—a wide expanse of gray, and knew I had Bradley in sight. The sense of relief was wonderful. I even took comfort in the rising stress level, because Larry and I were now inside crowded terminal airspace, and although the controllers were watching over all of us, we still had to watch out for each other: "Everything happens," as my first instructor said, and we didn't want any of it to happen to us.

Now the frequency was crowded: Bradley Approach had handed us off to the tower controllers, who were issuing landing instructions to a turboprop and a USAir jet and acknowledging an initial call from another USAir jet somewhere behind us. Bradley looked enormous. It had three runways arranged in a triangle, the longest of which was 24—over 9,500 feet, more than three times the length of the Marshfield runway. On the other hand, because of the heavy traffic, I knew we wouldn't have anything like the full length of runway 24 except in an emergency. The tower controllers would want us off of 24 as fast as possible to allow the jet behind us to land. While the normal final approach speed of a Piper Warrior was around 70 knots, a jet came in at almost twice that speed. If we wanted to land at Bradley, we had to be prepared to get out of the way.

Almost before I could catch my breath, Bradley had cleared us to land after the USAir DC-9. I could see it straight ahead, a couple of miles away, perhaps two miles out; the turboprop had already landed and turned off the runway. We seemed high. I glanced at the altimeter: We were still at 2,400 feet! I should have started a descent several minutes ago. Easing back on the throttle, I set the plane into a 6-degree descent at 120 knots as Larry glanced over.

"I should have started down earlier," I said a little frantically.

"No, no," he said. "This is fine. You need to keep your speed up. You can't do a seventy-knot approach here."

I didn't believe him. Even if we kept this rate of descent, we'd still turn onto our final approach well high of where we should be. I began to turn away from the USAir jet, planning to go behind him and gain some more room to lose altitude.

"Aim for the jet, aim for the jet," Larry cautioned me. "I know it doesn't feel right, but if you start to swing behind him you'll be way back of where you should be. And you've got another jet on your tail."

All of a sudden, flying a small plane between two jets for the first time in my life, trying to listen to Larry's words and the controller's words and my own instincts as I headed toward the runway, I felt an intense, enormous calm. This was perfect. This was exactly where I wanted to be. I belonged in this airspace, I knew what I was doing, and I would do exactly what needed to be done. Although it was a sensible moment to be afraid—afraid of screwing up, of losing control, of making a mistake—I was not afraid. Aiming for the USAir jet, I realized that Larry was right: The jet was already almost over the threshold of the runway, and I was actually aiming for the place he had been a couple of seconds ago. Picking a spot about a mile from the end of 24 as my aiming point, I expected to ease my descent and slow down to landing speed from then on. By the time we reached it, turning onto final, I was at 1,000 feet and 100 knots. I was just adding the first notch of flaps when the tower controller came on to tell me to keep my speed up; the USAir jet behind me was heading toward minimum separation distance.

"Keep the nose down, keep it down," Larry urged. We were lined up with 24 now, plowing in faster than I had approached before, but because we had already begun to add flaps it was necessary to keep the airspeed below 103 knots to avoid ripping the flaps off the plane. I thought about this for a second: There was no way I was going to touch down at more than 75 knots, no matter what was happening. I'd ask the tower to go around before going through with a landing I didn't like. We were a half mile out as I began to bring the power back to lower the airspeed to 70, but Larry motioned me to leave the throttle alone: "Not yet, not yet," he said. We were almost to the runway, showing 85 knots.

"Okay, cut the power now," Larry said, and as I did the airspeed began to bleed off just a little as we swung over the runway threshold: eighty . . . seventy-five . . . A second before the wheels touched I eased back on the yoke, touching down a little hard but not bouncing back up and not really flaring either, just rolling as the controller came on to tell us to exit the runway "without delay" and taxiway Echo appeared just ahead of us on our left. I was braking fairly hard to bring the ground speed down fast toward the end of our roll, until, by the time taxiway Echo appeared, we were within a decent turning speed. We rolled off the runway and held our position. In a few seconds the tower controller would hand us off to the ground controller, who would tell us where to taxi and park. Just then the roar of thrust reversers filled the cockpit, and the USAir DC-9 that had followed us in thundered past us on 24. Larry glanced at it, then at me.

"That was a great approach," he said. "You were very cool."

"It felt fine," I said. I was surprised at how much I meant it.

Later, in the pilots' lounge at Bradley, walking around to look at various announcements and cabinets full of equipment, I thought about what it was like to feel no fear. Before that moment I had known I was going to land at Bradley, but some-how I hadn't really *decided* to; it was just something that was going to happen. When things got tight in the air, however, I knew I had to get down, and Bradley was where I was going to land. It was in my hands. Yet it wasn't a matter of ego, not something I was proud of. It was a moment of furious intensity, one in which I felt once more as if I were living on the edge of the wing, feeling the plane through my body or my body through the plane; this was who I was. What was there to fear? In that sweep of confidence, nothing mattered but the moment; I was free of the past. The abuses of childhood, the miseries of religion, the searing sorrow of death and loneliness—all these were gone. In their place was something simpler, more direct, which probably alone deserved the name of life. I thought again, suddenly, of Clinton in *Dolphin Island*, as I had been doing so often over the course of the summer. Was this moment of confidence the one that had landed him on the hovership? Did it bring him, indirectly, to the island and the man who would finally care for him? His confidence and mine were the same, I thought, and I realized why Clinton's life spoke so powerfully to me: It was a model of a kind of promise I might one day realize.

And then I laughed. Clinton was fictional, the product of a writer's imagination. As much as I had identified with Clinton as an orphan, as a child in search of someone to affirm the worth of his life, I could not stay with him now. For I, a real human being, could not escape my past, and what I called life was inevitably more than that crystallizing moment of fearlessness I had just known. Perhaps all life ultimately directed itself toward that fearlessness, but no one, I thought, could simply escape into it. I had earned that moment through months of study and practice and euphoria and disappointment; how much more practice would it take to make such moments less rare? The mind of Arthur C. Clarke might have allowed Clinton to invent his father, but for me the invention would have to be more a matrix of experience—not a particular man, a loving scientist, but an airplane and a body of knowledge that would allow me to see more clearly the man I might be. Behind that airplane and that body of knowledge was a real father, shadowy, detached, who might have been different but was not. The "father" I invented could never finally erase that simple tragedy, and yet the real father might still be back there somewhere, I thought, secretly applauding what he had set in motion.

Chapter Eight

THE PARENTAL
VOICE

I take off alone for Westerly, Rhode Island, on August 13. A direct flight from Marshfield to Westerly would consume barely forty-five minutes, but the course for that flight would keep me away from some of the most beautiful scenery on the East Coast, including Newport and the southwestern shoreline of Rhode Island. I choose instead a more elaborate route, crossing over the airports at Plymouth and New Bedford, then turning toward Newport State and on into Westerly. Flying the coast, I ought to be able to see not only Martha's Vineyard but also Block Island, that wind-wracked haven guarding the entrance to Long Island Sound. The day is calm and sunny, a foretaste of Indian summer. Once in the air, climbing to 2,400 feet over Marshfield, I entertain the fantasy of heading west and flying for as long as the fuel and weather hold out.

It's good to be alone in the cockpit again. As much as I've come to like Larry, I'm beginning to realize how rare my times alone are. I'm in 44949 today, a plane whose history I share in some small way, and as I scan the cockpit instruments I'm reminded again of how these moments of aloneness play into that strangely erotic companionship I first felt in 44847. Every piece of this plane is attuned to rhythms of the natural world, the earth and sky. Although at times the solitude of the cockpit has been deafening, today I hear that deeper rhythm, deeper even than the bass thrumming of the engine, and recognize it as a sound to defeat loneliness.

Although I'm headed somewhere I've never been before, the companionableness of the plane makes it difficult to escape the feeling that this flight is a kind of homecoming. Perhaps it's also a matter of the route. I've lived near an ocean since I was six weeks old. At some level I must have decided to learn to fly near an ocean because there alone could I feel my own life reflected below. John Hay writes about a similar experience in his book *The Bird of Light*, which I discovered recently. The book first caught my eye because it focuses on the life cycles of terns in the Cape Cod National Seashore; I was sure that, not too far in the future, I would be making an approach to the single runway in Provincetown at the very tip of the Cape, swinging out over the ocean and flying in low over the northern dunes, and I wanted a feel for the life and landscape there before coming. But Hay's book is also about the life of the planet, including human beings, who despite their best efforts have not yet spelled the end of nature. Hay writes about the psychic importance of the ocean better than any contemporary author I know. "The unchanging rhythm of night and day, the rolling beat of the tides, in and out like our own breath, is eternally reassuring," he says. His words confirm what I already sense, the kinship of my body and the ocean more than 2,000 feet below. "At the same time," he adds, "we are born with a restlessness which is as close to fundamental nature as any of our ideas about it." It is not enough to have a job, a house, even a family, if all of these become versions of some *thing* that locks you down to a place in which you can barely struggle, barely breathe. The heart asks for more. "We reflect a planet that is never at rest," Hay says. "We respond to its daily moods, its often violent extremes, with passionate uncertainty, always searching for solutions to an inner hunger we are unable to control."

When I first began to realize, a relatively short time ago, that the physical world had its own secrets, I thought of the world as another opposition: To find those secrets I had to leave my faith behind and take on a different life whose roots lay firmly in the earth. But that now seems wrong as well. That is not what my father did, I think, or rather not what he tried to do. His heresy about our cat, who knew that it was time to die, was ringed with an admiration for the unknowable. Every time he rose into the air, he faced forces he could calculate to an extent but never fully know; there was always something new to discover, a new relationship between wing and lift. And yet terror lay heavily anchored behind this promise of knowledge. It's no wonder that parting became his main mode of behavior, as it still is. Perhaps his greatest achievement will be to make himself a parting from the earth before he actually leaves, so that he will be a kind of heavier-than-air angel, a creature with substance but no mass, a man with no feet in the grave. If fewer and fewer people know he exists, if he can—rarest of all accomplishments—outrun the demons that haunt him, will he still be truly human? It is hard to justify saying good-bye to him in this way.

There is a suspicion, Hay writes, that young terns arriving in a particular territory "may not be there simply because they followed a colony as it settled in. They may be returning to sites where they last heard a parental voice. It is in *place* that life starts out and is sustained in the memory."

220

"In place" . . . but in which places did I hear a parental voice? It was always around me, of course, and yet I can scarcely bring it to mind except on those odd occasions when something more than a voice broke through—a way of speaking at once verbal and physical, as when my mother held me in her arms while I screamed from the ear infections from which Christian Science could not heal me, or when my father shoved my rowboat into a whitecapped channel. But mostly I hear it now, in a small plane in the air, a place I never shared with either of my parents.

What gives this plane the power to invoke those associations? It may be—because I was never confident of the love of people—that I first learned really to trust in places. To a young boy people could promise perfection, yet be strikingly imperfect; they could speak of the power of love to heal, yet retreat when love did not heal. But no landscape ever did such things. On the beach in Avalon, I dashed in and out of the ocean, bodysurfing on large waves following a nor'easter, emulating Clinton's great ride. Then I ran up into the dunes, threw myself down, and rolled around until the sand clung heavily to my wet body and I emerged with something like an animal's coat, thick and matted. Though the ocean and sand and sea and sky said nothing to me, they also promised nothing; I could simply wrap myself in them. And they were absolutely reliable. Although I might have to leave them, they would never leave me. That is why, now, they still seem to me to be something called "nature," something different from yet akin to humankind, and why even the vastly stupid human assaults on nature have not spelled its end. But that is also why I want to protect the natural world: It is a home to all our creatureliness, a parental voice for anyone who has ever felt orphaned by human beings.

But if creatureliness were all that I was after, why did I

choose to seek it in a plane? I laugh at myself. How could place really be enough? I found comfort in places, but it was the comfort of an angry orphan, a child at sea, and what I wanted was the true voice of the parent herself—or himself. I wanted to hear the words of the man who loved the earth, and yet for whom earth was not enough. I wanted him to tell me where he had heard his parental voices, and what drove him away from them. Was it the fear of death, or was it some deeper confidence that life revealed its secrets to people who dared to leave? And did asking always mean leaving? In Sunday school I was often startled by the passage in Matthew in which Jesus says that he is come "to set a man at variance against his father, and the daughter against her mother, and a man's foes shall be they of his own household." The standard interpretation has to do with matters of faith: Those who fall under the sway of Jesus' teachings inevitably will pull hard against those who do not. But I wondered if the verse applied in a different way to my own family, to many families, in which a quest for true love—rather than romantic love—exposes every human failing, wounds the seeker so much that he has to leave, and yet binds him to those who seem to wound him. So much of religion came with promises of sweetness and light, but the reality of it seemed to me harsh: Love was not what it looked like most of the time. Sometimes love was an abject silence; sometimes love was a breaking down of everything that had been called by the name of love. And sometimes, all too rarely, love was the presence of a soulmate or, failing that, the place where a soulmate had once been. If you loved your life enough to ask what it meant, love might lead you away from all that you had loved, yet some thread—call it a parental voice—might still remain to keep you steady in the night.

The voice of an air traffic controller comes on to alert me

to traffic at eleven o'clock, altitude unknown. On this flight I'm using the Ocean approach controllers, based in Providence, to keep a radar eye on me and warn me of anyone else flying nearby. Because I'm a VFR flight rather than an IFR one, however, the controllers have to handle me on a "workload permitting" basis: If, as they separate and sequence the IFR traffic, they happen to see a potential problem near me, they'll let me know. In this case, the other plane is also VFR and either doesn't have an altitude-encoding transponder or isn't using it, so Ocean Approach knows only that it's somewhere nearby. Scanning the sky in quick glances all around the eleven-o'clock position, I see no one for a few seconds; then I notice a Cessna passing quite a ways below me. No problem. I radio Ocean to tell them I have the traffic in sight. The frequency falls quiet again for a few moments.

After a few days of fiddling with my intercom, I realized with a sudden burst of self-deprecation that it was nothing like an amplifier, and that all I had to do to get music to come out of it was to run a cable from the earphone jack in my tape player to the intercom itself. Now I have Rickie Lee Jones's *Pirates* playing clearly through my headset, interrupted only when Ocean Approach checks in with a traffic alert. Flipping the tape over at the end of the side, I come back to the deep, descending notes of "We Belong Together," a song I first heard in Massachusetts but associate mostly with California. As Jones sings, I remember what it meant to be home—the fog rolling over the coastal range into San Francisco at exactly this time of year, the long, brown grass of the Sonoma coast easing its way down to the coastal cliffs. The coast below me is not that coast, yet the words of the song combine them somehow in my mind, and I begin to remember how everything that is left behind is not necessarily lost: John Hay was right about that.

Crossing Worden's Pond, a major landmark south of Providence, I begin to look for Westerly. I'm a few minutes too early, but as I begin to swing out to sea and lose altitude I catch sight of the field. Like Marshfield, Westerly has no tower, so I'm announcing my approach on the unicom frequency, 123.0. About four miles south of the airport, over the Atlantic and just beyond the beach, I turn back toward the runway at pattern altitude and announce my intent to make a 45-degree approach to the downwind leg. As I do this, I realize my forty-five looks a little sloppy; it's more like a 60-degree approach, and I'm going to have to make a fairly sharp turn soon to line up with the downwind leg. But that seems okay. A shiver of amazement begins to ride my body: I'm about to land alone, having flown somewhere I've never been. Although I'm only about seventy-four miles from Marshfield, I might as well be in Alaska: I've never seen this place before, I know only numbers—runway lengths and compass headings, field elevation, unicom frequency—and yet this place is a reality below me, hard earth and sand and sea, and when I touch down I will have dropped into a slightly different part of the world with a confidence I could not have imagined even recently.

A Beechcraft Bonanza comes on the frequency, announcing its approach to the downwind leg. I look behind me on both sides, just to make sure he's not running me down; I look off to the left and right. As I look around I notice I've lost a little altitude, flying now about 100 feet below the pattern. Not good. The Bonanza comes on again, saying he's about at midpoint in the downwind leg. *I'm* at the midpoint of the downwind leg. "Beech Bonanza . . ." I begin.

At that moment the Bonanza zips over my head going the other way, about 100 feet above me. I look up, stunned. Then

I'm horrified. What did I do wrong? Glancing at the runway, I think I'm a little far out for the downwind leg; I shouldn't have turned so soon from my approach. But no—the runway looks to be about where it should be in relation to my plane. Functioning more or less mechanically now, frightened, I slow the plane down, lower the flaps, prepare for a turn to base.

"Piper Warrior, this is the Beech turning onto the downwind. Still don't see you. Where are you?"

"Turning onto the downwind"—the phrase sticks in my mind. This guy was flying *upwind* in the downwind leg. That's why he flew right over me. If I hadn't been a little low, he would have plowed right into me. What the hell was he doing? Did he think he was too far out to be officially in a downwind leg? Maybe; still, flying parallel to the downwind in the opposite direction, so close to the actual downwind, wasn't much of a standard procedure.

I sigh. I still don't want to fight about these things. Is it because I'm so new to the air? My first thought, I notice, is to blame myself.

"Westerly Bonanza," I say, "Warrior four-four-niner-four-niner is just turning left base for runway two-five." In a few minutes I'm down, tying down the plane as the Bonanza taxis up to the green-clapboarded Westerly terminal. A small group of people, two men my father's age and their wives, comes over to greet the Bonanza pilot as he climbs out. It looks as if they're all going up for a sight-seeing trip. Nice people, nice pilot, from what I can tell; they've all been alive a long time. I wish them luck, knowing it's not enough. Inside, a few minutes later, having a cup of coffee at the restaurant, I think about this so-called homecoming and laugh to myself a little ruefully. The parental voice may call us back, but doesn't guarantee that we'll arrive safely. It's funny how that used to worry me so much. Now, however, I'm beginning to realize that I was never as afraid of losing my life in an airplane as I was afraid of losing my soul.

II.

*I*t is possible to romanticize virtually everything about flying. I do this myself, or rather struggle not to do it, for behind most romantic notions is a core of truth too threatening to appear in its own right. If I can get past the romance, I can find what I need. But this is not always easy. Flying is adventure, eros, homecoming; it is both a thrill and a route to self-discovery. This is romance; what could be better? What other truth is there?

But in flying, as in love, there is darkness and risk, and while both have meaning, neither is particularly attractive in its own right. To fly a small plane out over the Atlantic, then down to a seaside airport, may sound lovely and beautiful, but it may also be an occasion for accident and death if another pilot happens to be flying carelessly in the same airspace. The FAA, which takes an extremely dim view of large planes flying into each other and goes to exceptional lengths to prevent such catastrophes, takes an almost equally dim view of small planes colliding: Pilots' licenses are routinely suspended for such adventures as flying upwind in a downwind leg. Where risk exists, what matters most is a pilot's ability to manage the risk as much as possible. To live and work smoothly and carefully in the face of death is to fly well, and while this may have romantic connotations, the real prospect of a fatally stupid maneuver tends to make pilots—most pilots—unwilling to drop the veil of romance over whatever it actually means to them to fly.

In a small plane, the engine may fail; someone else may run into you; you may make an approach to the wrong runway of some airport; you may fly into bad weather, lose control, and spin into the ground; you may run out of fuel; you may get lost and forget how to find yourself again. These are a tiny fraction of the number of real dangers in the air, and good pilots seek regular retraining and flight instruction to ward off dismal fates. Yet no amount of training can compensate for how well a pilot knows himself and likes himself in the cockpit. Alone and in trouble, he or she may slide quickly from self-deprecation to panic, and then nothing and no one can help. Something more than self-regard is as urgent in the cockpit as proper training. If you are short on self-love, you will either begin to learn it in the air or give up flying. To fly without it is very quickly to be lost.

I have often been afraid of becoming lost. Where others seemed to have a self, a lodestone of angry egotism, I had language, and when I was growing up it was possible to become lost simply by saying the wrong words. It amazed me, as an adult, to read in Mary Austin's autobiography that she identified something inviolable in her life, an "I-Mary," from the age of four. I could not imagine doing that. And yet, somehow, I did, just as my father routinely disguised or muted the strength of his character. But if you live for years with an image of yourself as significantly damaged or weakened by life—and if the truth, your truth, actually lies elsewhere—then "becoming lost" is not simply a matter of screwing up again, of demonstrating another failure. To a child who fears his life, getting lost on the way home from school may be terrifying, but so may the prospect of finding his way safely. The more he succeeds, the more he is lost to that eviscerated identity he carries around with him. If he shows weakness, if he loses his way, he behaves predictably, and solicitous adults rush to his aid at the same time they regret his inability to cope. If he shows strength, he loses his way in a much larger sense, because he confounds those solicitous adults who see themselves as losing power over him. The second kind of loss is by far the more dangerous, but it is also crucial to any real self-discovery, any real homecoming.

Perhaps getting lost physically was always terrifying to me because it both confirmed my need for failure and my need for escape. Either of those needs I might handle at any given moment, but not both; together they were too volatile. To prevent them from ever conjoining, I made sure I was as unlikely as possible to become lost. I memorized maps, routes; I spent hours in grade school drawing precise freehand maps of the United States, with cities as carefully placed as my estimates allowed. My heroes were early explorers, not—I thought at the time—for their adventures, but for their maps: Drake, Vespucci, and Champlain fascinated me because of their audacious determination not to get lost. During my brief career in the Boy Scouts, I quickly mastered orienteering, in part because I loved the topographic maps we used. Compasses and lines were not language, but could place me in the world more precisely than any language I knew, and no one in my religion could complain that I was learning to read maps. There was safety in an isogonic line.

Ironically, perhaps, this interest in map reading began to lead me directly toward that other kind of lostness even as it kept me centered in the world. As I mastered the art of charting a course, I started to understand that I was not a cipher, or a person who existed only in others' eyes. But what was *I*? Someone with a place in the world? Someone who deserved to be vibrantly alive simply by virtue of his human life? These were reckless thoughts, and I shoved them away from me, along with maps. I stopped reading maps when I was thirteen.

Now, reading them again, I see that old controversy in quite a different light—more abstract in some ways, in others far more personal. Although I grew up in a society with fathers and mothers, the larger roles into which they played—the patriarchies and matriarchies of their lives—were much more important than I once recognized. My father reluctantly fulfilled all of the obligations of business, mortgage, and family entrenched in a patriarchal society, but my family was matriarchal, and its source of power lay in a larger matriarchy, Christian Science, whose Mother Church watched over us all. My mother coveted, if not my father's life, then my father's apparent power, not seeing how his role as a businessman crippled him. Effectively denied his freedom to work and to earn money, she sought power in other ways: Her church and her children would keep her from getting lost.

But to guarantee her this safety, we children had to be obedient to the power behind her, which meant that Christian Science had to be our way, our truth, and our life. When my older brother and sister rebelled, they deprived her of the one weapon she wielded against a society that made her feel worthless. Someone would have to obey, someone sensitive enough to the power battles to know that another rebellion would be fatal to my mother, and someone who implicitly would be willing to sacrifice his life for hers. It appeared that I would be that person.

But there was something in me as strong as my cat Siddhartha, as strong as my muted father, and too wily to be used as a sacrifice to a religion that promised my mother so much and failed to deliver. I hated that part of myself, but it was there. It told me that I would, indeed, as Jesus said, have to lose myself to find myself, and that in this process I might lose everything I loved. If I struck out on my own, I might shatter the crystal underpinnings of my mother's life and ruin an apparently pristine relationship with my church. If I struck out on my own, I would never be able to go back: The home I had grown up in,

229

including the vision of the world it conveyed, would be lost to me, and I would—as my father so long ago implied—have to fall back on whatever resources and ingenuity I possessed. But what I did not know then—what neither my mother or father taught me—was the possibility of grace descending upon one who is lost. "A spirit comes to a destitute person in a form he can recognize," my friend Katherine McNamara once told me, quoting a Koyukon wise woman from Alaska. To be lost is to catch a glimpse of the whole.

My New York sectional chart shows Windham, Connecticut—my next cross-country destination—as an airport about seventy miles east of Marshfield, with several good landmarks on the way. North Central State Airport, in Rhode Island, is visible from several miles north or south of my course, allowing me to work back to the right heading if I lose my way. Dayville Airport, although small, lies midway between North Central and Windham, further confirming my route. Because I'm anxious about such a long flight inland over rural terrain, however, I decide to chart a different course, using the Putnam VOR as my main course guide. Putnam is about fifty-three miles west of Marshfield on a heading of about 277 degrees; I'll be able to see North Central on the way to the VOR, but not Dayville. Windham itself lies about twenty miles southwest of the VOR. I plan to leave Marshfield on the appropriate course heading, tune in Putnam on 117.4, and fly directly to the VOR. When I reach it, I'll simply head down to Windham. Whatever chance of getting lost might otherwise come into play on this trip, I can't lose with VOR navigation. On August 25, the day of the flight, I have Larry approve my route and climb into 44847. This trip, at least, should be completely straightforward.

And it is, for about thirty minutes. Once outside of the Boston TCA, I climb to 4,500 feet to give myself a margin of safety in case the engine quits. Cities give way to towns and then isolated houses; forests cover more of the landscape than I would have imagined. An occasional railroad track or high-tension line snakes through the landscape, emblematic of civilization and danger to me, since both would destroy my plane if I tried to land near them. Both have landmark value, of course, and yet I don't need them. With the VOR tuned to Putnam, the course deviation needle deviates hardly at all when I fly 277 degrees. I'm right where I should be. North Central passes south of me, an irrelevant but pleasant verification of my route.

I haven't brought my Walkman today, so there's no music in the cockpit, but the beautiful light and the crazed Plexiglas windshield of 44847 allow me to drift a little into my own thoughts, or nonthoughts. When I focus again, a few seconds later, on the aircraft instruments, everything looks fine—except the VOR. With remarkable suddenness the needle has swung off to the left, which probably means I'm north of the ground-based signal. Checking the directional gyro, I find I've slid into a slight turn to the right, flying at about 285 degrees. No tragedy; I swing back slightly below the original course, 270 degrees, to bring the needle back in line.

But the needle doesn't come back to center. In fact it swings even farther out to the left. This could mean two things: It could mean I drifted off for more than a few seconds, allowing the plane to slide significantly off course; or it could mean I'm actually right over the ground-based signal, causing my navigational radio to become erratic. What should I do? I could turn even farther southwest, say 260 degrees, just to see what happens. If the needle begins to swing back to center, I'll know that I simply let myself fly northwest for too long. On the other hand, glancing at my timer, I see that I've chewed up about the right number of minutes to be over Putnam. It would make sense that my VOR is behaving this way. What I should do, then, is turn on course for Windham and wait to pick up a 250-degree "from" signal from the VOR.

Two choices. I glance at the timer again. Really, it's not *quite* time for me to be over Putnam. It's more likely that I let the plane fly too far northwest. Turning left to 260 degrees, I fly for one minute on that heading while waiting for the needle to return to center.

It doesn't; it also doesn't flip over to a "from" reading. I can feel the sweat beginning to accumulate on my brow. Looking down at the ground, I can see a couple of lakes off to the north, and a highway, and lots of trees, but nothing else. It dawns on me that without a clear signal from this navigational radio I have no idea where I am.

Suddenly I'm fighting claustrophobia. I'm stuck up here! The more I look at the ground, the more outrageously foreign it appears, like a museum exhibit gone awry. There is no place for me down there. The phrase sinks into my flesh like a bullet. I was never any good at being a human being, and now I'm lost, goddamn it, and the ground below is as different from me now as a person is from a dark angel, but I have no miracles, not even dark ones, to call on.

I glance out at the horizon, always too far away, and fumble with my sectional. What can I do? I can fly north, south, east, or west. "Great, Tom," I say to myself out loud in a voice rich with self-loathing. "Great insight. You're beginning to panic." It's true; I am. If I fly north, I might eventually find the Worcester airport; if I fly south, which is what I'm more inclined to do since I'm already doing it, I could go for a long way without finding anything. I could wind up flying out over Long Island Sound. I could run out of fuel and crash into the water.

This entirely practical realization breaks the spell. I left

Marshfield a little over a half hour ago with four hours and forty-five minutes of fuel on board. I could fly *back* to Marshfield, turn around and fly back to Putnam, doing this whole course again, and still not be low on gas. Fortunately for me the world operates not only on language but also on gallons per hour and air and fuel mixtures and engine RPMs, and these can come to my rescue when language cannot. I sigh, look down at the ground, then down at my sectional, thinking.

Let's say, I say to myself, that when my VOR needle went off to the left I actually was over the Putnam VOR. That means I'm now several minutes west of the VOR, but north of my course to Windham. The sectional tells me that a second ground-based VOR—Norwich, at 110.0—is relatively nearby. Since I have two navigation radios, I could tune one to Putnam, one to Norwich, and see where on the map the two signals converged. In fact, I could set the omnibearing selector on the Norwich radio at 11 degrees "from," set the same selector for the Putnam radio at 245 degrees "from," and wait until the needles in both VORs centered. At that point I would be directly over Abington, only a few miles away from Windham. But this solution, as neat as it is, freaks me out: I don't trust these radios right now. What I need is some earthbound confirmation of my position—a town or another airport.

Turning sharply southward, I decide to try to find Dayville. It's not the smartest thing to do, but if I can find it I can turn to a course heading of 300 degrees for a bit over two minutes, then turn back on course for Windham. The model for this recovery is my trip to Southbridge. There, with Larry in the cockpit to help quell my anxiety, I used a rule-of-thumb method of self-recovery, and it worked. I'd like to do the same thing again if I can; I won't have to deal with the VOR at all if I don't want to. After a few minutes of flying, however, I begin to see how pointless this all might be. I could fly around in ever-widening circles until I did, in fact, use all my fuel, and never see Dayville. On the other hand, if I tune in one of the radios to the Putnam VOR again, setting the omnibearing selector for 210 degrees "from," I can turn back toward the VOR when the needle centers, and this will—I think—take me directly over Dayville.

As I do this, the needle centers almost immediately. I remember to breathe for the first time in what seems like minutes. Dropping the nose of the plane slightly, I see a small town and, incredibly, an airport with a dark asphalt strip running southeast-northwest—Dayville! Turning northwest to 300 degrees, I fly for about three minutes, then turn to 245 degrees, the Windham course heading from the Putnam VOR. As I turn the omnibearing indicator on my VOR from 210 degrees to 245, the needle centers: I'm on course again.

In what seems like seconds, the Windham airport shows up. Its long perpendicular runways, along with a third closed off for use as an aircraft ramp, make it blessedly difficult to miss from the air. Announcing my downwind and base legs, I ready the plane for landing, gliding to a relatively smooth touchdown. This is Windham, I say to myself as I taxi the plane to the general aviation office, not quite believing I managed to find it.

A man comes out from the office as I climb out of 44847 after parking it.

"You do know you're at *Windham*, Connecticut, right?" he asks pleasantly. I stare at him for a minute. Is he clairvoyant? Does he know what I've just been through?

"Oh, yeah," I say. "You bet."

"I just wanted to check," he says with a slightly ironic smile. "You were announcing an approach to *Westerly* the whole way in. Come and get some coffee if you want it."

I'm about to chew myself out for this stupid mistake, but then stop. It's actually an interesting error. I must have been more frightened than I realized. Yet, running back through the whole scenario, I anchor myself in the essential facts. I was lost. I began to panic. Whether or not I actually stopped myself from panicking is unclear, but it feels that way: I looked for physical realities in which to place my hope, and found them. I thought of various solutions, choosing one that was not necessarily the best, but it worked. I'm here. I'm found. It's an incredible luxury, much like recovering from a serious illness or surviving a motorcycle accident or—or what?

I look around the airport, savoring the humid air. Something is not quite right, and yet I feel more whole than I have felt in many months. Walking back to 44847 with a cup of coffee in my hand, I give in to the urge to pat the plane on its cowling, thanking it for what it is, for what I did. In some larger sense I may be more lost now than I have ever been, and yet the present victory is real and sweet. I will not give it up.

III.

As if in compensation for the relative drama of the first two solo cross-countries, the next excursion—to Worcester Airport—is utterly uneventful. The smooth flight, however, clears me for the final cross-country, a distinctly more complex trip. The FAA requires that applicants for a private pilot's license fly at least one cross-country excursion whose total distance is at least 300 nautical miles, "with landings at a minimum of three points, one of which is at least 100 nautical miles from the original departure point." What that means in Marshfield terms is that I'll be flying to Albany, New York—both a major commuter airport and an Airport Radar Service Area, an ARSA—

and, after stopping for coffee and fuel, head down to New Haven before returning to Shoreline Aviation. The mileage to Albany alone will be as much as the total round-trip mileage of any of my previous cross-country flights. Total time in the air will be around four and a half hours. It's a lot to plan, a lot to think about. The other flights showed that I could make my way around the terrain, deal competently with air traffic controllers, and even find myself when I was lost. But this trip is the final dividing line: A life in the air ultimately means distance and travel, and to earn the first you need to earn the second.

It's also true that, after completing this trip, I'll almost be ready for the private pilot's practical test, the check-ride, in which an FAA-designated examiner—probably Lew Owen in my case—will decide whether I'm finally qualified for the license. After the Albany–New Haven run, there's not much left to do, I tell myself. This is it. It seems almost impossible to believe, and as nervous as I am about the flight itself, I can't help looking back with astonishment at the route I've traveled these past two years. The astonishment goes a long way to ease the anxiety.

On the evening of September 10, the day before the flight, I call the Bridgeport FSS to get an outlook on the weather. It sounds okay: probably a high cloud cover with scattered clouds below 6,000 feet, winds from north-northwest at 10 to 15 knots, and an AIRMET for light to moderate turbulence. Although I'm not wild about the AIRMET, I've flown under such conditions before. If my stomach won't handle it, I'll land at some intermediate airport and decide then whether to continue or go back to Marshfield. Filing my flight plans for Albany and New Haven calms me; I must be ready for this trip.

By the time I get down to Marshfield at eight A.M. on the eleventh, however, the sky above the airport is dark, and the wind whips in from the northwest with an ominous gustiness. There are only three of us at the airport this morning—Peter, one of the other flight instructors, who's going to sign me off for the flight to Albany; Cecil Horton, one of the FAA accident-prevention counselors; and me. The other students scheduled for morning flights have either canceled or decided not to show up. I take a walk around the ramp to feel the weather and decide what to do. Although Belmont was also overcast when I left this morning, it seemed like more of a fog cover to me, and now, looking north to Boston, I see the hint of a clearing—pockets of deep, clear light between or behind the clouds. It's hard to tell, though, from the ground. Weymouth has just reported a 2,500-foot ceiling. Perhaps the best thing to do is to go up and look around.

Although I've never flown with Peter, I admire his reputation for carefulness; his students invariably speak highly of him. He and I confer as Cecil heads down to his hangar, readying his Cessna 152 for a trial flight.

"It's a little rough up there," Peter says. "You've got a ceiling, so you can go take a look if you're up for it. I'll check again with Bridgeport. If you don't like how it looks, wait for another day. Don't shove off unless you're sure the weather's good all along the route."

That sounds fine to me. I head out to 4347H, the first plane I ever met at Marshfield, as the wind whips the corners of my parka against my waist. It seems clear that a cross-country flight today won't work, and while I'm a little relieved I'm also uncharacteristically disappointed. I was ready *today*. I think of the NASA astronauts, settling into the space shuttle for three or four hours in preparation for a launch, only to clamber out again because of a fuel leak or a computer glitch or the possibility of a thunderstorm. Who has it worse? I smile—silly question.

The plane checks out okay. I pull out my sectional, my navigation log, my pocket calculator, and my timer; all set. The sky above has grown darker even as I've sat here. Getting up and down again may be enough excitement for today. As I start the engine, preparing to taxi, I see Cecil's orange-and-turquoise 152—known locally as the Howard Johnson plane—heading down the taxiway toward runway 24. Although technically there's not much Cecil can do to help me if I need help, it's good to know he'll be in the air with me. I may be able to talk things over with him on the unicom frequency if there's any question about staying or going.

Beginning my roll a few seconds after Cecil slips smoothly into a crosswind takeoff, I shake and bounce into the bumpy air. Though it's not the worst I've ever flown in, it's certainly not comfortable. I can't see Cecil, but he's already said he's not staying in the airport pattern, whereas I am; he's probably above pattern altitude by now. As I climb, the dark cloud above me seems smaller, more localized. Boston itself is distinctly sunny, and the clouds in that direction look high and hazy. Could I fly around this bad weather and head for Albany?

Cecil comes on. "Hey, you know, it's not bad up here," he says. "This thing's gonna blow through in a few minutes. Looks like clear sailing up north." I know what he's saying; it's the closest he's ever come to wishing me good luck. Checking with Peter, who confirms Cecil's observation with data from Bridgeport, I climb to about 2,000 feet, then head northwest. In about five minutes the skies clear. I'm on my way to Albany.

The first seventy-six or so miles are a straight shot northwest to Orange Airport, near the northern border of Massachusetts. I stay below 2,500 feet for the first forty miles, not only because of the cloud cover but because of the Boston TCA. By the time I reach Sterling Airport, about twenty-five miles southeast of Orange, however, I've climbed to 4,500 feet. At this altitude I'm slightly below a scattered cloud layer, just as Bridgeport forecast, and turbulence is a problem: The air is almost always bumpier below a cloud layer than just above it. Why not go higher? Visibility is no problem; I'll climb to 6,500. Informing the Boston Center controllers of my intentions, I receive an acknowledgment with the reminder to "maintain VFR." What else would I do? The climb among scattered clouds requires slight turns to maintain minimum clearances—500 feet below a cloud, 1,000 feet above, and 2,000 feet on either side—and as I ease up to the higher altitude I feel somewhat like Jack ascending the beanstalk, climbing around and around in a kind of muted wonder, not knowing how it will look at the top. At 6,500 feet, I'm above the cloud layer, which now appears relatively flat and undulant, like an Iowa landscape in the winter snow. The air even looks thinner up here, the light clearer and a little tinny, like a fine voice played on a Victrola. I have a slight headache from the altitude.

Although I'm relying today primarily on pilotage and dead reckoning to carry me to Albany, I also have the VOR tuned to Gardner, a ground-based signal about twelve miles east of Orange, to confirm my course. With the omnibearing indicator showing a course of 310 degrees, more or less the course I'm flying, the course deviation indicator swings about 5 degrees off to the right. This is exactly what I want, since the Gardner signal is slightly to the right of my course. Partly because everything is going so smoothly, I'm having minor fits of anxiety. This is the middle of my journey. If I get sick or frightened here, I can't easily get back to Marshfield, nor can I get to Albany with any greater ease. A crisis of confidence would be a crisis. I try to talk myself past the anxiety by looking at each instrument in the cockpit, reminding myself of what it does and what it's supposed to tell me, and by looking outside as far as I can see. This is almost jet territory, and I think of being a passenger on all those TWA flights I took when I was relatively happy in the mid-1980s. The biggest difference now is that I'm not a passenger. Far off to the west, a lone jet, probably a DC-9, heads down into Boston. As it turns out, he's on the same frequency I am, so I can hear his conversations with Boston Center. I'm part of that world now, and it charms me, thrills me. I don't have to be afraid.

It begins to dawn on me, however, that the clouds below me look denser than they did a few minutes ago. I'm having a hard time admitting to myself what this means. Glancing down, I see a couple of small lakes, a town, and a small airport—Gardner—almost directly below me. The VOR course deviation indicator has centered, telling me that I'm now slightly north of my intended course. More disturbing is how little of the town I can actually see. The airport itself, a place much like Marshfield, is clear beneath a wide patch of blue sky, but clouds make the town and its surrounding countryside a strange puzzle in which the missing pieces form a greater whole than I can sketch in my mind. Bridgeport said scattered clouds, not a broken cloud layer. Oh well. Perhaps this is just an isolated phenomenon, not unlike the cloud under which I took off an hour or so ago. I could call the Bangor or Burlington Flight Watch on 122.0 for a weather update, but it's hard to imagine I really need it. There's no drastic change, after all—just a little thickening.

Five minutes later I begin to sense the larger risk. The cloud layer is now fully formed below me, eerily like a setting for a fairy tale or faded adventure story. I remember a movie I saw once as a child about mail pilots who flew earlier in the century, holding themselves above the cloud cover while waiting for a break big enough to reveal a landmark. My situation is not yet that bad, but bad enough: I can see the Orange airport now, but only because of a relatively lucky break in clouds that must cover 70 percent of the sky below me. On the other hand, looking closely for other landmarks and routes down through the clouds if an emergency arises, I realize I'm still technically VFR. If the cloud cover doesn't get worse, I can swing into a gradual descent shortly after the Boston Center controllers hand me off to Albany Approach. If broken cover turns to overcast— then what? At the fringe of my mind I can see several alternatives, but none I want to admit to myself at this point.

The Orange sighting is important because it marks my last course change before Albany. Swinging slightly to the left, picking up a 295-degree course heading, I tune in the Gardner VOR for a "from" reading; the Albany VOR won't be usable until I'm within nine nautical miles of the field, so I'll have to rely on Gardner for now.

I lose sight of the ground. There's nothing below me but low turrets of cotton, a fantastic child's castle. Having complained to myself about the idiocies of other pilots before, I'm reluctant to confess my own; for the time being I'm fine, I'm VFR above the clouds, and things may change when I'm closer to Albany. Still about fifty miles out, I call Boston Center to ask whether it's about time for them to hand me off to Albany. The controller sounds vaguely surprised. He tells me he's working on that handoff right now.

How far am I really from Albany? I'm not sure. Although Albany Approach will probably give me a position report when the handoff comes, I hate to feel as if I'm effectively lost until they check in. While I know I'm on course, I don't know *where* on the course I am, and although it occurs to me to call Boston Center and ask, I don't want to sound stupid. It's one of the oldest pilot errors in the book—the desire to appear in control, or not to cause trouble, at almost any cost—and I'm falling for it. And I know it. But I'm still not ready to admit to serious trouble.

A few minutes later, when Boston hands me off to Albany, I learn that I'm thirty miles east of the airport. A few openings in the clouds show distinctly hilly terrain—the Massachusetts Berkshires—and my navigation log tells me I ought to be nearing Harriman and West Airport, another landmark. The landscape looks like an old Kodachrome slide from which most of the pigment has peeled away. Every now and then I catch a swatch of dark green, or the scattered red and gray and brown of a town. I must be somewhere between Williamstown and North Adams. The broken cover shows no signs of retreating to scattered clouds, and Albany is getting close. If I don't try to get underneath the clouds now, I'm going to have to confess my predicament to the approach controllers and have them vector me down, a procedure tantamount to an admission of VFR failure. Just off to my left I can see a deep break in the clouds, like a winding staircase down to the rugged ground. Calling Albany, I tell them simply that I'm descending to 3,300 feet on account of clouds. Their acknowledgment is routine.

As I reduce power and trim the plane for descent, I find I'm going down steeply with sharp banks left and right to avoid the clouds. I'm watching my attitude indicator as much as the clouds and the ground below, making sure I'm not banking past 60 degrees. The vertical speed indicator shows a drop of almost 1,000 feet per minute; it's difficult to keep the airspeed below 126 knots, the maximum speed for normal flight. Although the plane can fly above 126 knots in calm air, turbulence may bounce it around enough to cause structural damage. Because I'm fairly sure to encounter turbulence on the way down, I have to watch the speed carefully. Yet even with the throttle almost all the way back, the needle hangs on to 126 with a constant upward shiver. Feeling the throttle at the low end of its quadrant reminds me of another risk, the possibility of shock-cooling the engine. A prolonged steep descent with the power at idle will cool the engine so rapidly that the cylinder heads could crack. Getting down thus becomes a kind of seesaw game in which I pull the nose up and open the throttle a little whenever I see an upward break in the clouds. The only blue sky around me is straight up, but I can still see patches of ground. Although the terrain directly below me looks flat, the ground seems to rise both west and east; I must be flying down into a valley. Glancing at my sectional as I bank the plane left and right, I remember I'm among a series of mountain ranges. Mount Graylock is somewhere nearby, but I forget how tall it is and the plane is bouncing around enough that I can't quite see where it is on the map. My eyes do focus, however, on the easternmost mountain range along the border of Massachusetts and New York, in which the high point is supposed to be 2,798 feet. That's good; if I level off at 3,300 I should be below the clouds but enough above the highest terrain to plot a safe route into Albany. Somehow I don't notice the large number in bold blue ink just above the 2,798-foot elevation. That number is "41"—a so-called critical elevation—meaning 4,100 feet. Somewhere near where I am, something rises almost a thousand feet higher than my new intended altitude.

In the break in the clouds off the right nose of the airplane, I suddenly see an airport—it has to be Harriman and West. I can also see portions of a town just north of it, which must be Williamstown, and a river right below me. Although I'm south of my intended course now, I'm almost down to 3,300 feet. The problem is, I still haven't reached the base of the clouds.

"Four-three-four-seven-hotel, I've lost you on radar."

243

The controller's voice is chillingly urgent. In a flash I realize I must have dropped behind a mountain range. He can't read me; he's calling to see if I'm still out here.

He thinks I've crashed.

Glancing up, I see a winding route back up through the clouds. Giving the plane full power, I begin a climb at the best angle-of-climb speed, sixty-three knots. More than anything now, I want altitude, and if I hold this northerly course heading I'll be pulling away from the higher peaks to the south. I call the controller to tell him I'm climbing back to 6,500 feet on account of clouds. When I get back there, if the cloud cover is still bad, I'll declare an emergency.

The flight back up to altitude, though bumpy, is astonishingly peaceful. With every foot of altitude I feel as if I've been given back my life. That feeling rides in tandem with a visceral shock at what might have happened. It's then that, glancing again at the sectional, I see the large blue "41" and realize the danger I was in. According to the sectional, Mount Graylock was about two miles south of my course at 3,688 feet. I didn't see it—but would I have seen it? I realize I've just created a classic scenario for the kind of accident one is supposed to learn to avoid in ground school.

At 6,500 feet, about twenty-five miles from Albany, I see something remarkable. The sky clears almost completely just beyond the last ridge of the Berkshires; the clouds stop as if held by an invisible fence. I can see Albany clearly. The relief is physical: I cry out to myself in gladness.

I call the Albany controller as I put the plane in a gentle descent. It's a slow moment at the airport, so I receive no vectors or altitudes. There's a jet on final approach, and another that's just come on the frequency; I'll be second to land. The approach controller hands me off to the tower controller, who reminds me to keep my speed up. No problem; I can't wait to get on the ground.

The only problem is that, while I can see Albany just fine, I can't see the airport at all. Checking the sectional repeatedly as I sink through 5,000, 4,000, 3,000 feet, I notice the airport's location a couple of miles north of the city, across a major freeway. But it's difficult to say exactly where the northern edge of the city *is*; the suburban sprawl is considerable. Spotting a fairly tall brick building that looks like a reasonable northern marker, I aim for it. I'm at 1,500 feet now, a couple of minutes out; the tower has cleared me for landing. I still can't see the airport. The tower reminds me that I have a jet on my tail. I need to land and exit the runway "without delay."

Slowing the plane down to a relatively high approach speed, flying a northwesterly heading, I'm on a right base to runway 1, which is still invisible to me. This is ridiculous. On each of my previous cross-countries to major airports, I've seen the airport long before landing. In a second I'll have to call the controller, tell him I don't know where the airport is, and go around in a hurry; otherwise one jet pilot, and possibly a controller as well, is going to be mighty upset. Turning to the final approach heading, preparing to go around, I suddenly see the runway. It's right in front of me now. As I line up with it, I notice that it seems slightly lower than the surrounding businesses and houses. Perhaps the suburbs camouflaged it, or perhaps—who knows?—it's one of those legendary airports you can always spot *after* the first flight. Another cry of relief, then a landing so ordinary it's deeply anticlimactic. I pull off at the first exit, wait for the tower controller to hand me off to Ground Control, and breathe the heavier air of grace.

After the flight to Albany, the rest of the trip—everything that was worrying me earlier in the morning—seems routine. I fly in clear skies at 7,500 feet from Albany to New Haven; the air is gusty but not unpleasantly turbulent. Flying almost due south to the Pawling VOR, I turn southeast after about thirty-three minutes, being careful not to confuse the Tweed–New Haven airport with Sikorsky Memorial Airport at Bridgeport, a few miles west. New Haven is reporting winds from 340 degrees at fifteen knots, gusting to twenty-five—not the best news for a small craft. The tower clears me to land as I drop down to 800 feet. There's no other traffic in the area—also potentially a bad sign. Flying a right downwind to runway 32, I pick up both a powerful tailwind and a series of wild gusts; turning onto base, I drop 10 feet, climb back up, then rise suddenly by 25 feet. The upwind wing pitches down sharply, then back up. Focusing on the plane and the instruments, I feel an old anxiety creeping up my back. To hold it at bay I remind myself how I would have felt a year ago in weather like this. It's almost worth a laugh, but now the updrafts and downdrafts require my entire attention. Lining up with runway 32, I hold the plane slightly sideways for the crosswind, adding power quickly to correct for sudden downdrafts. Then, just as I approach the runway threshold, I cut power to land, and the air seems to disappear below me. I'm in a powerful downdraft, falling like a rock. Thrusting the throttle forward, I barely manage to keep the plane from slamming down on the runway. The plane settles back down quickly in the stiff headwind. I'm down and safe, if slightly rattled, in New Haven.

Now the most difficult part of the flight is over. Ahead, I remind myself as I eat the lunch I bought in Albany, is the southern New England coast, with the eastern tip of Long Island to keep me company. Despite the haze, visibility is twenty miles; I'll be able to see Montauk as I fly over the Connecticut coast. The balance of land and sea delights me. I've come back to the kind of place I most love, emblematic of Avalon—and, I realize, of Summerton as well.

A bit under an hour and a half later, after having spent almost five hours in the air, I see the long spit of Duxbury Beach and switch over to 122.8, my home frequency. "Marshfield Traffic, Warrior four-three-four-seven-hotel is four miles south on a forty-five to runway two-four," I announce, so happy to be home that I don't even worry how difficult the crosswind landing may be. Here, too, the gusts are high, but they're also coming almost perpendicular to the runway; it will be a maximum crosswind landing in the Warrior. I'll do fine. Checking my watch, I realize I'm coming in at almost exactly the time I told the folks in Marshfield I'd be back. It's a happy feeling.

Keith, who's been monitoring the unicom, comes on with an airport advisory. Then a pause, and a quick shift from professional to personal—he wants to know how I'm doing. I smile; he's a good guy. "Everything went fine, Keith," I radio back. "It was a great trip." And somehow, although the approach to 24 is bumpy and gusty, I'm unphased; the landing is soft and smooth, full of its own kind of happiness.

What was there to say? That I almost got caught in clouds outside of Albany? That I might have crashed into a mountain? That I hit a sudden downdraft over runway 32 in New Haven and nearly slammed onto the runway? All of these might have been worth discussing, but somehow they seemed exhausted as topics of conversation the minute I brought them up. I knew what I had learned about flying from the trip—more than I had learned from any previous flight; I knew what I would do and not do in the future, I knew what I would watch for. But mostly I knew that I had done something I would have described to myself as impossible a short time ago. As I hung around the airport, talking with Keith and Larry about the trip, looking out the big picture window at the windsock and all the planes on the ground, I felt delighted to be a human being. It had been a long time, I suddenly realized, since I had last known that delight.

NIGHT
FLIGHT

*T*hen, it was early October, and the life I had tenuously held together began to fall apart. At least it looked as if it were falling apart, and friends and acquaintances, watching from the outside, read it that way when they talked with me or at me.

In ordinary daily life, disaster is disaster: A plane crashes, people are killed, and the cataclysm ripples outward among the living like water from a poisoned pond. In the life of the heart, however, what seems like disaster may not always be so. For so long I had lived fearfully, taking halfhearted steps to break free, learning to survive. I did not understand that a good life, for me, would be one in which I could think and act with confidence, deciding where I had to go not on the basis of how successfully I would please others but on how much of my own heart I could find along the way.

Airplanes were the emblem of my heart; they could lift me away from what oppressed me, enacting in real life the wizardry of my imagination, but they could also crash and kill. To live well, I had to trust their world. If I could trust, I might learn what my father most wanted to teach me; if I could not, I would always be the one acted upon, the man swinging in all directions because he had never found a high ground from which to defend himself.

Learning to fly could not, by itself, radically alter my life, but the demands it made on both my strengths and my fears were so elaborate that I could not fly for long and remain the frightened, hopeful person I had been on arrival at MIT in 1988. Touching down on the Marshfield runway in mid-September after five hours of cross-country flight, I was in some ways more intimately acquainted with the world than I had ever been, and also angrier at it. How had I let so much of my life slip beyond my grasp?

In October I moved out of the rundown apartment I had shared with Lesley and Nathaniel and Georgia. I had reached an end with words. I could give Lesley no further encouragement with her stalled dissertation, I could listen to no more complaints and criticism, I could no longer bear to hear my failings so clearly spelled out. If my role in this household was to succeed at being a failure, I would no longer have it. It was unbelievable behavior for me. Several of our mutual friends withdrew from my life and advised Lesley to "change the locks and get a lawyer." There was no doubt that my move, as precipitous as it was, threw my world and Lesley's into chaos. Although the last three years had been horrible, we had thought we could see a way through it. Now the future was interpretable.

I moved into a cheap rooming house in Cambridge, close to MIT and reasonably close to Belmont, where I would return four days a week to take care of Nathaniel and Georgia. My room, though large, was in the back of a labyrinthine building whose dark narrow corridors smelled of old fried fish, canned soup, and sweat. The kitchen down the hall had two hot plates and a refrigerator but no sink. Dishes were to be washed in the communal bathroom sink, an old china basin in a pink-tiled room. Long ago someone had put up cotton curtains with fake lace fringes; they had yellowed and stained with time, complementing a decor of black grout whose crevices sprouted mildew in several interesting shapes and sizes. The kitchen and bathroom were uncleanable and uninhabitable, but the breeze that came through my room windows was soft and sensuous. I could sit by the windows and read, or grade my students' work, or write. This, it seemed, was where life would begin again. It was a hell, a refuge.

As the full weight of my move descended upon me, I realized how desperate things were. We had had no money before; in fact, we were thousands of dollars in debt. I had no intention of abandoning Lesley or Nathaniel and Georgia, but this meant that all but a small fraction of my salary had to go to them. I had almost nothing to live on. The people at the doughnut store on the corner knew me as the man who came in with forty pennies counted out for a regular doughnut and a cup of water. I could write myself yet another credit card check, getting by for perhaps another month, but that was no answer. I was sick of being in debt to other people. The right thing to do was to crawl home and beg forgiveness, as some well-meaning acquaintances pointed out, but this I would not do. If I were to survive—if there were to be, really, an I—it would have to exist with more clarity and independence than it ever had before. Curiously, at this point, I was more ready to die than I was to give up.

Then MIT, which for three years had been the catalyst of my despair, began to shift. A new chairman in my program, who saw the inextricable links between personal and professional life, took a serious interest in my difficulties and found a limited but important way to help. My first book brought in a small royalty check, and with this, along with some other income from writing, I was able to forestall financial collapse. When the rooming house became unendurable, I managed to find an apartment without a lease—a virtual impossibility in Boston. In early November, when I moved into the apartment, I recalled for the first time in many years what it was like to have a place of one's own. In this quiet place, on a blue-collar street behind Tufts University in Medford, I could concentrate on my writing and my teaching more clearly than I ever could at home. The result, ironically, was that I had more time to take care of Nathaniel and Georgia than I had when I was actually living in Belmont.

And Lesley was changing incredibly rapidly. The bleaker her academic work had become, the more determinedly she had devoted herself to it, yet the devotion could not compensate for something in her life that had been lost. It seemed that her heart was divided, but any attempt to discuss this brought a harsh response. Although I was the target of her frustration, I also knew there was a vibrant creativity within her that I had not seen for years; suddenly it began to resurrect itself. When I first met her she had been a poet, a quilt-maker, a botanist. Now, although she suffered profoundly, poems once again came in a rush from her pen, and when I returned to take care of the children I sometimes saw sketches for beautiful new quilts. The passion of this work began to spill over to her dissertation—a finishable creation, as these new weeks passed, rather than a monster.

Then the University of Iowa, on whose informal yes I had placed so much hope, made a formal job offer. I could leave Boston in June if I wanted to; I could start over. As helpful as the new chairman had been, MIT still seemed too risky. It had not given me clear evidence that it knew how to value people.

Although I could see how that might be changing, I was no longer willing to stake my future on that possibility. I knew that I was free to go.

Now, months later, it seems astonishing how much was in flux, how much of my muted soul—and Lesley's—was finally demanding attention. Then, however, events seemed to be taking place in a maelstrom of sadness, and although I felt that, to some extent, I could control what I set in motion, I quickly realized how simpleminded that notion was. Among other things, my move had unleashed my own storm of anger. Furious at having lived for so long like a slave to others' desires and to my religiously endowed need to be "purified" of the human condition, I vowed to do nothing unless I could see how it confirmed my own nascent life. I was by turns relieved and outraged and appalled at having moved out. Nothing in my past gave me any guidance, except for the fragments of a hope that had not quite died—learning to row, dreaming of bush flying in Alaska, reinvoking my father's life, learning to fly. I could still fly, I told myself. I could still fly.

One former student of mine, who watched my transformation at close range, tried her best to wean me away from what had wounded me and bring me into my own life, and hers. Over tea, within the cocoon of music we both loved, we talked about our hopes and frustrations, or just sat silently, grateful for the solace. To me she came as a benediction. Her vision of her life connected powerfully with my own fragments of hope, and as we began to dream together I caught a glimpse of the people we might become. But I was angrier and more disoriented than I knew, until I became a burden even to her. Too much was dark in my life, and my efforts to call down the lightning only increased her uncertainty. I began to see myself as a risk, a person too volatile to rescue.

The *Airman's Information Manual*, which covers more than one might ever want to know about flying, also includes a section on why *not* to fly. It lists divorce or marital separation among the top reasons for staying out of a cockpit. I knew this. But if I stopped flying now, after having come so far, I might lose my one-handed grip on what was left of my life; that would be a real, not an apparent, disaster.

One afternoon in late September, before the worst of the crisis had hit, Larry and I were going over my logbook down in Marshfield. Larry kept flipping the pages back and forth, looking increasingly perplexed.

"There's still a lot of shit you haven't done," he said finally.

"Like what?"

"How about hood work?" The FAA required at least three hours of instruction in flight by instruments alone. This was known as "hood work" because the student pilot wore a large visor or hood over his forehead to keep him from being able to see outside the plane. The instructor watched for other traffic; the student tried to keep the plane level, or in coordinated turns, by referring only to the attitude indicator, the altimeter, the turn coordinator, and a couple of other instruments. It sounded fascinating to me, but neither Donnie nor Steve had had me try it, no doubt because I was having enough trouble flying when I *could* see outside the plane.

"What about night flight? No night flight? What about recovery from unusual attitudes?"

"What's that?"

"It's a kind of hood work. You close your eyes, put your head down, put your hands in your lap. I put the plane in some kind of unusual attitude—a steep banking turn approaching a stall, a diving turn, whatever. Then I tell you to open your eyes.

You have to get the plane straight and level using only the instruments."

"Sounds like fun," I say wryly.

"How come you haven't done any of this stuff? You should have done night flight before you did your solo cross-countries." Larry looks annoyed, then sighs; it doesn't matter. "We'll start next week."

On October 7, I arrive at Marshfield around seven-thirty in the evening. Although the green-and-white rotating beacon cuts a wide swath of sky above the eastern edge of town, I find the barn dark when I drive into the lot. Has Larry forgotten? I bang on the door. There's a light on in the chief pilot's office, Larry's office, but no one answers. I bang again. Larry appears in the office doorway, gives me a slightly sour look, then walks slowly to the front door. Opening it gently, he points at the knob as I start to enter.

"The door," he says, "is unlocked."

"Oh."

Larry flicks on a light near the main counter in the waiting room, and I stand there jotting down notes as he describes the differences between day and night flight. I notice he seems to be watching me rather carefully. Finally he reaches for the unicom microphone, clicking it quickly five times. Suddenly the dark night beyond the window is alive with light: A double row of white dots streaks through the blackness where the runway should be, and deep blue lights seem to hover in space just above the taxiways.

"Pilot-controlled lighting," Larry says simply. "That's what it looks like when you click your microphone. Three clicks in five seconds for low intensity, five clicks for medium, seven for high." He pauses. "You don't seem all here tonight. What's up with you?"

I take a breath to calm myself down. "I think I'm moving out," I say.

Larry stares in a funny combination of comprehension and disbelief.

"Moving out of Belmont?" he asks. "Holy shit. Are you sure you want to fly tonight?"

"Yes," I say. "Very much."

The coastal evenings already are quite cool. My windbreaker is too light for the chill air, and I've forgotten my gloves; my hands shake as I take samples of fuel from the fuel strainer, and cold gasoline pours over my fingers. It seems as if I'm doing everything wrong. Forgetting to set the flaps before starting the preflight, I climb back into the cockpit to pull up the flap handle, then scrape my leg and nearly fall on my face when I catch my pants cuff on the footrest just below the wing. Larry is also going around the plane, checking it out, watching me. I'm shivering by the time I settle into the cockpit.

The darkness has made this a foreign place. After turning on the master switch, I realize I don't know which switch controls the lighting on the instrument panel. I can hear the gyros spooling up, but I can't see the attitude indicator or the directional gyro; the compass above my head is dark. Scanning the panel with my flashlight, I see something briefly reflected in the glass in front of the instruments. Strangely elongated, it's half face, half light. I don't even recognize myself.

Larry hops in beside me, sighs, plugs in his intercom, then shuts the door. "That dial or knob or whatever you want to call it to the left of the master switch controls the panel lighting," he says, knowing from experience what's most on my mind. "The dial on the right side controls the VOR lighting. The left dial also turns on the navigation lights—red for port, green for starboard." I flick the two dials on, experimenting with light levels. The panel lighting seems annoyingly faint to me.

"Why don't you get the engine started so we don't run down the battery?"

The propeller is a whirring darkness before me as the engine spins to life. For the first time in ages I worry that this plane may get away from me. My movements are jerky, haphazard. Fumbling for the checklist, I drop it to the floor, then bang my head on the control yoke as I reach down to find it.

"Hey!" Larry's voice is not harsh, but commanding. "Easy, easy. It's your first night flight. Night flying *is* different. Everything's gonna feel strange for a while. Just mellow out a little."

After doing the run-up on the dark ramp beyond the main hangar, we taxi in silence toward the departure end of runway 24. Suddenly Larry begins to tell me a story.

"You know, a lot of pilots won't talk about stress," he says. "Macho. I worked with a guy like that once. One day we were flying, he says, 'You know, if you got a problem, just put it out of your mind. Keep your personal life out of the air. That's what it means to be professional.' Know what? I actually *believed* him." He laughs ruefully. "What a stupid jerk."

"Who?" I ask suddenly.

"What?" says Larry. "Hey—pay attention. The point is: No one flies without problems. You have to learn how to fly *with* the problem, think about it, talk about it. I had to do that," he said. "I'm still doing that. You know about me and marriage."

I pause for a second, glancing at him. "I guess I don't."

"Let's go up in the air," he says, glancing around for traffic as we reach 24. "We'll do some maneuvers, and we'll talk."

Within a few minutes of takeoff, it's clear I'll win no prizes for flying tonight. I take off too steeply, seesawing up to pattern altitude as I adapt to flight by instruments and by the appearance of the night terrain. Nothing looks familiar. I can guess where Duxbury Harbor is by the intense darkness below me, but Duxbury Beach is equally invisible, and it takes a few minutes to see the tiny pinpoints of light in the windows of houses out on the strand. Shopping centers, to which I pay scant attention when flying in the daytime, become beacons of civilization at night, glowing like stranded spaceships in the middle of the semirural darkness of Kingston and Plymouth. Since I don't know where the shopping centers are in relation to anything else, however, I feel as if I'm flying through a kind of junkyard of old spaceships, as Captain Picard did in a recent episode of "Star Trek: The Next Generation". It's hard for me to get my bearings. Boston looks like the city of Oz, hazy and crystalline on this beautiful night, but I'm short on landmarks over nearer ground.

"Why don't you head toward Plymouth?" Larry suggests.

Looking around to where Plymouth Airport usually is, I see only a large black hole. We must already be south of it. Glancing over my shoulder, I notice a set of white lights, like runway lights. They don't look exactly right, but they're close, and I'm new at this: Must be Plymouth. I begin to bank to the right.

"Where are you going?"

"Plymouth."

"Where is Plymouth?"

"Right over there."

Larry looks at what I've been glancing at.

"Ah-ha. There seem to be a lot of little cars on the runway."

Looking more closely, I realize I've confused Plymouth with yet another shopping center. Larry chuckles.

"Believe it or not, planes have actually landed in shopping center parking lots at night," he says. "Pilots for major airlines have landed at the wrong airports. This is how it happens.

Plymouth is actually right over *there.*" He points southwest until
I can make out the dim white lights, so much paler than shopping center lights, that indicate a runway. Slowly I'm getting my
bearings.

From time to time, as we fly, Larry tells me about his past.
It's rockier than I realized, but similar in many ways to my
present. In the relative darkness of the cockpit, through the
muted clarity of my headset, I hear his voice almost as if it were
a voice in my own head, or a voice I had come to know
well—the voice of a brother, perhaps, who had been away a
long time but had not lost touch with the rhythms of his
younger brother's life. I smile slightly to myself: Larry is actually
seven years younger than I am. But he's earning the role of the
older brother tonight. He intersperses observations on muddling
through personal crises with comments on distance perception
and runway approaches.

I do six takeoffs and landings, of which only the fifth is any
good. Larry has to get in on the first two to keep me from
plowing into the ground, and on the sixth, as my weariness
shows, I yank back hard on the yoke at the last moment, just
barely keeping the nosewheel from slamming onto the pavement. Larry clears his throat.

"Try to keep it simple," he says. "Remember, as you cross
the threshold, shift your gaze down to the red lights at the far
end of the runway. That'll give you the perspective you need.
It's actually easier than in the daytime, if you just trust it. Okay,
let's go in."

He gives me an appraising look as I take off my headset,
wiping the sweat from the headband and earcups. "So, what're
you gonna do now?" he asks.

"I'm going home," I say. "I'm tired."

Larry stares out the windshield into the blackness.

"Look, what you're going through, it's the kind of thing where people just stop flying for six months. It wouldn't be the end of the world if you did that."

"I know," I say, "but I don't want to stop."

"Okay," he says after a minute. "You didn't do great, but you did okay."

Two weeks later, having moved into the rooming house in Cambridge, I'm back for another night flight. By rights everything should be even worse than before, yet I feel strangely serene. Larry notices the difference the minute we get into the cockpit.

"Boy," he says, "for a guy whose marriage is breaking up, you really seem sharp tonight. What's different?"

The question brings down the facade of language I'd made to comfort myself. I'm not serene at all; I'm angry. I'm furious. I'm outraged at the past four years, at my marriage, at my job, but the anger goes deeper—deeper than anything I can say. I am fed up with my life, with who I am. And yet, far from being out of control, I feel almost exhilaratingly focused—even, in a strange way, happy.

After takeoff I climb out smoothly, nailing seventy-nine knots on the airspeed indicator, beginning my turn to the downwind leg at 700 feet. Leveling off at 1,000, I hug the runway; one of the problems last time was that I strayed wide of the runway on downwind, screwing up my timing on base and final. I realize tonight that, as miserable as I was last time, I learned far more than I expected. Having lived through a comedy of errors, I'm determined not to offer a repeat performance.

We glide gently down to 500 feet as I finish the base leg, keeping the airspeed indicator right on 65 knots. It's almost as if I'm walking the plane down to the runway. Final approach is quiet, an easy drop of 500 feet a minute. As my landing light illuminates the "24" on the runway threshold, I shift my gaze to the far end of the field, where two brilliant red lights warn me of the end of the runway. Easing back on the yoke, I hold the nose off until the main gear squeak lightly on the almost-invisible asphalt. We're down.

"Huh," Larry says, obviously surprised. "Okay, let's go around again, and we'll try some emergency stuff."

This time, in the downwind leg, Larry flicks off the landing light. "You've just had a landing light failure," he says, "one of the commonest problems of night flight. You've still got the runway lights, but you won't be able to see the surface of the runway. Just remember, the surface is about a foot *below* the runway lights. Don't try to land even with the lights or you'll flare high."

No problem. Although I'm listening to Larry, I'm beginning to understand that something *is* different about tonight: It's as if I can see beyond my own sight. I can locate things that ought to lie just beyond my vision, and I can feel the right course and altitude for the plane as if both were part of my sinews, my marrow. It's such a wonderful feeling that I don't worry much about not being able to explain it. What I know is that, the more I test it, the more certain I am of it. Everything beyond this plane and this approach, every problem that lies waiting for me back in Cambridge or Belmont, falls away from my life right now, and something else takes over. I have been calling it anger, and there's a fury to it I recognize, but now anger seems less and less like the right word.

As we come in on final, I can see the runway lights but not the runway itself, yet I know it's there. I can see in my mind where it must be, a foot below the lights. As I cross the invisible threshold I look again to the far red lights, ease back on the yoke, and squeak the plane down in darkness between two rows of white lights.

Larry nods, not so much with approval as with curiosity. "Not bad," he says. "Let's go back up."

This time we leave the pattern for a few minutes, hoping that no one else on the frequency clicks his or her microphone three or five times. The runway lights will go off by themselves after about fifteen minutes, and Larry wants this emergency landing to be without runway lights. At one point I glance down to see the pale white-and-blue dots of light around my home field. A second later, glancing again, I see nothing but darkness.

Larry flicks the plane's landing light back on. "You've got a landing light this time, but you can't see the runway. You know it's down there somewhere. Look carefully."

I can't say that, in this darkness, I can actually *see* the airport, but I notice what seem like darker and lighter shadows, and the dimly lighted, slightly curving road just north of us I recognize as Ocean Avenue, heading down to the sea. If I really couldn't see the runway, I'd estimate its position about a half mile south of the avenue. Then I'd line the plane up for an approach until I detected some familiar landmark, or until I yielded to blindness and went off to look for a different airport. But I can, somehow, see the runway, or rather feel it: I know where it is. Floating downward in the base leg just beyond the seaside houses, I turn to final over what looks like an undifferentiated stretch of marsh. The green-and-white beacon above the barn is still flashing; I keep it in the right center of the windshield as I drop the plane through the darkness. Watching the altimeter, looking for the ground, I'm alert to the electricity in my fingers for signs that I'm wrong. My right hand is ready to push the throttle full forward. But then, as I expect, "24" appears suddenly in the narrow reach of the landing light, I ease the yoke back without the benefit of red lights at the far end, and the plane touches gently down on the unlighted asphalt.

Larry nods to himself, like a doctor making a complex diagnosis. "Okay, let's go up again." Leaving the runway lights off, we ascend from darkness to darkness.

In the downwind leg, Larry asks me how I'm doing. Catching his gaze, I see concern and admiration in his eyes. I just nod.

"This is the last thing," he says. "No runway lights. No landing light. You've had a complete in-flight electrical failure, so you have no panel lights. You can't see your airspeed or RPM, there's no attitude indicator or directional gyro. There's no nothing. The only thing on the ground to help you is the airport beacon. Think you can do it?"

"Sure."

"Listen," Larry reminds me carefully, "this is a *simulation*. If anything starts to feel wrong, go around; flick on any lights you need. I'm right here watching."

"I think I'll be fine," I say. I remember my old talk with Donnie about feeling a plane down, about how the instruments are crucial when your instincts lead you astray. Then I had thirteen hours of flight time; now, with fifty-five hours, I don't have a great deal more experience, but enough to know what a plane really feels like when it's descending too fast or when it's too high or too low or when it's about to stall. Then I was happy to try to fly without instruments. Now I'd much rather use them, but if this is an emergency, then so be it.

Darkness to darkness; no light in the cockpit, only one beacon on the ground. A slight differentiation in shadow tone distinguishes the runway from the marsh around it. I cut the RPMs to what sounds like 1,500, wait for ten seconds for the speed to drop, then add flaps; I trim the plane for what feels like a normal descent. We're going down a little slowly. I cut the power further, pull the nose up to bleed off more speed, then drop the nose slightly, turning to base. Another notch of flaps. The runway is there, I know it, I can feel it in my toes, in the tips of fingers that even now ease the control yoke slightly forward, feeling for speed and altitude. We must be doing about seventy knots—slightly fast but okay. The dark roofs of houses pass below me, their creosoted blackness becoming the mottled darkness of marsh, bracken, alder, birch. In a flash I catch sight of a ribbon of dark light, the stream near the threshold of 24. Looking ahead, I see a black rectangle like a hole in the ground, a long trough with no other dimensions. Hold off, hold off; let the darkness look as if it's going to swallow you. Suddenly it's rising around me as I ease back on the yoke, and the Warrior putters a few inches above the runway until it squeaks down on the main gear, just as it has done each time tonight. I have landed a blind plane in the blind, having seen only and exactly what I needed to see.

"I'll be damned," says Larry, a shadow on my right. He flicks on the instrument lights, the landing light, the runway lights. The sudden brightness all around me is almost disappointing.

"Let's go up again, do a few maneuvers, and call it a night."

For the rest of the flight I'm riding in the radiance of night sight, knowing I have seen and done things I had not thought possible. If only I could transfer these skills to the rest of my life. As much as I had mastered emergency landings, I felt more the recipient of a skill or a form of grace than a master of it. Was this kind of grace always arbitrary, or was there—I catch myself wondering—some truth to the core of my religious upbringing, in which one form of healing is a vision of clarity through the darkness? I feel no rush of gratitude for an indwelling spirit, no abiding peace of the kind described in testimonies of healing in my old church. On the contrary, I feel more of an abiding anger. Yet *anger* is not quite the right word. It is as if God Himself were angry, in a sustained fury that amounted to a new way of seeing ordinary things. I would be protected, this gracious anger said. "Can I trust that?" I ask myself. "What does it mean?" "It means," a voice seems to say, "that you can land safely in the darkness." That will be, I realize, the nature of my life for months to come. I see what I have been given.

"You know, when you're having an off day you don't fly . . . well, *horribly*," Larry says when we're back on the ground, "but you fly like a typical student. But when you're on, you fly as well as anyone I've ever seen." Larry, I've come to learn, hates compliments—either giving or receiving them; they tend to ruin his jokes. Realizing what he's done, he makes a scene of clearing his throat and pounding himself on the chest, then warns me against getting cocky. "I want you confident for the check-ride, but not overconfident, you know what I mean? You're still damned new at this."

I thank him and smile. Although I've asked Larry about the FAA check-ride several times, this is the first time *he's* brought it up. I must be getting close. Hold on to the darkness, I tell myself, hold on.

II.

"How are things at home?" Larry asked one day in November after I'd returned from an hour of practice over Duxbury Harbor.

"Which home?"

He smiled wanly. "I meant, 'How's it goin'?' "

"It sucks."

"You and Lesley, you think you'll get back together? I

mean, sometimes these things blow over. . . ."

"I don't think so."

"Ooo-kay," said Larry cautiously. "Been thinking about the check-ride?"

"Next week," I said. "As soon as possible."

Larry and I stared at each other for a few seconds. "I'll call Lew and see when he's available," Larry said. "I'll let you know the date."

Larry set a date with Lew Owen, the FAA-designated examiner: I called Larry back a couple of days later to cancel it. I was tired and angry; my life was a raw wound, and no one seemed to know how to heal it. I did not. Flying had been an act of Shiva, breaking down my old modes of dealing with the world even as it had begun to put new ones in place, but now life in the air seemed to be spiraling toward life on the ground. On any given day I never wanted to see an airplane again.

But I couldn't let go of this. It wasn't just that I didn't want to give up; I was trying to learn something, and I realized that I hadn't learned it yet. Somehow this check-ride hurdle had to be crossed, or I would always be stuck as a student, on the far side of whatever knowledge waited for me.

Clouds and high winds stormed away the Indian summer as the days grew shorter. Frost clung to the windswept Marshfield grasses in the early morning, and pilots now were brushing away light coats of frost from the wings and horizontal stabilizers of their planes. The engines that only a few weeks ago had started after a couple of pumps from the throttle now required full-scale priming. I felt as if something were dying. Or maybe I was. Maybe I had hung on too long, flown too much without really knowing why I was in the air. Maybe I hadn't realized how deep the anger within me was, how dark and confused it could be. Maybe I was asking too much, asking for a more meaningful life. Maybe my mother had been right: Life was a matter of working hard, being good, and keeping a lid on things.

"No," I heard a small voice within me say, perfectly quiet, beyond anger. "No." I called Larry and asked for a check-ride date for November 18. Lew Owen himself called a couple of days later with a confirmation.

I was out of sorts when I arrived at the airport that morning, not angry or upset exactly but foggy. The day itself was a little strange, a throwback to summer, with unseasonable warmth and a layer of brown smog ringing the Boston skyline. After a cup of coffee, I went over a few last-minute details with Larry before Lew checked in at around eight-thirty. He would phone in his request for a flight plan, then show up at the airport about a half hour later. I was to have the flight plan ready at that time; he would inspect it, and the exam would be under way.

I had seen Lew several times since I had first met him almost a year and a half ago. Among his many duties, he gave safety seminars at various airports in the Boston area, and I had attended a couple of these. His geniality and care for his fellow pilots always won my admiration. It was clear that he earned their admiration as well, and, more important, their affection. They would come up to him after his talk, clasp his hand, discuss family or friends or the finer points of flight. There was something almost ministerial in his manner, I thought. Going to a Lew Owen safety seminar was a little like going to church, and I found myself feeling both educated and, in a way I didn't understand, forgiven afterward. It wasn't a forgiveness that had anything to do with flying. It was just a feeling of lightness, of things being better. He could do that; other people had noticed it about him. The flight instructors at Marshfield held him in universally high regard as an examiner who would judge students respectfully. He knew his job and did it well, they said, but he also really seemed to love the people he flew with. Despite my anxiety about the check-ride, I was looking forward to going up with him.

Lew called in right on time with a request for a flight plan direct from Marshfield to Groton, Connecticut. In half an hour, right about when Lew walked in the door, I had finished drawing the course on my sectional chart and completed the flight plan form. Despite feeling as if I were running a few seconds behind the rest of the world, I was satisfied with my work. This was true even though I also knew I had done two unorthodox things with my course plotting. Instead of drawing a straight line from Marshfield to Groton, I had drawn a line south along the Duxbury beach for what amounted to five miles; then I drew the course down to Connecticut. After several cross-country flights, I had found that I simply got my bearings more successfully after climbing to my planned altitude and flying parallel to the beach for three minutes. This was idiosyncratic, but it worked for me, and I couldn't see why it wouldn't work for Lew as well.

My other unorthodox method had to do with a slightly different matter of drawing the course. Because the sectional chart was printed on both sides—everything more or less north of Cape Cod on one side, everything south on the other—I had to figure a way of making the course line continue accurately across the edge of the chart. I knew there was an overlap of two minutes of latitude between the two sides of the chart. This made it possible to mark the location of the first airport on tracing paper, then flip the sectional over, align the bottom two minutes of latitude on the tracing paper with the top two minutes on the sectional, and draw a straight line from the airport on the tracing paper to the second airport. Somehow, to me, this seemed too complicated, although my alternative—

which had to do with measuring course angles from a single line of longitude on different sides of the chart—was probably more complicated and possibly less reliable. Again, however, I thought I'd explain it to Lew and see what he thought. We might have an interesting discussion of course plotting and map reading.

Lew settled into the desk chair in the chief pilot's office at Shoreline to examine my work. Before he began, however, he made sure to ask me how I was feeling; we traded a few stories about flying, about life as a designated examiner, about teaching at MIT. He was trying to put me at my ease, I knew, but I thought I detected a gruffness or strain in him. I began to feel uneasy.

He looked down at the sectional and frowned—the first time I had ever seen him frown.

"What's this?"

"It's my course to Groton," I said idiotically. Then I realized what he meant. "I tend to start cross-countries with a three-minute hop down the beach to get my bearings," I explained.

For a second he looked at me to see if I were fooling. Then he realized I wasn't. The frown deepened.

"No," he said. "Oh, no. This is *not* direct. I want a straight line from Marshfield to Groton." He continued to stare at the course.

"How did you draw this?" he asked.

I began to explain my method of congruent angles across a single line of longitude on either side of the chart, but he stopped me.

"There's a right way to plot a course across the edge of the chart," he said. "Do it that way. I'll give you a few minutes to redo the flight plan." He paused for a moment. "You understand that I could fail you right now?"

269

As I stared at him, astonished, I began to get that dirty, soiled feeling I had had as a child when I had not been healed or when I had disappointed my parents or when, less frequently, I had failed a test in school. But equal to this was the realization that I had completely misjudged the man sitting before me. I had thought of him simply as a lover of aviation, an immensely kind man who had devoted his life to flying, a man who had lived through a tragedy and who commanded the respect and affection of hundreds of pilots. It did not hit me until that moment that I was in the presence of a man who had lost his son in a plane crash. The man examining me on my ability to fly safely was a man whose son had died. Instantly I thought of Nathaniel; what would I be like if something happened to him? Would I ever get over it? It struck me in a blaze of light that one way you might come to terms with such an incomprehensible loss, if you were a flight examiner, would be to emphasize safety and precision above all else. The world could never be made safe or explicable, but human beings could take a specific number of steps to diminish the risk, and any step not taken—or taken in an unprescribed way—could be seen as a failure. Although Lew Owen was a kind man who loved flying, I was not being examined by a kind man who loved flying. I was being examined by a man for whom safety was, in a more personal way than I could comprehend, a matter of life and death.

Many times I had run this check-ride over in my mind—how pleasant it might be, how I might really impress Lew with my skills—but now I was taken utterly aback by my own misreading of the event. How often did I misjudge people? More often than I realized? I found my mind wandering back to Lew as I tried to plot a new course. I should have understood him long ago, I told myself. I should have seen this check-ride coming when I first met him. There was something romantic about him, I admitted to myself through nearly clenched teeth, when Steve introduced us; he was—I hated to use the word—a celebrity, the way survivors of tragedy are celebrities, and he became a kind of reverse image of my own experience. He had lost a son; I had lost a father. But now I saw that, although the events were parallel, they were not comparable. Looking too quickly for metaphors and analogies by which to organize my life, I had overlooked the exacting details of reality. Now I was in the midst of them, and although I might have been prepared for the check-ride itself, I was not prepared to think about my own myopia.

The course-planning fiasco was a microcosm of the rest of the exam. I was off base, off guard. I would explain various details of aerodynamics and flight systems to Lew; he would ask me a question, and I would draw a blank. What color was hydraulic fluid? I had stared at it in my Subaru often enough to know that it was red, but when he asked I could not say. What was the narrow plastic strip on the leading edge of the wing near the stall warning slot? It was, I thought, an airflow separator to interrupt the airflow near the slot as the wing approached a stall, giving the pilot that much more of a warning—but I could not explain it. What was the typical ceiling of an Airport Radar Service Area? I stumbled as I said what I had known for months, 4,000 feet above ground level. How wide are the inner and outer circles of an ARSA? Ten nautical miles and twenty nautical miles, I answered, knowing that I was wrong, but stumbling for a second before coming out with the right answer—five miles and ten miles. Each time I opened my mouth, Lew looked more worried. As we talked, it became relatively clear that I knew what I was doing, but something was preventing me from saying it. Lew knew and admired my flight instructor, and understood that he would not have recommended me for the check-ride if he hadn't thought I was ready. At the same time, I was behaving bafflingly. It was a relief, finally, to climb inside the airplane.

As we taxied out to runway 24 I explained the checklist and some of the important details about the engine—how much power it had on one magneto versus two magnetos, what carburetor heat did, when the auxiliary fuel pump should be on. Lew nodded.

"Let's see," he said as I paused for a moment at the end of the taxiway. "Let's start with a soft-field takeoff. We'll go up, stay in the pattern, and do a short-field landing."

I tensed. A soft-field takeoff was a little tricky. The idea was to get the nosewheel off the ground as quickly as possible to prevent it from miring itself in a patch of soft or rocky earth and flipping the plane over. To do this, you had to hold the yoke all the way back while giving the engine full power. The nose would come up quickly, making the plane feel almost as if it were flying, but the main wheels would still be on the ground. Just as the mains were lifting off—and just as the stall warning was coming on—you were to ease the yoke forward, letting the plane fly just a few feet above the ground until it gained sufficient airspeed to climb. The soft-field takeoff was a precision maneuver in which mistakes could be costly. Holding the yoke back a little too long would cause a stall, forcing the plane back down onto the ground in what might become a series of false lift-offs ending in a crash. But pushing the yoke over too early could force the nosewheel back down on the ground, possibly damaging the wheel and the propeller and, at worst, flipping the plane over at relatively high speed or ripping the engine mounts off the airframe. The key to a successful soft-field takeoff was absolute concentration, and that was exactly what I lacked today.

272

As we rolled down the runway, nose up, airspeed climbing to 45 knots, I thought I felt the mains leave the runway and heard just the slightest grumble from the stall warning horn. Easing the yoke forward, I felt the plane begin to sink and realized we were only a few inches, not a few feet, above the runway. I pulled back on the yoke just as the nosewheel scraped the surface of the runway; we went up again, hovered a few feet above the runway until we reached best-angle-of-climb speed, then began to climb. It was not a disastrous takeoff but it was also not, I realized, a successful soft-field departure. My eyes began to feel damp.

Lew glanced at me but did not comment. "Okay, let's see you set up a short-field landing."

The keys to landing on a short runway, I knew, were approach angle and airspeed. To get down on, say, a 1,500-foot runway in a Warrior, you needed to come in on exactly the right glide slope, neither too low nor too high; you also needed to come in slowly, between 5 and 10 knots slower than the usual approach speed. In the downwind leg I went through the usual checklist, flipping on the auxiliary fuel pump, pulling back the throttle, waiting for the airspeed to drop below 103 knots, adding the first notch of flaps. By the end of the downwind leg, however, the airspeed was only down to 85 knots, and we had lost virtually no altitude. "Hold on," I said to myself, "hold on. Don't go in fast." But we were shooting out over the Atlantic, noticeably beyond the normal end of the downwind leg, and the Warrior had lost barely 100 feet of altitude. Airspeed hovered just below 80 knots.

"But I have to get down," I argued with myself. "What will Lew think if I fly a sloppy pattern?" Cutting the power further, adding another notch of flaps, I began my turn to base and realized I'd been fooling myself: We really weren't way out over the Atlantic. We were pretty much exactly where we should be for the base leg, except that we were too high and too fast. I should have stayed longer in the downwind leg, I thought regretfully, but it was too late now. Oddly, the idea of going around and trying again didn't occur to me. Lew had asked for a short-field landing, and I was going to give him one. Pulling the nose up a little more, I began to seesaw the plane down toward final approach, keeping the nose high to bleed off a little airspeed, then dropping the nose to lose more altitude. By the time I was near the threshold of runway 24 I was slightly high and still flying at close to seventy knots—ten to fifteen knots faster than normal approach speed for a short-field landing. Flaring high to complete the fiasco, I didn't touch down until almost 1,200 feet of runway had passed below me. Although it wasn't a bad landing, I knew that if I'd actually been on a short field, I probably would have gone off the other end of the runway and crashed into mud, weeds, trees, or whatever happened to be out there.

"That was not a short-field landing," Lew said. "Let's try again."

We tried four times, of which three were worse than the first. The fourth landing, in fact, was one of the worst I had ever done as a student pilot; coming in more than ten knots faster than normal approach speed, I didn't touch down until halfway down the runway, and didn't turn off until the last taxiway. By this time I knew I had failed.

Lew glanced at me. "Few weeks ago, we had someone come in high and fast at one of the short fields in the area," he said. "Went right off the other end of the runway. Almost crashed into a house across the street. I couldn't pass you on what you just did." All right, I said to myself, let's just go inside and hang it up. No, damn it, some other part of me said, you give

274

up too easily. Don't invite him to fail you.

"I think I was a little nervous," I said nervously. "I think I could get the speed down if we could go around again."

"No," said Lew. "I'll have to retest you on landings. But let's see what else you know."

So I went back up with Lew, knowing I had already failed one part of the exam, knowing it was possible to spend more hours and more dollars in the air and do nothing but fail other parts of the exam, and mostly I wanted to crawl into a hole in the earth and not come out until the ground had thawed. I wanted to be a bear, or a fox, or a mole, like the mole in James Taylor's song about the underground life of the lost lover. But I was still flying this airplane, I still had a flight examiner sitting next to me, and there was more to do.

The first checkpoint on our cross-country flight was the town of Taunton, about twenty nautical miles from Marshfield on a course heading of 246 degrees. Climbing smoothly to 2,000 feet, I turned to my course exactly over the runway. Whatever else I had ruined, I told myself, I wasn't going to screw this up. Keeping the directional gyro just slightly beyond the 245-degree mark, I started my stopwatch. We'd be over Taunton in about twelve minutes.

Ultimately no one was able to explain what happened next. Lew thought I had mismeasured the course, although it turned out that I hadn't, and Larry thought I'd forgotten to align the directional gyro with the compass, although the two were aligned when we checked them back on the ground. I myself was ready to attribute it to anything, including bad karma. As it turned out, after about ten minutes we were not approaching Taunton but rather flying over southern Brockton, about eight miles to the north. Checking the sectional as I flew, I thought I could actually feel my heart sink in my chest, although it might have simply been the effects of turbulence. We weren't anywhere near where we were supposed to be. Nailing the plane to 2,000 feet, tipping the wings slightly left and right to improve my view of the ground, I began to think what to do next.

Lew looked agitated. "Where are we?"

"We're over southern Brockton."

"Where is that in relation to where we should be?"

I glanced at the sectional. "A little less than ten miles north."

"Well, what're you going to do about it?"

Suddenly I was tired of being the nice, screwing-up student pilot.

"Well, if you really want to know what I'd do about it, this is what I'd do. Our course is supposed to go just south of the Providence VOR. I'd tune in Providence, then fly until I intercepted the course again."

"You can't do that."

"Why not?"

"Because this is about pilotage and dead reckoning. Now what're you going to do?"

I was past the panic stage, past good behavior, past everything. I was angry at the man next to me. I could feel these words forming on my tongue: "You know what I want to do? I want to give up flying. Yup—I never want to get in a plane again. In fact, I'm going to stop flying right now. *You* fly us back to Marshfield. I'm through."

I almost said it. But something about the immediate problem kept bugging me. Technically we were lost. But in more ways than one I was tired of being lost, and if one way of getting found had been ruled out, then I'd try other ways. I wasn't going to end my flying career by being lost.

Studying the sectional for a moment, I realized that to

intercept Taunton we'd have to fly slightly west of south for six minutes. Figuring a course of 200 degrees, adding the westerly magnetic deviation for a course heading of 216 degrees, I turned that way, explaining briefly to Lew what I was doing and hoping my directional gyro wasn't the source of the problem. Glancing at the compass after I'd made the turn, I saw it bearing about 215 degrees. So far, so good.

Perhaps my manner had changed; perhaps for the first time I had seemed to take the plane out of the examination and make it my own, which—another thing I had not really understood—was part of the purpose of this check-ride. For the first time that morning, however, I had done something that satisfied Lew. I had been lost, and now I was found. He nodded a minor approval.

"Okay," he said as we were approaching Taunton, "let's check for other traffic, then do some hood work." I strapped the plastic hood onto my head as he took the controls for a moment. For myself, I had broken a spell with the episode over south Brockton: I had remembered how to fly. Consorting only with the instruments, I did better hood work than I had ever done before.

"Okay," said Lew, clearly pleased. "I can tell you're going to be a good instrument pilot some day."

From then on it was a different check-ride. I closed my eyes, put my hands in my lap; he banked the plane this way and that to disorient me, then put the plane in a steep climbing turn and told me to open my eyes. Instantly I saw the problem as the instruments reflected it; lowering the nose, leveling the wings, I brought the plane back to level flight. After several variations on this, we went on to airwork—shallow turns, steep turns, stalls. With these I had no problem. By the time we returned to Marshfield, I was beginning to feel as if I'd had the check-ride

I had imagined so often before this day. But that was, of course, only partially true.

Back on the ground, I parked the plane as Lew gave me a sad, quizzical smile and climbed out. "The airwork was good, hood work was good," he said. "I'm not sure what you did wrong on the cross-country, but you recovered okay. But I sure can't pass you on the landings. I'm going to go talk to Larry for a few minutes. Come in when you've tied down the plane."

Somehow I had pulled the latter half of the check-ride out of the fire, but that didn't erase my earlier performance. The fact was, I had not passed. I sat in the empty plane for a few minutes, reflecting on this. Then I gathered my headset, my chart and lapboard, stopwatch and calculator, my flight bag and my coat. I stepped out of the plane.

Ann was there. We skipped the jokes and wisecracks. She gave me a hug. "What *happened?*" she asked incredulously, walking me back to the barn.

"I don't know. I just couldn't get the plane down." I couldn't figure out what to say to her—or to myself. Did this happen because I was intrinsically a bad pilot? Did it happen because my marriage was coming apart? Because I had been lonely and stressed out for four years? Because I had left my religion? Because my mother had had cancer and I had not been able to save her through prayer? Because I was a bad person and deserved to fail? It was astonishing how fast the questions regressed to the basic sources of guilt in my life. What I wanted to tell Ann, as we walked in, was that having her come out to see how I felt was one of the most comforting things to happen in recent days, but somehow I couldn't say it. Perhaps she knew anyway.

The door to the chief pilot's office was closed when I came in. I got a cup of coffee and hung around in the waiting room for a couple of minutes, then knocked on the door. Looking a little grim, Lew welcomed me in. Larry looked—

It was hard to say how he looked exactly—serious, but a little proud too, and I realized that he must have been defending me, explaining me, making my case even though my case was lost. I felt a rush of admiration for him.

Lew turned to me. "I'm not going to fail you for the whole exam," he said. "But I'll have to retest you on the takeoffs and landings. You've just got to get your speed down on approach. Call me when you're ready."

I must have been steaming with anger—it must have been scorching my hair, my ears, and I wanted to say something that would blow everything, like "What the fuck do you know about how I fly anyway? You think you saw how I fly? What do you know about my life?" "But he *did* see you fly," a small voice pointed out to me, and I swallowed and told him that he'd see a different pilot the next time he came. We shook hands, and he was gone.

A few days later, after Larry and I had gone around the field several times for several different kinds of takeoffs and landings, Larry turned to me almost in annoyance.

"This is pointless," he said. "You can do this shit. You've been able to do it for months. I wouldn't call your soft-field takeoffs or short-field landings the best I've seen, but they're adequate. They're what you're supposed to be able to do for the private pilot's license. Now *do* them."

I did them. When Lew came for the retest, it was as if no time had passed between the last half of the first check-ride and this second one. We were on good terms—wary, respectful, professional. Although my soft-field takeoff was slightly sloppy, it was clearly a success; I nailed the short-field landing, coming in slowly and bringing the plane down almost without a flare.

Although we drifted slightly off the centerline as I approached, the landing was, as Larry had said, "adequate." As I came in for the final landing in turbulent air, a sudden downdraft forced the Warrior down toward the creek at the end of the runway. Lew's hand shot out for the throttle, but mine was already there; a burst of power brought us up again, over the runway threshold. "Damn!" I said as we touched down slightly hard, but the landing was safe. Lew gave me a more appraising glance than I had seen before.

"Ah, that tells me a lot, a lot about what you're like as a pilot," he said. "You might think that's your worst landing of the day, but you were right there on the throttle. Now that tells me a lot."

A few minutes later I was sitting in the chief pilot's office, watching silently as Lew typed out the temporary airman's certificate that would serve as my private license until the FAA mailed my permanent one. It was wonderful; there was nothing to be said; everything had been done. Each keystroke of Lew's portable typewriter sounded like a prison bar coming down on the cage of my life. The liberation wasn't just about flying, I knew, but it *was* about flying; it had come by way of flying. I could fly, now. I could leave.

"So how did that feel?" Keith asked me a few minutes later, as we talked about flying and Marshfield up in his office. I must have had some kind of radiance that day, or at least I felt it within me. It seemed to go back a long way, along a path of my life different from the one I had usually followed. It went back directly to that day in the car with my parents, to the De Havilland Beaver, to the rowboat in New Jersey, to the death of Siddhartha. All of these illuminated a different life, which I had not really lived. But I had sensed its light as I lived in its shadow, and now, for a time, I had the light as well.

280

How did it feel? I thought about my other conventional accomplishments—becoming a professor, getting a Ph.D., graduating from college. "You know, Keith," I said after struggling to figure out what I meant, "graduating from college was a big deal for me. There was a time when I actually didn't think I'd make it. But getting this license is better than that. Much better."

He smiled. "Makes sense to me," he said.

III.

"After great pain a formal feeling comes," Emily Dickinson writes, but what is that formality? Is it the absence of pain? Is it dignity? Or is it what is left when pain has worn away much of what we thought was essential about our lives, leaving us with selves so plain and direct that we almost don't recognize them as our own?

Now, in late January, my mind seems to move more slowly, like an animal coming out of hibernation too soon. The ground is still covered with snow, the air is cold, there is too little to eat. But a slow mind is formal, less prone to grief.

What had I thought to do, I ask myself carefully, with flight? Was it to be an interesting story, a small compensation for a life crushed with cares and obligations? Would I be able to think about my past through it, make contact with the ghost of my father, explore the possibilities of eros, all with no more consequence than the act of writing words on paper?

I was fooling myself. I thought I knew what I was doing; I thought I knew at the outset what I would discover. The deprivations and achievements I saw in my past were volatile, but I could handle them. I was wrong. When I finally began to love this life, treating it with the breadth and honor it deserved, looking for connections to the man who had suffered before me, rediscovering the intuitive knowledge of my body, the intellect could no longer keep things safe. The life exploded; the story exploded.

How shall I put it back together? Wrong question: It won't go back together. What has exploded blew apart for a reason, for many reasons—because it was a false life, or because its powerful parts were built on quicksand, or because I did not know where in my past to look for strength. Perhaps I know a little better now than I did before. Those isolated incidents, seeming aberrations in which my father was so heavily implicated, are now central, and perhaps I have finally learned what he was trying to teach me. It may be that the love he offered me—the love of parting—was not really a matter of parting after all. We seem to come around again to a common ground, he and I, although we may never be able to explain this to each other.

What is left? *I* am left—a more mercurial creature than before, less well behaved, but also somewhat more likely to say what I mean, to trust myself, to take risks not simply because of the inherent danger but because of the possibility of a more expansive life. My children, Nathaniel and Georgia, are strong and beautiful, and are with me perhaps even more tightly than before, if only because the upheaval of the fall confirmed our preciousness to one another. Yet I have come to see how much I distrust families—how hard it is for me to be in one, how hard it is for the old wounds to heal. I will not be absent as my father was absent, but I harbor some of his resistance to the power others held over him. There is such anger in that resistance! It builds and builds like pressure between tectonic plates. I take some comfort in knowing that human beings will not forever endure intolerable lives, although I know that in fact this is not true; generations of human beings can, and still do, endure

intolerable poverty and dislocation. But I console myself with
the power of a certain kind of anger, a ground-breaking shift
along the fault lines of the heart. I wish my father had been able
to do more of that ground-breaking.

Late last night an unforecast storm dropped several inches
of snow on Marshfield, and the runway this early morning
remains unplowed. It is a beautiful sight—a long, unblemished
expanse of white, harboring only a few tracks of hares and
coyotes.

The wings of 44949 are covered with small islands of ice,
which I must carefully scrape and brush away. Even a light
coating of ice can change the shape of the wing enough to cause
a significant loss of lift; too many planes have crashed because
the pilot figured a little ice on the wing wouldn't matter. As I
crack and scatter bits of ice, I glance out at the expanse where
I know the runway to be. A takeoff and landing in snow—what
might that be like? I smile, thinking of young pilots asking the
same question in Alaska two generations ago, walking the landing strip to search for ice or rocks. How much different it would
be there; snow and ice would be semipermanent features, and
takeoffs and landings on any unpaved and some paved fields
would require tire-mounted skis. Pilots may travel a long way,
yet the best of them, I've learned, fly well in part because they
come to know their terrain intimately. To "leave," my constant
ambition, is actually to relearn topography, the signs of gradual
slopes and sudden uprisings, the nature of grasses and soils, the
characteristics of local storms. To leave is to return, to learn how
not to be a stranger. But I have been a stranger to the earth
virtually all of my life.

As I finish brushing the last bits of ice from the wings and
horizontal stabilizer, I hear the chunky roar of a twin-engine
plane and, glancing toward the threshold of runway 24, I see a

Piper Comanche on final approach. This is worth watching carefully. Although there was ice on the wing of 44949, there isn't necessarily ice on the runway; the air has been very dry here recently, and this storm came through suddenly. I would lay a bet, as the Comanche pilot clearly would, that the runway beneath the snow is relatively dry. But we could both be wrong, and if we are, he and his beautiful plane may go skidding into a snowbank.

I can hardly hear him touch down. One second he's in the air; the next, he's leaving tire trails in the snow. No skidding—no trace of ice, at least where his tires have touched. Pulling off the runway where the pure flatness of the snow signals a taxiway, he rumbles over to the barn and shuts down. Although he's a stranger to me, he's already told me what I need to know.

Doing the run-up on 44949, idling down the taxiway to the end of runway 24, I feel already as if I'm floating on some exceptionally buoyant, beautiful surface—something as calm as a benediction, but also a *thing*, a body with mass and shape and color. The snow is the air made visible. I love its formality, its taking form.

Though the sky is overcast, the air is clear, visibility high. As I climb I can see Provincetown, sparkling dully under dull clouds, twenty miles away. But I don't want to leave the pattern yet. I want to land. Once, months ago, I landed at night when I could not see the runway. Now, in daylight, I cannot see the runway, cannot find its centerline or its beginning or end, but I know where it is and I know where I want my wheels to touch down. Why is it that, when something obscures the most important thing from my sight, I can somehow see it more clearly than before?

Downwind, base, final . . . the plane glides down at 65 knots, a ptarmigan coming into a snowy field. The whiteness a couple of hundred feet below me seems to absorb the very human, metallic sound of my idling engine. The quiet grows larger, not smaller. Out of the corner of my eye I catch a bird cutting across the wildlife sanctuary just south of the airport—possibly a short-eared owl after a night of hunting, or a northern harrier. He vanishes into a thicket as I approach the invisible runway. Lower, lower—there is no surface, no definite place on which to fix my sight, and yet, glancing forward a ways, I see or feel where the pavement should be, easing the yoke back as the snow muffles the idling engine still further. I hover, flaring almost like a creature over the white air below me, waiting for the sound of wheels touching down.

No sound. There is the fact of the wheels in the air, and the wheels down, as I idle along the runway toward the taxiway. The landing is silent, as silent as hawks' talons grasping an alder branch. I glance over at the trees dividing the airport from the sanctuary. Among them are nests I cannot see, homes to animals I have known in glimpses, creatures who know life in a way not quite foreign to me. I do not envy them, but today, landing in the silence of fallen snow, I have a benediction of harshness, a cold quiet that makes at least some of the past fall away and leaves me with a life, eyes that can see and a body that can feel, an airplane, an uncertain future—and a kind of healing that seems to inhere in all bodies until they can no longer be bodies. I pull back onto the ramp, cut the engine, and let the quiet fill the cockpit. Opening the cabin door, I catch the sharp chill of the air. From somewhere, the cry of a hawk cuts through the sky like light. What is flying about? "It's about leaving," said the NASA astronaut, but healing comes less with leaving, I think, than with return. John Hay's terns go back to the place where they last heard the parental voice; people may return to a place even farther back, a place in the heart before it was wounded by ideas and loves that could not save it. Is there such a place? There must be. Perhaps it looks and feels like this, or like the other side of the line of trees, the sanctuary across the divide. I have seen the other side of the divide from the air, and now, I tell myself, I must get there on the ground.

ABOUT THE AUTHOR

Thomas Simmons is the author of *The Unseen Shore*, about his experiences growing up in a Christian Science family. A professor of nonfiction writing at the University of Iowa, Simmons has published articles in *The New York Times Magazine*, *The Christian Science Monitor*, and *Parenting*.